ROUTLEDGE LIBRARY EDITIONS: DISCOURSE ANALYSIS

Volume 9

FOCUS, COHERENCE AND EMPHASIS

FOCUS, COHERENCE AND EMPHASIS

PAUL WERTH

LONDON AND NEW YORK

First published in 1984 by Croom Helm Ltd

This edition first published in 2017
by Routledge
2 Park Square, Milton Park, Abingdon, Oxon OX14 4RN

and by Routledge
711 Third Avenue, New York, NY 10017

Routledge is an imprint of the Taylor & Francis Group, an informa business

© 1984 Paul Werth

All rights reserved. No part of this book may be reprinted or reproduced or utilised in any form or by any electronic, mechanical, or other means, now known or hereafter invented, including photocopying and recording, or in any information storage or retrieval system, without permission in writing from the publishers.

Trademark notice: Product or corporate names may be trademarks or registered trademarks, and are used only for identification and explanation without intent to infringe.

British Library Cataloguing in Publication Data
A catalogue record for this book is available from the British Library

ISBN: 978-1-138-22094-2 (Set)
ISBN: 978-1-315-40146-1 (Set) (ebk)
ISBN: 978-1-138-22461-2 (Volume 9) (hbk)
ISBN: 978-1-138-22465-0 (Volume 9) (pbk)
ISBN: 978-1-315-40182-9 (Volume 9) (ebk)

Publisher's Note
The publisher has gone to great lengths to ensure the quality of this reprint but points out that some imperfections in the original copies may be apparent.

Disclaimer
The publisher has made every effort to trace copyright holders and would welcome correspondence from those they have been unable to trace.

FOCUS, COHERENCE AND EMPHASIS

PAUL WERTH

University of Brussels

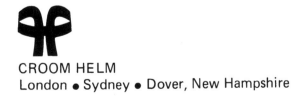

CROOM HELM
London • Sydney • Dover, New Hampshire

© 1984 Paul Werth
Croom Helm Ltd, Provident House, Burrell Row,
Beckenham, Kent BR3 1AT
Croom Helm Australia Pty Ltd, First Floor, 139 King Street,
Sydney, NSW 2001, Australia
Croom Helm, 51 Washington Street, Dover, New Hampshire 03820, USA

British Library Cataloguing in Publication Data

Werth, Paul
    Focus, coherence and emphasis.
    1. Discourse analysis
    I. Title
    415   P302

ISBN 0-7099-2790-8

Printed and bound in Great Britain
by Billing & Sons Limited, Worcester.

LIST OF CONTENTS

List of figures and tables

Preface and acknowledgments

Part I: Generalia

1. INTRODUCTION: BRINGING THINGS INTO FOCUS
1.1 The field of scrutiny	1
1.2 A programme	4
1.21 What do we know about texts?	4
1.22 What do we need to find out?	6
1.3 Defining terms	7
1.4 Aims and structure of the book	13
NOTES TO CHAPTER ONE	14

Part II: Setting up the system

2. DISCOURSE
2.1 What IS a discourse?	16
2.2 Summary: the properties of discourse	24
2.3 Sentences, propositions and semantic notation	25
2.4 Sketch of a model of D-grammar	31
2.5 Review section	33
NOTES TO CHAPTER TWO	33

3. CONTEXT
3.1 Linguistic and extralinguistic context: competence or performance?	34
3.2 Review section: context-of-utterance	36
3.21 Immediate situation	37
3.22 Towards a model of situation	38
3.3 Frames and scenes	41
3.4 States-of-affairs	44
3.5 The common ground	53
3.6 Relevance	57
NOTES TO CHAPTER THREE	58

4. CONNECTIVITY
4.1 Introduction	60
4.2 Cohesion	60
4.21 Anaphora: a first glance	61
4.3 Collocation	65
4.4 Connectors	69

4.5 Coherence	72
4.51 An informal analysis	73
4.52 The coherence constraint	75
NOTE TO CHAPTER FOUR	76

5. THEORETICAL CONSIDERATIONS: SHARPENING THE FOCUS

5.1 Constraints in general	78
5.11 Review section	78
5.12 Coherence constraints: general considerations	80
5.2 Positive coherence and synonymy	83
5.3 Negative coherence and antonymy	87
5.4 The coherence constraint: precise formulation	89
NOTES TO CHAPTER FIVE	93

Part III: A text-grammar

6. EMPHASIS

6.1 Emphasis-placement: an illustration	95
6.2 Is emphasis a surface-structure phenomenon?	97
6.21 What a phonological account must do	97
6.22 A possible phonological account of emphasis	98
6.23 Some counterexamples	100
6.24 Summary: emphasis-interpretation from surface-structure	103
6.3 Is emphasis semantic/pragmatic in nature?	104
6.31 What a semantic/pragmatic account must do	104
6.32 Rules for emphasis	105
6.33 Arguments for the semantic/pragmatic nature of emphasis	110
6.4 Nature and behaviour of Reduction	111
6.5 Nature and behaviour of Accent	115
6.6 Nature and behaviour of Contrast	118
6.7 Review section	119
NOTES TO CHAPTER SIX	126

7. CONTRAST

7.1 Contrast on grammatical items	131
7.2 Contrast on lexical items	144
7.3 Summary: Contrast on grammatical and lexical categories	147
7.4 Semantic properties of sets	147
7.5 C and negative coherence	151
NOTES TO CHAPTER SEVEN	163

8. ANAPHORIC CONNECTIVITY

8.1 Resumé of anaphora	166
8.2 Reference	168
8.3 Types of anaphor	174
8.4 The role of emphasis	179
8.5 Anaphora as coherence	186
8.6 Reciprocal anaphora: two views	187
8.61 The view from G-B	187
8.62 *Each*	193
8.63 *Other*	196
8.64 Quantifier-floating	197
8.65 Reciprocals in complex sentences	200
8.66 Ambiguity of the phrasal form	204
8.67 Reciprocals and discourse	205
8.7 Anaphora and coherence	206
NOTES TO CHAPTER EIGHT	211

9. SYNTACTIC VARIATION: GETTING MOVEMENT INTO FOCUS

9.1 Introduction: "Movement" in recent grammatical models	213
9.2 Topic-comment articulation: review section	214
9.21 TCA and emphasis	217
9.22 The TCA constraint	218
9.3 Syntactic effects: summary of predictions	221
9.4 "Unmoved" structures	222
9.41 Behaviour of stress in unmoved structures	222
9.5 Passives: predictions of TCA constraint	229
9.51 Contexts with and without passives	231
9.52 Why passivise at all?	236
9.6 "Emphatic" constructions	240
9.61 Examples of emphatic constructions in context	243
9.62 Why cleft or pseudo-cleft?	253
NOTES TO CHAPTER NINE	257

10. CONCLUSIONS

10.1 Summary	259
10.2 Implications	260
10.3 Empirical evidence for emphasis	265

BIBLIOGRAPHY AND AUTHOR-INDEX	269
SUBJECT-INDEX	283

List of figures and tables

Fig.	1.1	Text and Discourse	6
	1.2	Emphasis as a function of prominence	8
	2.1	Lexical connections in passage (2)	19
	2.2	Lexical connections in passage (1)	21
	2.3	A model of D-grammar	31
	3.1	Context-of-utterance	36
	3.2	Scale of possibility	45
	3.3	Scale of personal experience	45
	3.4	W_3 – the common ground	47
	3.5	A model of conversation	56
	5.1	Derivation	78
	5.2	Coherence in a text-grammar	81
	5.3	Van Dijk's global coherence constraint	82
	5.4	Antonymy	88
	6.1	Emphasis as a function of stress	95
	6.2	X-bar representation of (9a)	106
	6.3	Emphasis as a function of anaphora	109
	7.1	COMP structure	140
	7.2	Contrastibility	147
	9.1	Topic-comment pattern	217
Tab.	6.1	Emphatic structure of (9b)	107
	6.2	Emphatic structure of (10b)	108
	6.3	Thematic vs. semantic centrality	117
	8.1	Reference and possible-worlds	172

Preface

PREFACE AND ACKNOWLEDGMENTS

We take it that there are at least two kinds of reasons for studying linguistic, or indeed any other kind of, regularity. The first is the same as the answer given traditionally by British mountaineers when asked why they want to climb some forbidding mountain peak: "because it's there". John R.Ross in a paper (1975) on linguistic methodology, has an amusing metaphor in which he compares linguistic research to that kind of deep sea exploration which pulls up weird monsters at random from the depths, exclaims over them, and throws them back. We may refer to this first approach as the observational-descriptive. The second type of reason for studying linguistic regularity is for the light it throws upon the cognitive structures and properties of the human organism, and how at the same time it may help to confirm what is independently known about human cognition. This we may call the explanatory motive.

Observations and descriptions may or may not be advanced within the framework of an explicit theory (although it *seems reasonable to suppose that at least some inexplicit pretheoretical principle of what counts as admissible data is necessary). Explanations, though, must be couched within an explicit theory, since a true explanation cannot occur except as a set of facts independently confirming a consistent hypothesis.

In what are often thought of as "the bad old days" of traditional and structuralist grammar, it was frequently maintained that descriptions were sufficient grammars — grammatical theory was no more than a discovery procedure for finding descriptions. The idea that a grammatical description could, or should, correspond to anything "real" ("psychological reality") was derided at the time as the "God's Truth" approach to language, having little more value than Biblical ideas of prelapsarian purity. All that, however, was changed by Chomsky, who showed conclusively that not only must the study of language be theoretical, but furthermore, the goal of any linguistic theory must be explanation.

Preface

By "language", however, Chomsky has always meant **sentences**. One can describe the linguistic behaviour of sentences, but the ultimate goal is, as we have seen, to explain linguistic behaviour itself. This is normally done in terms of restrictions on rules which are said to reflect cognitive limitations of the human mind. However, as yet, we have very little direct evidence of such cognitive limitations, so postulating them as explanatory evidence is a little previous. We want to suggest that more accessible explanations may be found in **text-linguistics**.

The study of texts (i.e. sequences of connected sentences) has been rather differently treated in mainstream linguistics. Early work by Zellig Harris in the 1950's was descriptive and methodological, in the structuralist tradition. But in generative grammar, we have seen the rather strange spectacle of people hotly defending the explanatory power of sentence-grammar, while hotly denying the possibility of anything more than description for texts. Discourse analysis is a possible and for some purposes useful exercise — but because most systems of discourse analysis lack a real generative component, they tend to degenerate into mere taxonomies, (e.g. the work in Tagmemics, and in the Hallidayan tradition).

We want to show that a generative text-linguistics is nevertheless possible, and not only that, but actually essential in explanatory generative grammar. Notice we said text-*linguistics*. We are not claimimg that a text-*grammar* is possible; in fact, we would claim that this would be a misuse of the term "grammar", for the following reason: one of the metatheoretical distinctions drawn in linguistic theory is between **weak generative capacity** and **strong generative capacity**. Weak generative capacity is the capacity of a grammar to generate all and only the grammatical sentences of a language; strong generative capacity is the capacity to generate all and only the correct structural descriptions of a language. A grammar should display the latter property, for otherwise it would fail to distinguish between such sentences as *John is easy/eager to please*, or the ambiguity of *Visiting relatives can be boring* and so on. In this sense, a text-grammar is an impossibility, since we cannot generate the correct SDs for texts. On the other hand, it is quite conceivable that we could generate acceptable texts, given a sentence-grammar plus

Preface

constraints on the possible combination of sentences. A text-linguistics, then, is a sentence-grammar, enhanced by some way of controlling which sentences can go together. Why should anybody want to do this? Well, not only because textual regularities are there, but more importantly, because they have a crucial function in the working of sentence-grammar — they help to explain its operations. Exactly how this occurs we shall go on to discuss in the subsequent text.

This book has now been several years in the making, and publishers and fellow-scholars alike have long grown tired of enquiring after its progress. The years of its gestation have also witnessed a remarkable upsurge of interest in the study of text, with a journal, at least two series of collections and monographs, and probably twenty or thirty individual publications devoted to the field. My own thinking has naturally benefited greatly from this wealth of investigation and hypothesis, as will be reflected by the references in the book. Over the years of its making too, I have discussed most of its content at various times with people too numerous to mention individually; I hope they will accept this collective gesture of thanks. Whatever responsibility they may bear for the final outcome I will leave to them to assess. When I began the book, I was in the Linguistics Department of the University of Hull, and I received considerable encouragement from my colleagues there, not least from the Head of the Department, Erik Fudge. By the time it was completed, I had been several years at the Institut de Phonétique, Université Libre de Bruxelles. There, sad to say, I received quite the reverse of encouragement from the Director. Fortunately, the presence of Dr. Alain Bossuyt more than made up for this deficiency.

I would also like to acknowledge with thanks the help given me by Messrs. Croom Helm Ltd., the publishers, and particularly their representatives for linguistics, Nick Williams and Tim Hardwick; Roger Lass, who originally accepted my proposed outline for the book; the Belgian Fonds Nationale de la Recherche Scientifique, whose grant no. 1.5.334.82F has enabled me to conduct the research project described in the final section of the book; the Survey of English Usage and Survey of Spoken English, for permission to use extracts from their *Corpus of English Conversation* (Svartvik and Quirk

Preface

1980); and finally, my wife, Kitty Jacobs, whose many sensible suggestions have contributed greatly to the general organisation of the book, and whose other suggestions, perhaps less sensible, but undoubtedly more interesting, have contributed enormously to the general wellbeing of the author.

TECHNICAL NOTE: This book was written and set on a BBC microcomputer, equipped with a "Wordwise" word-processing ROM. For technical reasons, brace-brackets have been printed as columns of single-line braces (}), and Greek letters have been either spelt ('alpha', 'theta'), or else replaced by Roman equivalents. Logical symbols have been spelt out and printed in italics (*All, Included-in*).

Paul Werth,
Brussels, Dec. 1983

FOR
KITTY
GABBY
ABBY
AND
SAM
OR
ZOE

Bringing things into focus

Chapter One

INTRODUCTION: BRINGING THINGS INTO FOCUS

1.1 The field of scrutiny

In its comparatively short lifespan, generative linguistics has conventionally concentrated on a range of data whose boundaries are restricted to the single sentence. Thus, faced with such sentences as those in (1), generative linguists have had no hesitation in recognizing each and every one as perfectly acceptable[1]:

1. (a) *Most* people *enjoy brandy* after *dinner*
   (b) *Most* people ENJOY [brandy] after [dinner]
   (c) [Brandy] is [enjoyed] by *most* people after *dinner*
   (d) It's BRANDY that [most] people [enjoy] after [dinner]
   (e) What MOST people [enjoy] after [dinner] is BRANDY
   (f) [Brandy], *most* people *enjoy* after *dinner*

On the other hand, there are sequences that would often be regarded either as unacceptable outputs of sentence-grammar[2] (henceforth, S-grammar), or else as possible outputs, but only at the expense of a considerable machinery of special rules and constraints:

2. (a) *Have a brandy she DID
   (b) *JOHN, the FISH
   (c) *You'll find it BEHIND
   (d) *PUT it

From the viewpoint of the autonomous S, i.e. the single-sentence output of an S-grammar, the examples in (2) show two kinds of difficulty:
   a. where there is a syntactic infelicity of some kind, that is, a sequence which cannot be generated in a standard grammar; examples include unorthodox word-orders such as (2a), and deviant complementisation as in (2c,d)

[1]

Bringing things into focus

    b.   where there is an information-gap of some kind: particularly the zero-anaphora type of example, as in (2b), but also to a lesser extent, the indeterminate pronoun, as in (2c,d). The latter type presents problems of interpretation rather than derivation.

However, in certain circumstances, the judgments indicated by (*) can be reversed. These circumstances always involve specific **CONTEXTS**. Note that in all cases, it is the second S with which we shall be concerned.

3. (a) The Russians invaded Afghanistan — @*Most* people *enjoy brandy* after *dinner*

    (b) George enjoys malt whisky after dinner — @[Most] people ENJOY [brandy] after [dinner]

    (c) What do people like to drink after dinner? — @[Brandy] is [enjoyed] by *most* people after *dinner*

    (d) Most people enjoy brandy with their breakfast — @It's BRANDY that [most] people [enjoy] after [dinner]

    (e) Most people enjoy brandy with their breakfast — @What MOST people [enjoy] after [dinner] is BRANDY

    (f) Tell me about people's drinking habits here — @[Brandy], *most* people *enjoy* after *dinner*

4. (a) You know Mrs. Goldstein said she was going to have a brandy? Well, [have] a [brandy] she DID

    (b) George, you bring the soup. JOHN, the FISH
or: George ordered the steak; JOHN, the FISH

    (c) Don't try looking for the artist's signature on the front of the painting. You'll [find] it BEHIND

    (d) Do you want me to throw the parcel on to the table or put it there? — PUT it

Perhaps we should complete this comparison by suggesting appropriate contexts for the responses in (1) and the cues in (3):

5. (a) Tell me about people's drinking habits here — Well, *most* people *enjoy brandy* after *dinner*

[2]

Bringing things into focus

(b) You don't have to FORCE that Remy Martin down you. After all, *most* people ENJOY [brandy] after [dinner]

(c) The brandy-producers have recently sponsored a market survey of their product. Apparently, [brandy] is [enjoyed] by *most* people after *dinner*

(d) Really? I heard there'd been a change to VODKA — No, no: it's BRANDY that [most] people [enjoy] after [dinner]

(e) And I've also read somewhere that after dinner, cocoa is gaining in popularity. — Nevertheless, what MOST people [enjoy] after [dinner] is *still* BRANDY

(f) Do Belgians drink a lot of brandy? — [Brandy], *most* people here [enjoy] after *dinner*

6. (a) The Russians invaded Afghanistan. They *claimed* to have been *invited in* by the *regime*

(b) George enjoys malt whiskey after dinner. *Most* people [enjoy] BRANDY after [dinner]

(c) *Most* people *enjoy brandy* after *dinner* However, rising prices are preventing them from INDULGING in this luxury

(d) Most people enjoy brandy with their breakfast — That's not true: what MOST people [have] with their [breakfast] is COFFEE

(e) Most people enjoy brandy with their breakfast — No, it's DINNER that [most] people [enjoy] [brandy] with

(f) Tell me about people's drinking habits here — *Most* people *enjoy brandy* after *dinner*

Given the appropriate or inappropriate context, therefore, perfectly grammatical (that is, S-grammatical) sentences may be rendered unacceptable (that is, D-ungrammatical). On the other hand, S-ungrammatical, or S-semi-grammatical, sequences may turn out to be perfectly D-grammatical. One of the aims of this study, then, is to provide an explanation for such facts as these, and indeed to attempt what amounts to a definition of the term "appropriateness".

What we are investigating here is essentially the semantics of discourse. This crucially concerns what we conceive of as the "flow" of information

[3]

Bringing things into focus

through a linguistic sequence, and how it is deployed and manipulated by contextual factors. To put it simply: why do particular types of context demand particular forms of successive sentence structure? Why are particular linguistic forms appropriate to particular contexts, and inappropriate to others?

The answers to such questions are not simple, and moreover, they are extraordinarily far-reaching in terms of their consequences for the theory and practice of grammar. We shall maintain in the course of this book that the restrictions involved are essentially semantic-pragmatic in nature, though actually manifesting themselves at all linguistic levels:

(i) phonetic/phonological (e.g. stress, intonation)
(ii) syntactic (structural variation)
(iii) semantic (information-structure, reference, deixis)
(iv) pragmatic (interaction, implicature).

1.2 A programme

1.21 *What do we know about texts?*

"We" in this section heading refers not to "we native speakers of English", or some other language — who in a sense "know" everything there is to know about the grammar of their discourse. Nor does it refer to "we the author", but to "we the community of linguists". Surprisingly, perhaps, the short answer to the question is "very little"; we are hardly in a position to do much more than chart our ignorance. However, this rather glib response is also true of almost every other area of language, a fact which is presumably due to the complexity of the phenomena themselves as well as the inaccessibility of the biological and psychological systems underlying them. Yet it is also true of trans-sentential studies (as of semantics, for example, too) that, historically speaking, they have been even further hindered by the structuralist *diktat,* due to Bloomfield originally, that only the structural elements of sentences form the proper concern of linguistics.

Likewise, the generativist legacy has been

[4]

Bringing things into focus

equally stifling, with its insistence that sentence-sequences fall under the heading of performance. Obviously, it is true that sentence-sequences (or rather, utterance-sequences) are performed; but this is no less true of individual sentences (or rather, utterances). Just as a sentence, with its grammatical description etc., is the more abstract representation of an utterance, so is a text (a sequence of sentences) the more abstract representation of a discourse (a sequence of utterances). Thus, utterances and discourses are performed, in real time and in actual situations, but sentences and texts are their abstract symbolic representations. The generativist position, then, in regarding sentential facts as representational, and part of competence, but suprasentential facts as phenomenal, hence part of performance, is thereby confounding two levels of abstraction.

If we can therefore set aside these traditional objections to our field of study, perhaps we can attempt to formulate a consensus view of the commonly accepted assumptions underlying the study of text and discourse. Let us consider the following:

A – Sequences of utterances (and the sentence-sequences underlying them) are not simply random collections.
B – They display connections which are both syntactic and semantic-pragmatic in nature.
C – They occur in relation to practical situations.

(A) is of course the *sine qua non* of text-study, and in consequence it might seem trivial to spell it out. However, centuries of traditional language study based on sentences, together with the anti-text strictures of structuralism and generativism, have combined so powerfully as to foster the popular presupposition that grammar IS sentence-grammar. Sentence-sequencing is then dealt with, if at all, under some other branch of study, be it rhetoric, macrolinguistics, or performance. Often enough, indeed, its study is postponed indefinitely. (A) says, then, that an S-grammar alone is insufficient to account for the non-random character of sentence-sequences.

(B) introduces an assumption about the

substance of this non-random character. As it stands, (B) is neutral on the question of the relative importance of syntax vis-a-vis semantics, all gradations of which have been argued for[3]. Our own contribution to this debate will argue that many apparent syntactic characteristics are profoundly semantic-pragmatic in nature.

(C) is probably at one and the same time the most obvious and the most problematical of these assumptions. Clearly, an essential component of the production and comprehension of discourses and the investigation of texts is the wider context in which they occur and/or relate to. Yet at the same time, our ability as linguists to analyse, categorise and account for situations in general terms is extremely limited.

Nevertheless, this shortcoming is in itself no excuse for rejecting the study of discourse/text in principle (as do, for example, Katz and Postal 1964). Recent work on this area of experience has, moreover, produced some very encouraging lines of enquiry. We may cite the work of Minsky 1975 and Charniak 1975 on "frames", of Schank and Abelson 1977 on "plans" and "scripts", of Lakoff 1977 on "linguistic gestalts", and of Fillmore 1982 on "frame semantics" and "idealised cognitive models". In the spirit of this work, let us now, for the time being, take over the term "**frame**", defining it as follows: frames are to actual situations as texts are to discourses and sentences are to utterances. In other words, texts occur in frames, while discourses occur in actual situations: see Fig. 1.1.

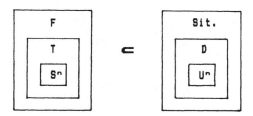

FIG. 1.1

1.22 *What do we need to find out?*

Let us assume the positions A, B, and C outlined in the previous section: we may now call them **sequentiality, connectivity,** and **contextuality**,

Bringing things into focus

respectively. We return to their more detailed description in Chs. 2 and 3, but for now we shall confine ourselves to outlining the further issues they raise.

Since sequentiality (or syntagmaticity) is also a basic property of syntax, one question we shall ask is, how compatible is the study of texts with extant S-based theories of grammar? We will argue that the interconnections between sentence, text and context should be used to test the explanatory power of this or that model of S-grammar.

Connectivity (or **COHERENCE**) is, we shall claim, the single most important principle of textuality. However, we need to establish exactly what the ground-rules of connectivity are; we also need to know what the machinery is by which it takes place.

Finally, we want to investigate how texts plug in to frames. What, in other words, is the machinery of contextuality?

To summarise, therefore:

    A - For sequentiality: how compatible is text-
         linguistics with sentence-linguistics?
    B - For connectivity: what are the principles
         of sentence-connectedness; and what is the
         machinery of this relationship?
    C - For contextuality: what are the principles
         and mechanisms of the text/frame
         interface?

1.3 Defining terms

The term **FOCUS** is used in this book mainly as a non-technical term referring in a shorthand way to a whole area of linguistic interest, namely that section of the discipline which concerns itself with the deployment of sentences to present information. It is also occasionally used, again non-technically, to mean something like the "object of attention". A third use, perhaps its most common one currently, is more technical, and we will return to it directly.

Some of the terms used, however, (and notably 'focus' itself) have been used in recent linguistics in sometimes wildly differing senses. We shall, therefore, briefly and informally describe them here, before defining them more rigorously in the body of the book. In order to create some sort of perspective for this enterprise, let us first state some general assumptions.

[7]

Bringing things into focus

We conceive of linguistic utterances as activities of message-production which crucially respond to contextual factors. We therefore need a mechanism which will feed these contextual factors into the sequence of linguistic forms making up the messages. Both the contextual factors and the messages are ultimately made up of "information": that is to say, they are always potentially expressible as sets of semantic propositions. Nevertheless, contextual information ("pragmatic presuppositions", and the like) has, for practical purposes, to be kept separate from message information ("sentence-meaning", etc.). Areas of overlap do exist, however, notably in 'reference' and 'deixis'. It is a major thesis of the book that **the different forms of sentence occurring in texts are motivated in large part by the unfolding patterns of information proceeding through the discourse.**

Within this broad framework, then, we may represent a discourse as made up of a sequence of propositions whose content is not random but interconnected. The connections occur both between separate bits of message information and between message and contextual information. This, in fact, is where the mechanism spoken of earlier takes its effect. Information is deployed in a discourse in such a way as to ensure **connectivity.** The mechanism of this deployment is here collectively termed **EMPHASIS,** and is of two kinds: **prominence,** for material which for some reason is made to stand out, and **non-prominence,** for recessive material. As we shall see, prominence too is bivalent: we need to distinguish **ACCENT** and **CONTRAST.** Non-prominence includes "inert forms", which do not take part in emphasis, and **REDUCTION.** We can sum up the relationship between all these terms in a tree:

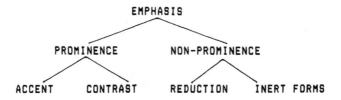

FIG. 1.2

Bringing things into focus

The two prominent types of emphasis are very often conflated under the term **focus**. This use of the term occasionally occurs in the present book, sometimes when referring to the work of others who do not draw the distinction, and sometimes because it is useful to refer to Accent and Contrast together.

Accent seems to be of two broad types: **information-accent** and **attention-accent**. The first of these provides for prominence on freshly-introduced semantic material, or, particularly in questions, for structural gaps where semantic material is not available. **Attention-accent**, on the other hand, occurs on previously- occurring material (which would normally fall under Reduction) when for some reason it has to be re-Accented. This might happen either from some sort of casual variable emphasis (e.g. the French *accent d'insistance*, or in certain individual styles), or else, and more importantly, to renew the present relevance of some "decaying" information. In this latter case, attention accent is presumably simply a special form of information-accent; it also then usually functions as a structural device for subdividing the discourse (cf. Lesgold et al. 1979, on "backgrounded information").

Reduction is associated with repeated semantic material, (which may be words, but need not be), when it is subsequently used with no special prominence, but merely, as it were, to keep the information in the "current file". Since in such cases there is a crucial link between a previous and a subsequent item, Reduction is an **anaphoric** operation. We shall also see that the information thus linked may be related in other ways than by straight identity.

When an item has **Contrast**, we must assume that there is a previous piece of information which in some way has a negative relationship with the Contrasting item. Since, therefore, such items necessarily have an at least implicit connection with another piece of information in the discourse, they too, like Reduced items, are fundamentally anaphoric. This shared property will be seen to have important implications.

We can briefly exemplify these notions in the following short dialogue. A fuller characterisation will have to await Chapter 6, where we in fact make use of primarily spoken data. Nevertheless, since spoken data always represent a particular choice of

[9]

Bringing things into focus

emphases on a given occasion, there is nothing particularly privileged about it, except for its spontaneity. Any competent speaker of the language, however, is fully capable of reproducing discourses which are coherent in terms of their emphasis, since this presupposes his ability to relate them to some standard situation. Thus reading aloud written texts is successful to the extent that it appropriately reflects their coherence.

> 7. "Heigh-ho! What a bally awful day", sighed Bertie, squinting out of the window.
>   "It does appear to be somewhat inclement, sir", agreed Jeeves, "though the meteorological prognostication for tomorrow suggests that the awfulness will be even more bally then. If I may say so, sir", he added.
> (With apologies to P.G.Wodehouse)

Accented items here are, roughly speaking, those which have been freshly introduced into the discourse. It follows, then, that items at the beginning of a discourse are rather more likely to be Accented than items occurring later on. It is, nevertheless, possible for early items to be non-prominent, as we shall see in later chapters. In (7), the words bally, awful, and day, in Bertie's utterance would certainly receive Accent (we are not considering the narrative inserts "he added" and so on). So too would Jeeves' words meteorological and prognostication. The word does, however, perhaps demonstrates attention-accent rather than information-accent. Awfulness and bally in Jeeves' speech, however, will be Reduced, since they essentially repeat Bertie's words. Inclement, too, is Reduced, though obviously not through mere repetition, but rather because it repeats a meaning instead of an actual form (i.e. 'inclement' = 'awful'). Contrast is exemplified in Jeeves' words tomorrow (as opposed to 'today' implied by Bertie), and more (as opposed to the lesser degree stated by Bertie). Many questions still remain unanswered, of course: these will be dealt with in subsequent chapters.

DISCOURSE, like focus, may refer either to a subject area, or function as a term within that subject area. In the first use, it refers to the linguistic level above the sentence, considered as

[10]

Bringing things into focus

an object of study. In the second use, it denotes a unified set of one or more sentences, connected semantically, and (ideally) representing a completed utterance. The term has also been used somewhat promiscuously to refer either to the concrete sequence of sentences, or to the abstract structure underlying them.

TEXT, however, has come in recent years to be used more or less exclusively for the abstract, underlying form of a connected sequence —that which a grammar is concerned with. We can therefore arrive at the reasonable proportion:

utterance : sentence :: discourse : text

However, since our primary concern here is not so much with text or discourse-grammar itself, but only with some of its processes and their effects upon sentence-grammar, we shall tend to use the terms interchangeably. Nevertheless we will return to the distinction between text-grammars, arguably the only reasonable grammatical model, and S-grammars, which we claim are deficient in crucial ways.

MOVEMENT was originally a Standard Theory notion for a syntactic operation involving a transformation of permutation, especially of NPs. The term 'movement' and indeed the whole notion of transformations has come into serious doubt in much recent generative literature. Some linguists seek to account for such phenomena by generation in the base component. Others attempt a lexical account of syntactic constructions. Equally, one may regard the forms in question as syntactic variants, having certain distributional characteristics, resulting from different possible influences, among them contextual ones. We shall, on the whole, continue to use at least the terminology of movement, while preserving an agnostic position on the question of their derivation. The variants in question include:

8. LEFT MOVEMENT
   (a) **Topicalisation:** Peterson, Tatum would have approved of
   (b) **Y-movement:** Peterson, Tatum would have approved of
   (c) **Clefting:** It's Peterson who Tatum would have approved of
   (d) **Wh-movement:** Who would Tatum have approved of?
       The pianist who Tatum would have

[11]

Bringing things into focus

       approved of comes from Montreal
  (e) **Tough-movement:** Tatum's approval was hard
       to get
  (f) **L-dislocation:** Peterson, Tatum would have
       approved of him
       Tatum, he would have approved of
       Peterson
  (g) **Adverb-preposing:** Almost certainly, in
       his later years, Tatum would have
       approved of Peterson
  (h) **Dative movement:** Tatum would have given
       Peterson his approval

9. RIGHT MOVEMENT
  (a) **Rhematisation:** Tatum would of Peterson
       almost certainly have approved
  (b) **Extraposition:** It is almost certain that
       Tatum would have approved of Peterson
  (c) **R-dislocation:** He would have approved of
       Peterson, Tatum would
  (d) **Particle-movement:** Tatum would have
       backed Peterson up

10. LEFT-AND-RIGHT MOVEMENT
  (a) **Pseudo-cleft:** ((The) one) who Tatum would
       have approved of is Peterson
  (b) **Pseudo-relative:** The man who Tatum would
       have approved of is Peterson
  (c) **Passive:** Peterson would have been
       approved of by Tatum
  (d) **Psych-movement:** Peterson would have been
       acceptable to Tatum

We shall take the position that these are not
merely "stylistic variants", but that the difference
between them is motivated by the informational
requirements of the discourse. We distinguish two
such requirements: one, arising out of position in
the discourse; two, having to do with impact in the
discourse-act. More specifically, by "position" we
mean the status of the constituent elements of
sentences (or, rather, of propositions) in the flow
of information in the discourse. By "impact" we
refer to the manipulation of sentence-structure in
order to facilitate the flow of information. We
shall be trying to substantiate these rather broad
claims with particular reference to the passive, and
to clefts and pseudo-clefts in Chapter 9.

[12]

Bringing things into focus

1.4 Aims and structure of the book

Fundamentally, we shall be concerned to chart the relationship between connectivity, contextuality and emphasis, and see how far this takes us in the explanation of linguistic theory in general. To do this, many apparently disparate areas have to be examined, and obviously in some cases our examination will have to be somewhat perfunctory. Dotted throughout the book are brief review sections whose main purpose is not historiography, but rather orientation: they attempt to provide for the reader a perspective upon the given topic. It should also be stated at this point, in view of the sometimes bitter in-fighting which occasionally affects the discipline, that our purpose, in the pages which follow, is never to denigrate this or that theory, but merely to track down those (elements of) theories which are consistent with the facts adduced, and the hypotheses proposed.

In very general terms, our approach falls into the category of the "functionalist view of language". We hold, that is to say, the view that language is a purposive instrument, whose properties reflect the expressive needs of speakers within given situations. Such needs may, of course, be manifold and mixed, but we pursue the thesis here that the basic need which explains textuality is the requirement of "relevance". If a discourse/text is relevant, then it has managed to reconcile speaker-meaning with contextual-background.

From Ch. 2 onwards, the book falls into two parts. Part I is concerned with the examination of those properties of situation, language, and language-theory which are required in an explanatory theory of text as briefly delineated in the previous section. Accordingly, Ch. 2 looks at the notion of "discourse" itself, demonstrates its non-randomness, and proposes a model within which a D-grammar might conveniently operate. Ch. 3 examines the notion of context, and brings together several strands from current work in artificial intelligence, logic, and pragmatics which in our view should feed into a theory of situational context. Ch. 4 then investigates the central principle of the system, namely, the notion of connectivity, or as we subsequently term it, COHERENCE. Ch. 5, finally, confronts the principle of coherence with recent linguistic theory, based not on systems of rules, as

Bringing things into focus

in classical generative grammar, but on systems of rule-constraints.

Part II then develops and applies the version of text-grammar proposed here. Ch. 6 contains the operational core of our approach, elaborating the notion of emphasis and organising it into a systematic device for the realisation of coherence in texts. Ch. 7 presents a closer scrutiny of the most complex of the three types of emphasis, namely Contrast, looking at it both syntactically and semantically. Ch. 8 takes up the connective phenomenon of anaphora, and attempts a unified explanation in terms of coherence and emphasis. Ch. 9 does the same with phenomena of a more apparently syntactic nature, namely the so-called processes of movement in English, though concentrating on three in particular. Finally, Ch. 10 summarises our proposals, considers their implications, and outlines a programme of research to provide experimental evidence consistent with them.

NOTES TO CHAPTER ONE

1. When necessary, examples will be marked for emphasis, a technical term of this book, which will be defined later. For the time being, this marking should be understood in terms of superficial stress. Thus, *italics* = normal stress, CAPITALS = contrastive stress, and [brackets] = reduced stress. Unmarked items are either predictable (as in the case of "weak impersonals", such as <u>people</u> or pronouns), or else do not enter into the emphatic system at all. The sigil (@) means "highly improbable as a discourse-continuation", (*) means "highly improbable as an isolated instance", and either of these judgments may be tempered by one or two question-marks, as indeed may examples bearing neither (@) nor (*). We generally assume that any context supplied is itself initial, and hides no surprises.

    In general, we shall mark emphasis only as far as is necessary for the purposes at hand. Similarly for the predictable cases: from time to time, we shall explicitly mark their Reduced stress when this is relevant to the point being made.

[14]

Bringing things into focus

2. Wasow (1979: 3 sq.), discussing examples like:

    (i) *Learning that John₁ had won the race surprised him₁

    (where the subscripts indicate anaphoric reference), dismisses attempts to make them grammatical, given a suitable context. He remarks that such facts are irrelevant to the question of anaphoric relations within the sentence. This observation should be considered along with Wasow's later speculation (p.147) that anaphora is a discourse phenomenon. Thus the coreference between John and him in (i) when embedded in an appropriate context results not from a direct anaphoric relation between those two items, but from separate relationships of anaphora contracted between these items and elements of the preceding text. Cf. Kuno 1972, Bolinger 1979, Carden 1982, and the discussion in Ch. 5, fn. 7 (p. 94 below).
3. See, for example, Grimes 1975, Halliday and Hasan 1976, de Beaugrande 1980, Hoey 1983, Longacre 1983.
4. For a similar use of the term focus, cf. Yule 1979. It should be stated at this point, to clear up any possible confusion, that our present usage of these terms is rather different from our previous usage (e.g. Werth 1977, 1980a, 1980b). This is chiefly to avoid dependence on the term focus itself, since as we shall see, the best-known current usage of this term (in Chomsky 1972) confounds two quite distinct phenomena (here, Accent and Contrast).

    In our previous usage, focus was one of these (viz. Accent), but since Chomsky's examples are all of Contrast, the linguistic community at large tends to use focus to mean 'Contrast'. We therefore avoid it as an operational term in this work.

[15]

Discourse

Chapter Two

DISCOURSE

2.1 What IS a discourse?

Just as a native speaker is capable of making judgements about the acceptability (or even perhaps the "grammaticality") of sentences, so too is he capable of making judgements about the textuality of discourses. He is capable of deciding, that is to say, whether a given sequence of sentences forms a connected text, or whether it is merely a random list. This can be very easily demonstrated.

Given the following two passages, all parts of which have been taken from the front page of a British Sunday newspaper, the native speaker of English and even the minimally fluent non-native speaker can easily decide that one is continuous and the other not. (For reports on similar experiments in the recognition and production of discourse, see Hoey 1983):

1. Mr. Reagan did not offer a solution of his own. The baby was never walked out in a pram, but was always taken in a carry-cot. A police-patrol spotted him driving a car, and gave chase. The motion which the General Council agreed today will go before the TUC Congress this week, and will be overwhelmingly carried. The body is now expected to be buried in Spain.

2. Fred, the hungry alligator — bar attraction of the Mill Hotel, Alveley, Salop — is dead, having bitten in half the electric heater which warmed his six-foot tank. Hotel owner Mrs. June Hodson said: "It's quite unheard of. Now we'll have to get another baby alligator; Fred was good for business. We're going to have him stuffed

[16]

Discourse

so he's in the deep freeze at the moment".

The ability to discrimimate between connected and unconnected stretches of language is presumably fairly basic, and is closely related, we would postulate, to the ability to assess meaningfulness within sentences; or, put differently, the intrasentential connectivity between words and phrases. We will argue that connectivity at both levels — that is, both between and within sentences — is crucially semantic, and that the obvious formal links which exist are in fact the overt manifestations of semantic connections. This is, let it be said, not a view shared by all: in fact, most current approaches assume that it is the formal connections which are prior and "more strictly linguistic".

Before extending our discussion further, let us take a preliminary look at the two putative discourses in (1) and (2). We shall first examine their 'connectivity', an intuitive notion which we shall try to define subsequently. We will also observe that the situation, i.e. the physical and conceptual background, is of crucial importance. The passage of continuous discourse is, of course, (2), though we may note in passing that by some criteria it is perhaps a good deal less likely than passage (1).

Taking (2) first, then, the reader will immediately notice, perhaps unconsciously, that there is a clear thread of meaning running through the whole piece. Each sentence has an obvious topic, and the topics have a reasonably clear connection with each other. Further examination enables us to break the passage down into two sections (which we will call 1 and 2), the first consisting of a complex sentence with an interpolated appositional parenthesis, the second consisting of a quotation-introducing clause plus three sentences, two of them non-simple. (We shall number the section-parts 1-1 etc., and the thematically important items within these will be 1-1a etc.).

     3.(a) 1-1a: Fred, the alligator
             1-1b: is dead
             1-1c: having bitten...heater... tank
             1-2a: bar attraction
             1-2b: of the Mill Hotel,...
             2-1:   Hotel <= 1-2b> owner Mrs. Hodson
                   said <2-2 to 2-6>

[17]

Discourse

```
2-2:   It <= 1-1> is quite unheard of
2-3:   We  <=  1-2b>  will  have  to  get
       another alligator <i.e. than 1-1a>
2-4:   Fred <= 1-1a> was good for business
2-5:   We  <=  1-2b> are going to have him
       <= 1-1a> stuffed
2-6:   He <= 1-1a> is in the deep freeze
```

The most striking connections here are semantic in nature, forming a network of **cross-reference** in the passage. Section 1 contains a high proportion of new information, while section 2 contains a high proportion of reference back to section 1. Furthermore, as we shall shortly see, the semantic connections are not just confined to anaphoric links of the kind indicated in (3a), that is to say, broadly speaking to signals of identity. There are also important lexical and logical links, to which we will return presently.

But let us first examine passage (1) in the same way. We find a very different situation:

```
3.(b) 1:   Mr. Reagan did not offer a solution
      2-1:  The  baby was never walked out in a
            pram
      2-2:  but [the baby] was always taken in a
            carry-cot
      3-1:  A police-patrol spotted him
      3-2:  and [the patrol] gave chase
      4-1:  The General Council's motion will go
            before the TUC
      4-2:  and [the motion] will overwhelmingly
            be carried
      5:    The body is expected to be buried in
            Spain
```

Passage (2), as we have seen, contained two networks of back-reference, namely that referring to the alligator, and that referring to the hotel. Furthermore, these two items were explicitly related to each other in the opening sentence. Passage (1), on the other hand, contains only three clear cases of back-reference, all of them intrasentential and all realised by zero-anaphora (cf. Ch. 8). There is no clear topical connectivity, unlike passage (2), where all the sentences were "about" either the alligator or the hotel. For (1), though, the topics are: Mr. Reagan, a baby, a police patrol, a motion of the General Council, and a body; and although the possibility of some semantic connection between

[18]

Discourse

these items exists in principle (as we shall presently discuss), it would evidently be of a somewhat perverse and occasional nature.

Turning now to another aspect of semantic connectedness to which reference has already been made, we may examine the passages for evidence of lexical links, or **COLLOCATION**. (The term is used more or less in its Firthian sense, cf. Firth 1951, Halliday 1966, McIntosh 1961, Mitchell 1971). In order to obtain an informal picture of the word-word connections in passage (2), a type of semantic field diagram (Fig. 2.1) may be constructed, with alligator and hotel as its twin nodes.

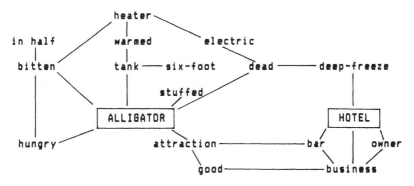

FIG.2.1

It must immediately be said that an unlabelled diagram such as Fig. 2.1 would be inadequate as a semantic notation, if that were what it was intended to be. Nevertheless, the reasons for that inadequacy are interesting in themselves, and point the way to the type of analysis that we shall subsequently be attempting. First, the relationships between the connected items in the diagram are of many different kinds. Some seem to be grammatical, in the sense that the items occur in a grammatical relationship, such as Subject-Predicate, (e.g. alligator-dead). Others are more purely semantic (such as hotel-business), while still others are situational or cultural, reflecting socio-cultural assumptions or expectations (e.g. stuffed-dead). We shall argue that these are all ultimately semantic-pragmatic.

A second reason for the inadequacy of Fig. 2.1 has to do with another property of collocation in

Discourse

the Firthian sense: over and above the semantic relationships between words just referred to, there is another type of bond which reflects the probability that certain pairs or sets of words will occur together. Most students of collocation in the tradition of Firth (such as the ones cited above) seem to have assumed that it is a relationship between pairs of words. However, it is fairly clear that most, perhaps all, high probability pairings take place within a more or less specific context, usually reflected by another word or words. In passage (2), for example, given the item <u>alligator</u>, the normal collocation expressing 'habitat' would be <u>swamp</u>, <u>river</u> etc., and one would expect to find the further context of 'tropical', or the like. However, given the alternative context of 'captivity', the collocation expressing 'habitat' will then be <u>tank</u>, with few alternative possibilities.

The network of interlocking relationships shown in Fig. 2.1 is, we claim, exhaustive for the passage, though as we have already pointed out, such diagrams cannot pretend to be more than rough indications of the relevant lexical connectivity in the text under consideration. There may, of course, exist other potential connections between lexical items, which happen not to have been selected by the producer of the given text as semantically important. For example, since the alligator was in the tank, and the alligator was also in the hotel, then the tank must also have been located in the hotel (assuming that hotels are larger than tanks). Furthermore, deep-freezes are usually electric. But these particular relationships have not been drawn in passage (2), nor do any important implications depend on them.

We may examine passage (1) for lexical connectivity in the same way; the result is shown in Fig. 2.2. Apart from the obvious lexical connections, it will be noted that there are several problematical links (marked with queried broken lines). By "problematical", we mean on the whole three types of indeterminacy. The first is **anaphoric indeterminacy**, and occurs when an anaphor (usually a pronoun) has more than one potential antecedent in preceding discourse, a situation which may easily arise in view of the limited intensional specifications of most anaphors. The second type is **descriptive indeterminacy**, when one expression may potentially function as an alternative description

[20]

for another expression. The third type, which is perhaps merely a special case of the second, is **polysemic indeterminacy**, when certain senses of two items are potentially linkable.

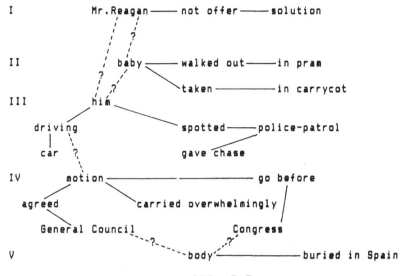

FIG. 2.2

Clearly, the only unquestionable connections occur within the "blocks" marked I-V, blocks which of course correspond exactly to the individual sentences of passage (1). The problematical links, if accepted, would have to be interpreted as metaphorical, pejorative, or otherwise marked. The reasons for this arise naturally from the Principle of Co-operation (Grice 1975).

Firstly, we may note that among the speakers of any language there exists a "drive to interpret": there is, that is to say, a strong presumption on the part of the listener/reader that any sequence of sentences of his language he encounters will in fact "make sense". If the individual sentences make sense, he will act on the assumption that they are also connected sensibly, until he is forced to accept otherwise. Thus a "climate" of interpretability encourages the listener to look for ordinary interpretations, and then extraordinary ones, before concluding that none are to be found.

Secondly, the normal devices of connectedness include **COHESION** (which we shall examine more fully

[21]

Discourse

in Ch. 4), and more specifically, **ANAPHORA**. An important property of anaphors is that semantically (i.e. intensionally) they are very non-specific: a typical pronoun will copy only the number and possibly gender of its antecedent. From the reverse point of view, therefore, any lexical item which satisfies those broad identity-conditions could potentially be the antecedent of that anaphor. This is what we have called anaphoric indeterminacy. (For a fuller account of anaphora, see Chs. 4 and 8). An example occurs in the third sentence of passage (1):

> 4. A police patrol spotted him driving a car, and gave chase

If (1) were a connected discourse, then <u>him</u> could refer to either of two possible antecedents, <u>Mr. Reagan</u> or <u>the baby</u> . The former of these fulfils the conditions of singularity (in the grammatical sense) and masculinity, while the latter is singular and could be masculine. We are therefore faced with a minor dilemma at this point: one anaphor with two possible antecedents. How do we go about reaching an interpretation? We first look around the discourse for further information which will help us to adjudicate between the possible interpretations. Information is propositional in nature, so we look at the propositions of which <u>him</u> is an element, and find two of them: *the police patrol spotted him,* and *him driving a car.* We now have to appeal to pragmatic knowledge, which informs us that practically any physical object as well as many abstract objects can be spotted (in the sense of 'perceived'), which does not help us much. However, pragmatic knowledge also tells us that of the two, Mr. Reagan is much more likely to drive a car, which enables us to reach a tentative interpretation of <u>him</u> in the third sentence of (1). Nevertheless, the reader will be very worried by the fact that there appears to be no other connection between the sentences of (1) — at the propositional level, for example.

Potential cohesive relationships of this sort, then, can apparently indicate semantic links which have in fact been forced by the indeterminacy of the pronoun. There are, moreover, other types of indeterminacy, as we have seen — for example, that brought about by **co-referring phrases**. It is a strong stylistic requirement of English, along with many other languages, that repetition should

[22]

Discourse

normally be avoided (and this may, of course, be the basic motivation for most cases of pronoun-anaphora). Yet in most discourses, the subject or topic is an item which has to be repeatedly referred to. There is, therefore, an inherent tension in discourses between the semantic need to refer to the same item continually, and the stylistic need to avoid repetition at all costs. Nevertheless, it is possible to refer to the same concept without either tedium or loss of specificity by using either (a) a virtual synonym (i.e. an alternative linguistic form having the same, or very similar, semantic structure), or else (b) a definite description (i.e. a locution referring to the same entity but in different terms). Our second and third types of indeterminacy distinguished above both fall into this functional category. Thus, Mr. Reagan might alternatively appear as one of (5a-f):

> 5. (a) President Ronald Reagan
> (b) The 40th American president
> (c) The former governor of California
> (d) The oldest American president since the War
> (e) The star of *Bedtime for Bonzo*
> (f) Mr. and Mrs. J. E. Reagan's oldest son,

and so on. Since such descriptions can make use of any attribute of the entity in question, and since any attitude to, or connotation of, the referent may independently be included, it follows that such phrases as those in (5g-k) too could equally well be descriptions of Mr. Reagan, given the appropriate time, situation, and opinion.

> 5. (g) The warmonger of Central America
> (h) The protector of democracy as we know it
> (i) That blithering idiot
> (j) The scourge of communism
> (k) The dangerous nutcase in the White House, etc., etc.

All of this is a preamble to the observation that sentences one and two of passage (1) could conceivably be linked by taking the baby to be a pejorative reference back to Mr. Reagan. Nevertheless, once again, the propositional evidence suggests otherwise: we may be reasonably confident that U.S. Presidents do not normally get carried around in either prams or carry-cots.

[23]

Discourse

Other forced intersentential lexical relationships might occur between <u>driving</u> and <u>motion</u>, and between <u>General</u> <u>Council</u>, or <u>Congress</u>, and <u>body</u>: thus, driving is a sort of motion, and a Council or Congress is a sort of body. Again, however, the propositional evidence is quite clear: <u>motion</u> in the sense of 'movement' cannot be agreed or carried; <u>body</u> in the sense of 'official group' is unlikely, except in some pejorative or metaphorical framework, to be buried.

2.2 Summary: the properties of discourse

We are by now in a position to summarise what in our view the main properties of a discourse are. Discourses contain links of reference (often, but not necessarily, realised by pronouns). We shall later (Ch. 8) talk about the phenomenon of **reference-chains** across a discourse. Discourses also contain collocational links, whereby lexical items enter into semantic fields by reason of their mutual expectancy (see also Ch. 4). Discourses also contain propositional relationships, i.e. between predicating items and nominating items (for further discussion of which, see the next section). Finally, discourses have to fit in with a relevant area of pragmatic knowledge (an extremely tricky concept which will be further discussed in Ch. 3).

It will be objected, and is of course true, that all of the properties given above as belonging to discourse, belong no less properly to sentences. Sentences may contain reference-links, collocational connections, propositional relationships, and may require pragmatic knowledge no less. But this is not surprising: sentences are a part of language too, and nobody would wish to argue that they are completely different from discourses. In fact, given that sentences (or rather, utterances) are components of discourses, it would be surprising if they did not display many of the same characteristics.

Nevertheless, discourses display all of these characteristics in a way that sentences can never, for obvious reasons, emulate: that is, across sequences of sentences. For this reason, it seems sensible to hold that these four characteristics are in fact properties of discourse — but since sentences inhere in discourses, they are also *ipso facto* properties of sentences.

[24]

Discourse

2.3 Sentences, propositions, and semantic notation

So far, we have been talking about textual study in terms of sentences: sentence-sequences, utterances, and so on. However, these constitute only one aspect of textual reality; other aspects, relevant to certain purposes, would include the phonological representation and the semantic structure. The second of these will in fact be the aspect which is relevant to our present purposes, although in Ch. 6 we will consider the claims of a surface-structure account of the phenomena we are interested in.

Each of the three levels we have mentioned may be represented in one or another notation, i.e. a method of expressing facts using symbols which are externally justifiable. Thus, phonological notation is based on phonetics, syntactic notation is ratified by mathematical principles of constituency and equivalence, and semantic notation is founded on logic tempered by conceptual considerations such as perception and belief. The twin keystones of classical logic are truth and consistency; those of the conceptual domain are perhaps comparison and contrast.

The orthodox truth-conditional semantics of philosophy in the last 100 years was developed mainly by mathematicians: Frege, Whitehead, Russell, Church, Tarski and Reichenbach, to name a few of the most eminent. Partly for this reason, this variety of semantic notation defines semantics narrowly, as being concerned only with the rules and properties governing truth-values. It is not concerned with problems of specifying sense, except insofar as it has a bearing on truth-value, nor with contextual or pragmatic factors. Truth-values in the classical theory are necessarily binary: True or False. Yet many semanticists, particularly those working with language, have for some time been arguing for a multivalent logic, with perhaps an infinity of values between 0 (False) and 1 (True) - cf. Lakoff 1972, McCawley 1981a, 1981b. Standard logic furthermore, stipulates truth-conditions: what must hold for a statement to be true, e.g:

6. John is a bachelor iff John is human & John is adult & John is male & John is unmarried.

[25]

Discourse

Each conjunct in (6) is taken to be independently verifiable, or in other words, corresponding to reality. This, together with a calculation of the effect on truth-value of conjoining with '&', allows us to compute the truth of the statement as a whole.

Straightforward though this account of sentence (6) sounds, there are nevertheless grave problems with it. Firstly, the question of verification: by what procedure must one verify the conjuncts of (6)? In real life, their predicates are, for a variety of reasons, extremely difficult to define. ADULT is a gradable adjective when used biologically, and may have different realisations of value 1 for different individuals. In its legal use, however, it is a simple binary. HUMAN must either be defined encyclopaedically as 'having two legs, such-and-such a chromosomal structure, reversible thumb, ...' etc., or else "emically" (Pike 1954) as 'non-bovine', 'non-equine', 'non-canine', ... etc. Neither of these enterprises is necessarily a finite project. MALE is seemingly for most intents and purposes a binary term, but in the real world it too, like ADULT, admits of different degrees of category membership, and has varying criteria for admission to the category. Finally, UNMARRIED may be defined according to several quite distinct and sometimes completely incompatible criteria, be they legal, religious or social.

Moreover, as if these problems were not enough, we find that the supposedly solid logical operator '&' also becomes extremely problematical when translated into the ordinary English conjunction and, since this latter can mean '& then', '& because', 'as a result of which', '& therefore', '& moreover', and probably several other possibilities too, (cf. Werth 1974 for some discussion of this). Finally, the whole statement (6) may in certain practical situations become extremely difficult to assess for truth value, even assuming the independent calculability of its conjuncts and operators. For example, what if the John of sentence (6) were John the 23rd? Popes are, of course, adult, male, human and unmarried: yet it somehow does not seem to be completely appropriate to refer to a Pope, or indeed to any Catholic priest, as a "bachelor". (The point is made in Fillmore 1975, 1982, quoted by Lakoff 1982).

In fact, there are many kinds of statements

[26]

Discourse

which are not objectively verifiable at all. The
following are quoted by O'Connor 1975:

    7.(a) Abortion is wrong
      (b) God created the world
      (c) Every even number is the sum of two
          primes.

(7a) is a value-judgement, (7b) a statement of
faith, and (7c) has not yet been proved. There are
many lexical items whose meaning embodies just such
a subjective evaluation as (7a):

    8.(a) This plant is a weed
      (b) Geoffrey is a confounded nuisance
      (c) Freddy is a hero

These all therefore lack a truth-value (which is to
say they cannot be assessed for one); however, they
clearly do not lack meaning. Then, there are many
cases of utterances in statement-form which however
are not statements:

    9.(a) I promise not to hit you
      (b) I wonder where Bill is
      (c) It would be nice if you brought some wine
      (d) I'm asking you to reconsider your
          decision.

Furthermore, there are many utterances which are
neither statements nor in statement-form:

    10.(a) Where's Bill?
       (b) Please bring some wine
       (c) Think again.

Set (9) are the performative(-type) predicates; (10)
are non-declaratives. Neither of them is susceptible
of a truth-conditional account, since "truth" is an
irrelevant assessment in their case. Consider (11),
for example:

    11. A: I wish you'd lose weight
       B: That's true.

We shall look at performatives again in Ch. 6.23.
    It seems then that there are considerable
difficulties with the standard methods of logic when
these are applied to real linguistic examples. It is
not the purpose of this book to put forward any

[27]

Discourse

proposals for logic, but it seems clear that any adequate logic of natural language will have to be multivalent ("fuzzy") and will have to work with imprecise cognitive categories (cf. Lakoff 1982).

We have been using terms like sentence and statement with regard to semantic operations. However, these may be inexplicit or misleading. We need a special term for the semantic expressions which carry meaning and which enter into our analysis. Logic has provided the term **PROPOSITION**, which is a "logical sentence" expressing a basic meaning-configuration, and consisting of a **PREDICATE** together with one or more **ARGUMENTS.** Arguments may be of several kinds: **DESIGNATORS** name individuals, and include proper nouns and singular definite descriptions; **VARIABLES** represent semantically empty argument slots, though they can be further defined in the proposition and "bound" by a quantifier; **PROPOSITIONS** may themselves be arguments in larger propositions. Predicates are verb-like, but will often correspond to an adjective, an NP, or a preposition in surface-structure. Furthermore, and this is an important point for our subsequent analysis, a surface noun or adjective, say, will contain one or more predicates, these corresponding to the semantic components of a componential analysis. It will be at the level of these predicates that our forthcoming mechanism will apply.

A fully-specified proposition is one which has the right number of arguments for its particular predicate, and of the right type (e.g. rumour requires a propositional argument). Furthermore, its arguments must be **CONSTANTS,** i.e. either designators or else quantified variables. This condition guarantees that a proposition either actually refers, or else is capable of referring. Nevertheless, we shall generally find it convenient to work with unspecified propositions, i.e. ones with unquantified variables: these are known as **propositional functions,** or PFs. In fact, our analysed examples will show that PFs represent the surface-form of many text-sentences rather adequately, in that surface-sentences are often unmarked for specification in themselves, though the specification is actually implicit in the context. This claim brings out an interesting discrepancy between logic and linguistics: among the class of designators are included the pronouns. Yet, as is well known to linguists, pronouns are often

[28]

Discourse

variables, whose specification is "filled in" by the processes of anaphora (cf. Chs. 4 and 8).

We shall actually be using the notion of 'proposition' in a way which classical logicians might frown upon. A quote from McCawley will elucidate the differences:

[I] use ...'proposition' to refer to a conceptual unit rather than to a function giving truth-conditions. To most modern logicians, a proposition is simply a function associating a truth-value to each state of affairs. Under that conception of 'proposition', any two self-contradictory sentences correspond to the same proposition: the function that associates the value 'false' to every state of affairs. As 'proposition' is used here, there are infinitely many different self-contradictory propositions, and any self-contradictory sentence can be said to express some particular self-contradictory proposition.

(McCawley 1981a: xiii)

PFs, then, denote the basic and more complex relationships of the conceptual system. The variables are empty slots awaiting complete specification, either by reference or by quantification. Yet we would argue (cf. Werth 1976: 16sq., 188) that the variables cannot be completely empty, and a fuller account would stipulate the type of semantic relationship i.e. the case-role, existing between a predicate and its several variables. However, this information has been omitted here.

Let us now complete this section by giving a semantic analysis of the propositions contained in a text-sentence. Except when completely necessary, we shall not analyse predicates below the level of the word. Predicates are thus defined as meaning-bearing elements, and are shown in capitals. Semantic predicates correspond not only to surface predicates, but to any meaning-bearing item. Non-meaning bearing elements, such as certain prepositions occasionally introduced for expository purposes, are shown in lower case. Anaphoric links are shown by bracketing the antecedent with a subscript index, this index reappearing at each point where a corresponding anaphor occurs on the surface (and zero-anaphora is counted as an

[29]

Discourse

occurrence). The same device is used for other types of head-modifier relationship, such as verb-adverb or noun-adjective; however, there is little danger of confusion in such cases. We shall, moreover, try to maintain the general syntactic structure of the surface. As an example, let us take a sentence from (2) above:

> 12. Fred, the hungry alligator, is dead, having bitten in half the electric heater which warmed his six-foot tank

(We have omitted the long parenthesis). (12) contains several propositions:

> 13. (a) Fred is dead
> (b) He was an alligator
> (c) It was (always) hungry
> (d) The cause was as follows:
> (e) He severed this thing
> (f) This was by biting
> (g) It was a heater
> (h) It was electric
> (i) It warmed something
> (j) This was his tank
> (k) It was six feet long

We can represent these separately:

> 14. (a) $<<FRED>_A <A\ -ALIVE>>_B$
> (b) $<A\ ALLIGATOR>$
> (c) $<A\ HUNGRY>$
> (d) $<B\ BECAUSE\ C>$
> (e) $<A\ SEVER\ D>_C$ (f) $<C\ by\text{-}BITING>$
> (g) $<HEATER>_D$
> (h) $<D\ ELECTRIC>$
> (i) $<D\ WARM\ E>$
> (j) $<TANK\text{-}of\text{-}A>_E$ (k) $<E\ SIX\text{-}FOOT>$

Furthermore, there is at least one chain of pragmatic presuppositions which is necessary to understand the causative link in (12):

> 15. If you touch an electric element with a sufficiently high voltage, you're likely to die
> 16. If you bite something, you touch it

Again, we can put this into exactly the same notation as (14). Instead of the standard logical

[30]

operator notation, we are using italicised English words. This should serve as an *aide-mémoire* that they are intended to have their "natural logical" values, rather than those of classical logic.

    17. *All* A: *If* <<ANIMATE>_A <A TOUCH B> <ELECTRIC-ELEMENT>_B>_C & <B HAS E> <<VOLTAGE>_D <D HIGH>>_E *Then* <C CAUSE F> <A -ALIVE>_F

    18. *All* A,B: *If* <A BITE B> *Then* <A TOUCH B>

Putting (17) and (18) together constitutes an explanation of Fred's death, and can be said to be derivable from the speakers' general knowledge in our culture.

The full expression for (12) will now look like this:

    19. <<FRED>_A <A <A HUNGRY> ALLIGATOR> <A -ALIVE>>_C <C BECAUSE D> <<A SEVER E> <<E ELECTRIC> HEATER>_E <E WARM G> <<G SIX-FOOT> TANK-of-A>_G>_D <D by-BITING> *presupposes: if* <18> *then* <17>.

We have not given (17) and (18) again in full, but have simply indicated their relationship to each other within a presupposition on (19). The examples that we actually analyse in the subsequent text will never in fact be as complex as (19), since we never analyse more than those propositions which actually contribute to the point we are making.

2.4 Sketch of a model of D-grammar

This is not the occasion to argue in detail for one text model rather than another, but in general terms, the sort of model suggested by the foregoing facts is one in which the constituent propositions (Ps) in a text are generated in series[1]:

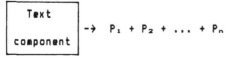

FIG. 2.3

Discourse

The connective '+' is rewritten into one of the logical or pragmatic connectives, & *(and)*, *or, if...then, implies,* etc. We will moreover propose a condition on the sequence of P's thus connected that their predicates be marked by emphasis under conditions which will emerge in Ch. 5. These essentially will operate by reference to the semantic structure of the preceding P's in the text and in the context. This proposal bears affinities with, and indeed is essentially a descendant of Van Dijk's (1972) global coherence constraint. We shall, however, try to show that the effects of coherence are farther-reaching than a mere condition of textuality.

Further questions do, of course, arise: assuming that each P in Fig. 2.3 is expanded by PS-type rules or dependency-rules etc., and then transformations, rule-constraints, relation-changing rules or the like, is each P taken to the surface or to some intermediate point before the ensuing P is dealt with, or are they somehow expanded simultaneously? In other words, is there any evidence that the coherency-relationship between Ps is necessarily at the level of phonetic realisation, surface, shallow, deep or semantic structure? Are there indeed different levels of coherence?[2] These are substantive and empirical questions which we leave for later research.

The relationship between repetition (and coherence) and stress-reduction (and emphasis) is one which is central to the thesis we will develop subsequently. The global coherence constraint of Van Dijk 1972, to which we have already referred, is the semantic circumstance whose executive machinery is that of emphasis. Emphasis, we shall be arguing, not only reflects the information deployment of the discourse, it also regulates the formal organisation of its constituent sentences. To demonstrate the truth of this claim, we shall in particular be examining the behaviour of the output of the group of rules once known as "movement transformations", (see section 1.2 above). If the transformational terminology gives rise to too many conceptual problems for the reader, it is not at all crucial. The same set of sentence-types may just as conveniently be represented as variant expressions of the same propositional structure, whose actual form has been motivated by contextual factors. We examine these contextual factors in Ch. 3, and look at their effect on syntactic structure in Ch. 9.

[32]

Discourse

2.5 Review section

Interest in the study of discourse has expanded phenomenally in the last decade. In 1976, the present author wrote that "the field of discourse is a well-, though not deeply-, ploughed one in European linguistics" (292). More or less completely ignored by American structuralists and generativists (including the present school of Chomsky), discourse-study in America by the early 70s was still a very minor interest, despite some pioneer work by Harris (1963), the tagmemic school of Pike (e.g. 1964), stratificationalists such as Cromack 1968, and "unclassical" generativists such as Lakoff (1973) and Karttunen 1971. Description and criticism of some of this work may be found in Werth 1976: 292sqq. An account of the study of discourse in the last decade (i.e. bringing Werth 1976 up to date) may be found in de Beaugrande and Dressler 1981: Ch. 2.

NOTES TO CHAPTER TWO

1. The essential nature of a text, therefore - as here presented - is a Markov series (cf. Brainerd 1976). Discontinuous texts, however, are perfectly possible, particularly in conversational discourse. Moreover, further structuring of texts, between the level of the initial state and that of P is often postulated, particularly in narrative and other literary forms (cf. Reid et al. 1968, for example). It might be, though, that in spontaneous discourse, any further structuring is determined by the subject-matter, the exigencies of turn-taking, etc.

2. For instance, it may be that certain stylistic devices affecting word-order (such as parallelism, chiasmus etc.) may be low-level re-ordering rules, not affecting the cycle or the major movement cases at all, and not, note well, conditioned by emphatic structure (though they might carry emphatic effect).

[33]

Context

Chapter Three

CONTEXT

3.1 Linguistic and extralinguistic context: competence or performance?

Most approaches to the question of context will normally make a distinction between linguistic (or verbal) context and extralinguistic (or situational) context. The notion of linguistic context is to some extent contingent upon the view that the domain of grammar is the sentence: the linguistic context is then the verbal surround of the given S which is presently under scrutiny. Small wonder, then, that linguistic context should figure not at all in a competence S-grammar, Standard Theory (ST), for example. The concept of a "given S", let alone its surrounding context, is clearly contingent upon the existence of some actual utterance (that is, some S actually in use). It obviously has no connection with making generalisations about the grammatical properties of some class *s* of Ss. If we then go on to accept the Chomskyan orthodoxy that language-in-use constitutes performance, we are forced to exclude context and its effects from the Theory of (Competence) Grammar. Otherwise, the rules of that grammar would have to cater for a potentially infinite input as well as a potentially infinite output. See Ch. 10 for some further remarks on competence and performance.

But what if there is incontrovertible evidence that those so-called competence rules ARE affected by facts of linguistic performance? Clearly, in such a case, it would no longer be possible to argue for the existence of a hermetically-sealed component of grammar answerable only to its own internal constitution (i.e. so-called "autonomous syntax"). This is precisely what we shall attempt to demonstrate in the ensuing chapters: the form of sentences is profoundly influenced by the contexts in which they are situated; the grammatical rules accounting for those sentential forms must therefore incorporate contextual information.

[34]

Context

This necessarily leads us into D-grammar. For some time now, the feeling seems to have been growing in mainstream linguistics that it is no longer feasible (if indeed it ever was) to divorce competence, narrowly defined, from performance, and to restrict one's attention only to that which can easily be formalised. As long ago as 1968, in a paper to the Linguistics Association, the present author sought to extend the current ST model to include a discourse capability, and in America in 1969, Gerald Sanders was arguing that the natural domain of grammar was not the sentence, but the discourse. Since then, the study of discourse has become almost commonplace (cf. next section).

So, assuming the necessity of D-grammar, we should now consider how to assess its adequacy as a grammar. The first point to make is that the notion of "grammaticality" applies rather uncomfortably to discourse[1]. In fact, a D-grammar is forced to operate in terms of probabilistic rather than absolute rules and judgments. Given that any sequence of sentences can probably, with a little imagination, be contextualised somehow, it would actually make more sense to assess discourses by reference to the probability of their extralinguistic contexts. Thus, the most easily acceptable discourse would be one relating to a completely standard context. The more effort that is required of the listener to find a suitable context, (assuming normal intelligence and language-experience), the lower in acceptability is the discourse.

The notion of linguistic context, too, necessarily undergoes a sea-change in a D-grammar. What is from the point of view of an S-grammar the linguistic context, is from the viewpoint of a D-grammar simply a possible output. In what follows, therefore, we shall rarely use the term 'linguistic context', but will normally substitute instead the term 'discourse'.

Let us now grasp the "performance" nettle: In an S-grammar, we do not need to know the actual lexical items chosen for a particular syntactic structure in order to be able to say something intelligent about that structure in general. In a D-grammar, by precisely the same token, we do not need to know the specific sentences making up a sequence in order to be able to say something intelligent about the sequencing of sentences in general. It is an error to suppose that one cannot

[35]

generalise about discourses, just as one can generalise about sentences. So, for example, if the meaning of any given sentence is describable in principle in an S-grammar, then so equally is the meaning of a discourse, which is made up of Ss.

But what S-grammars cannot in principle account for is the relationship between an S and its surrounding discourse. We shall be arguing that such relationships are essentially semantic, though they may manifest themselves formally (in word-order or intonation, for example).

We may now ask the question: what is the relationship between discourse and extralinguistic context (or "situation")?

3.2 Review section: context-of-utterance

Informally, we can divide the context of an utterance into three broad types:

FIG. 3.1

The notion of context in linguistics is one that is invoked more often than it is discussed. Within linguistics, it is probably fair to say that more attempts to capture the idea have been made in Britain and Europe than in America. In American anthropology and sociology, however, a considerable amount of "programmatic" discussion has taken place. The comparative neglect in American linguistics, however, is presumably another heritage of Bloomfield. Most of the attempts to provide a descriptive framework - rarely more - for situation have concerned the immediate situation (or "setting"). In linguistics, at least, (and this is evidently true of both Europe and America), very little work on the cultural assumptions underlying a language in society has ever been attempted. We do not undertake to repair these discrepancies here. The following merely reviews, and occasionally suggests, directions of study.

Context

3.21   *Immediate situation*

In Britain, J.R.Firth's outline for studying the "Context of Situation" (Firth 1950), arose out of a need first formulated in anthropology to be able to describe the situations surrounding language. Its original formulator, Bronislaw Malinowski, saw this in terms of cultural assumptions (1930: 301 sqq.). Firth's system was as follows:

> 2. A. The relevant features of participants: persons, personalities.
> (i) The verbal action of the participants.
> (ii) The non-verbal action of the participants.
>
> B. The relevant objects
>
> C. The effect of the verbal action
> (Firth 1950: see 1957: 182)

Firth's schema, though, apparently excludes cultural information, or rather, does not explicitly include it. Elsewhere, however, (e.g. 1935: see 1957: 32) he visualizes Context of Situation as embedded in the "Context of Culture".

In terms of Fig. 3.1, (2) clearly does, on the other hand, include information from the linguistic context under Ai. It also has information about the immediate situational context, i.e. A — but only if this is meant as a separate category from A(i),(ii). If A(i),(ii) are meant to be exhaustive subcategories of A, however, then the only situational information contained here concerns actions, some more of which is also included under heading C. However, the omission of the events leading up to the action is puzzling, unless they are included under Ai. These questions aside, though, the most telling problem in the schema is deciding, in a principled way, what is "relevant".

Firth's Context of Situation was transmuted and incorporated by Halliday and his associates into a theory of language functions (or rather, several related theories). Perhaps the most developed of these in practical terms is that of Sinclair and Coulthard 1975, in which discourse is a

[37]

Context

linguistic level between Grammar and Non-linguistic Organization. The exponents of discourse (and specifically class-room discourse) are, in descending order: LESSON, TRANSACTION, EXCHANGE, MOVE, ACT. These ranks are each linked to the next below through classes of the lower rank realizing structures of the higher rank. The three major acts (the lowest rank of discourse) are ELICITATION, DIRECTIVE and INFORMATIVE and they overlap to a considerable degree with the grammatical categories (realizing the rank of clause): interrogative, imperative and declarative. That the fit is not complete, however, can be seen by the common occurrence of, for example, interrogatives having a directive function. Sinclair and Coulthard therefore suggest two "intermediate areas² where distinctive choices can be postulated", (p.28): SITUATION and TACTICS. Tactics is more or less equivalent to part of what we called in section 3.1 the linguistic context, that part which deals with the "syntagmatic patterns of discourse" – though discourse surely has paradigmatic possibilities too. Situation, nevertheless, is said to include "all relevant factors in the environment, social conventions and the shared experience of the participants" (*ibid.*).

The resemblance to Firth's Context of Situation in (2) above is obvious. The difficulty, however, as Sinclair and Coulthard freely admit, is again to determine what is "relevant". Now, clearly, relevance depends upon your theory, explicit or implicit. So far, we lack a theory of situation: linguistics in this respect is today in a rather similar position to linguistics twenty-five years ago in respect of syntax. There are plenty of programmes (e.g. Slama-Cazacu 1961; Hymes 1964, 1971; Goffman 1964; Ellis 1966; Cazden 1970), some useful fragments (cf. the work on scenes, frames, etc., reported on in section 3.3), and even some taxonomic frameworks, some more comprehensive than others (e.g.Sinclair and Coulthard 1975, Halliday 1972).

But perhaps the historical similarity can help to point situational theory in the right direction. Pre-Chomskyan syntactic studies were orientated towards the description of the data: sentences, utterances, phonetic sequences, and so on. Chomsky's innovation was to show that the central mysteries of language were its acquisition and creativity and that these could not be explained without a general theory of all language. This was to allow the

[38]

Context

formulation of language-specific grammars, whose aim was to account for all and only the grammatical sentences of each language. But underlying all of these language-specific grammars was Universal Grammar, whose properties are founded on neurological characteristics of the human brain. Despite many changes in the methods, assumptions and concerns of syntactic theory over the last two decades, these fundamental aims remain unaltered. Situation study is in the pre-revelation stage now: attempts have been made to describe the data (participants, social conventions, settings etc.), with varying success, but all of this is in a theoretical vacuum.

The rest of this section, it is only fair to say, is highly speculative. If the analogy with syntactic study may be pursued, we now need a general theory of human interaction with situations, allowing the formulation of culture-specific situation-"grammars". The immediate goals of such a task would perhaps be to account for the possible components of situations in cultures, and the constraints operating on their combination. The further goal would be a Universal Situation Theory, relating human perceptions of situations and their interaction to properties of human cognition. The ultimate goal might then be to merge Universal Grammar and Universal Situation Theory into a single unified conceptual system. In view of the complexity, the infinitude and the ill-determinedness of the notion of "possible situation", it might be objected that these goals are impossible in principle. We need only point out perhaps that the widely-accepted goal of generative grammar was for many years stated as: "to account for all and only the grammatical sentences of the language". This was based on the no less complex, infinite and ill-determined notion "grammatical sentence", but was perhaps a necessary stage towards a better understanding of the units and levels involved in the task.

Perhaps our analogy will carry us further. Representing the process very simply, we can consider an S-grammar as building basic configurations and then running them through filtering rules. The function of the former is to reflect the underlying intensional relationships of the sentence, while that of the latter is to regulate its form. In just the same way, we surmise, we ought to be able to analyze situations into basic

[39]

Context

configurations of elements plus, perhaps, rules relating them to actual situations. But situational study is at an immediate disadvantage: the basic elements of syntax, whichever competing theory you favour, have been used and studied for centuries, so that they at least provide a starting point for setting up configurations. Situation has no such categories or elements ready-made — it must be the first urgent task of its study to isolate them.

Our own hypothesis (which we consider further in the next section) would be that the way in which human beings structure situations is semiotically equivalent to the way they structure language. This, in our view, does not derive from any notion of the primacy of language, but falls out because this way of dealing with externals is a fundamental characteristic of the human mind. If a universal conceptual system of the kind we have just speculated about is really possible, then it will require just such a high-level analogy as this to unify the different components. Let us consider what such an analogy might consist of.

Seiler 1970 points out that any semiotic system includes three basic notions:

> 3.(i)   categories (or: units, elements, constituents)
> (ii)   relations;
> (iii) properties (or: features).

Taking the above hypothesis one step further, then, we might apply (3) to situations with the following result:

> 4.(i)   "objects", material or abstract, discrete or complex, and including an "Ego";
> (ii)   "relations": see below;
> (iii) "predicates"; whatever is attributed to the objects

The relations might include relationships between:

> objects and space (location-direction)
> objects and time (point-frequency-duration)
> objects and modes of existence (quantification)

as well as those between objects and other objects:

[40]

Context

power (status, importance, property)
resemblance
order (pattern, class)

A special group might include possible relationships between "ego" and the other objects: perceptive, affective, moral and social relations. The "predicates" might include subdivisions of form (size, shape, structure etc.), presence or absence of mobility, (motion, growth, change) and causation. There might, further, be relations between objects and predicates: volition and manner come to mind. All of the foregoing is undoubtedly over-simple, and it is not really a proper part of the present work to develop a full-blown theory of situation. But theories of discourse clearly need a firm basis in such a theory, as do theories concerning language variety (register, "sociolect", etc.).

3.3 Frames and scenes

When we were talking about collocation (Ch. 2.1), we made the point that the situational context will usually affect the precise semantic relationships existing between lexical items in the discourse. The discourse itself at least partially reflects the situation in which it is embedded, as we have also seen. For example, within the type of style generally called "headlinese", the sequence (5) will vary in meaning (i.e. extension and, to some extent, intension, too), according to the general situation which the discourse reports.

5.   WEST'S BID FAILS

Given a discourse about international relations, <u>West</u> would normally refer to the Western world, and <u>bid</u> would probably mean 'attempt (to find a solution, say)'. A discourse about a card-game would probably entail that <u>West</u> referred to a particular position of play (i.e. to the immediate right of the dealer), and that <u>bid</u> referred to the number of tricks contracted for; while in a discourse about an auction, <u>West</u> might refer to a particular dealer or company, and <u>bid</u> to his offer. Other combinations are of course possible also.

These remarks about situation are intended to be no more than suggestive of its relevance for the

[41]

Context

study of discourse. What appears to be indicated is that situational context must figure in both the comprehension and the production of language. It should not, however, be assumed that these processes refer to situational information in the same way and at the same stage of their operation. We may assume, in fact, that situational considerations are more salient in the production-end of discourse, since in terms of its comprehension, a discourse presents itself to the listener as a finished unity. Within such a unity, furthermore, it becomes extremely difficult to separate out situational determinants from linguistic determinants.

In the last section, we referred to a number of attempts to capture the structure of situations, in order to be able to relate them iconocally or algorithmically to linguistic sequences. This work views the human handling of situations in terms of certain stereotypical arrangements: FRAMES (Minsky 1975), SCENES (Fillmore 1975), SCRIPTS (Schank and Abelson 1977), SCHEMES (Kintsch 1977), PLANS (Sussman 1973), and SCENARIOS (Sanford and Garrod 1981). These each deal with a different area of speaker-experience, from which, it is postulated, he stores a prefabricated set of expectations about that kind of experience for later re-use. Thus, frames catalogue contiguous objects in given situations: e.g. a fisherman on the bank of a river, holding a fishing-rod, a bait-tin, a landing-net, a small stool etc. Such a stereotyped list would explain, for example, the use of the definite article in:

> 6. There was a fisherman on the bank of a river setting up his equipment. He took a gentle out of the bait-tin and carefully fixed it on the hook. He flexed the rod, and when he was satisfied with his cast, he sat down on the stool and bit into a sandwich.

Scripts, on the other hand, encapsulate standard sequences of events, such as visiting the hairdresser, taking the driving-test, brushing one's teeth, or eating a meal. Each of these, in addition, incorporates a frame of typical objects. The other terms mentioned above all, in various ways, combine the two aspects of expected objects and standard events shown in frames and scripts respectively, to produce "enactments" of common, recurrent

[42]

Context

situations. Both speaker and hearer can refer to these stored routines, thus significantly reducing the strain on processing-time which would be necessary if situations had to be explicitly invoked every time they were present in the background of a discourse.

We would like to take these ideas a little further. Our first hypothesis (in line with our remarks in the previous section) is that situations are semiotically equivalent to propositions, in that they contain objects, concrete and abstract, having various states, attributes and relationships to each other and to other complexes of objects and relationships (cf. Werth 1976: 22; and section 3.4 below. See also de Beaugrande 1980: 80sq., and de Beaugrande and Dressler 1981: 95sq., for a similar, though more detailed, suggestion, also reminiscent of the classification in Roget's Thesaurus).

Our second point is that we may without loss of specificity amalgamate the above stereotypical situation-types into a single category of **SCENES**. The term is taken from Fillmore 1975, who more recently (1982), calls them 'Idealised Cognitive Models', or ICMs. Scenes will also necessarily display this semiotic equivalence, encapsulating typical situations just as propositional frames (Fillmore's case-frames) encapsulate typical "atomic" relationships — cf. Ch. 2.3 above. Furthermore, we can say that propositional frames, which are related to our PFs as a specification is related to a blueprint, are potential propositions waiting for specific use in a situation to activate them; in the same way, scenes are schematic outlines of situation-types,

> with many positions left blank...; later parts
> of the text fill in the blanks (or some of
> them, anyway), introduce new scenes, combine
> scenes through links of history or causation or
> reasoning, and so on. In other words, a person,
> in interpreting a text, mentally creates a
> partially specified world. (Fillmore 1975: 125)

Thirdly, from the chronicle of our entire experience, including the second-hand experience of education, reading, television, and so on, we build up a repertoire of scenes which embody our expectations of how different situations turn out. This repertoire is part of our conceptual system, just as the repertoires of verb-complementation or

[43]

Context

argument-structures are part of our linguistic system.

Fourthly, such scenes are activated in preference to the more painstaking construction of a discourse-specific "picture" composed of elements freshly put together for the occasion. In fact, we might speculate that it is hardly possible to compose such a picture without at least some prefabricated parts. This allows speakers and hearers alike to "pigeonhole" new experiences, thus saving valuable processing-time and energy.

The above ideas about scenes are still rather speculative, but a great deal of contributory research is going on at the present time in this general area of interest (cf. the authors cited above). Our chief concern, at the moment, however, is to put forward a plausible hypothesis as to the contents of a theory of situation. We therefore now turn to the notion of 'state-of-affairs'.

3.4 States-of-affairs

One of the problems besetting the development of a theory of situation is that people differ in their concept of what constitutes a "likely" or "unlikely" situation, or, to put it in more abstract terms, what constitutes a possible situation. Just as any theory of sentence-grammar must face the question of what a possible sentence consists of, so must a situation-theory construct a definition of "possible situation". Clearly, as soon as the matter is formulated in this way, we have to concede that each of us has his own personal experience of situations, but that there are many other experiences which we have never enjoyed at first hand, though we have every reason to believe that they do occur. Still other experiences may have actually happened to somebody else, but to us they may seem bizarre or far-fetched. Yet other sequences of events we may confidently dismiss as impossible. The notion "possible situation", then, is obviously a continuum of probability, cut across by the filter of personal experience, as respectively depicted in Figs. 3.2 and 3.3. We have shown probability in terms of percentages: in practice, however, we presume that speakers use something like a five-point scale:

[44]

Context

```
100% probable                          0% probable

<--ACTUAL----PROBABLE----POSSIBLE----UNLIKELY----IMPOSSIBLE-->
```

FIG. 3.2

```
PERSONAL EXPERIENCE
        SECONDHAND EXPERIENCE
              DISTANT HAPPENING
                     DOUBTFUL POSSIBILITY
                           IRRATIONAL EVENT  ------>
```

FIG. 3.3

The scale of probability, therefore, ranges from "not only probable, but actually existing", through "not actual, but entirely possible", and "though possible, very improbable", to "completely impossible". The scale of personal experience, on the other hand, really represents a cline of credibility: from "complete certainty", through "confident acceptance", "reluctant acceptance", and "incredulity", to "complete dismissal". Where on these scales a given event falls is thus partly a matter of evidence and partly of expectation based on personal knowledge. In fact, as we shall see, it is entirely assessed in the light of the same sort of mechanism by which the common ground is constructed (cf. the previous section on scenes, and section 3.6 below).

We have already seen in Ch. 3.1 that "situations" can be of many kinds, ranging in complexity from the state of the table in front of me as I enter this book into the word-processor, to the sociopolitical situation of Europe immediately before 1914. Furthermore, it is obvious, as Halliday and Hasan point out (1976: 21), that not every element of a situation is equally important, or even salient at all, for a particular event or discourse. So it is essential to be able to define, or at least refer to, those elements which ARE salient for a given purpose. For our present purposes, let us propose a "linguisticocentric" definition of situation: **the situation is the conceptual background of a discourse.** This background, as we have speculated in the above sections, may be

[45]

Context

considered to consist of conceptual objects (concrete and abstract, simple and complex), actions, processes, states and relationships. Since we are arguing that it is a systematic object essentially the same as a semantic structure, then it follows that it too can be expressed propositionally. Thus, to all intents and purposes, a situation is in fact equivalent to a set of propositions (cf. our earlier discussion of scene and subsequent depiction of common ground).

In any case, let us now assume that we can depict situations, including scenes, in terms of a connected set of propositions. This acknowledges that situations and texts are the same kind of objects. But what about the relationship between a text/discourse and the situation to which it relates?

A first point is that any text is related to at least two situations: it must itself necessarily occur IN some situation (let us call it w_0), as well as being ABOUT one or more situations $w_1....n$. Switching, at this point, to the terminology of Possible-World Theory[3]: w_0 (or World-zero) is what the speaker perceives of as the "actual world". "Being about" a particular world w_j means that the subject-matter of the discourse is situated in that world. The primary textual event of transmission occurs in the actual world, however that may be defined. But the subject-matter of a discourse may be about any conceivable state-of-affairs. In fact, we may regard it as one of the main functions of a discourse to set up and delimit some state-of-affairs w_j, within which each sentence is contextualised, and to the eventual depiction of which it contributes. The state-of-affairs w_j is what we shall subsequently refer to as the **COMMON GROUND**. We may think of it as a potential entity at the beginning of a discourse (perhaps in the form of a partially specified 'scene'), which gradually becomes "fleshed out" and more detailed as the discourse proceeds. The implied target of this process, however — a full description of w_j — is, of course, an idealisation. Consider the case of two old friends talking about their many shared experiences. In such a case, the common ground is not so much expressed as evoked, since for them the common memories already exist. For example, they might be talking about the South of France (= w_j in this case), and apparently apropos of nothing, one of them might say:

[46]

Context

> 7. I saw her only last week, as a matter of
>   fact

where her refers into some complex shared experience of the two speakers having to do with w_j, and evoked by that particular subject-matter. The point is that the necessary connections must exist, but perhaps only in the common consciousness of the speakers (cf. Clark and Marshall 1981 for the notion of "copresence" as a heuristic for mutual knowledge). The only check necessary is that such knowledge must be capable of specification if required; we shall assume this always to be the case.

Let us assume, therefore, that a world (or, a state-of-affairs) is a triple of situation, time and location. A situation, as we have already suggested, is a scene which consists of objects in states, relationships, processes and actions. Then, $w = s,t,l$, and $w_o = s_o,t_o,l_o$, i.e. the here-and-now situation. Any alteration in the coordinates of, say, w_o will lead to a state-of-affairs alternative to w_o. For example, a variation away from s_o (the actual situation as perceived by the speakers, under normal conditions), with t_o and l_o remaining as they are, would obviously yield a non-actual state-of-affairs. Correspondingly, keeping the situation stable, but transferring it to another time or place, will also transform it into another state-of-affairs. (See Lewis 1981 for a more careful account of a similar system).

Let us see exactly why this apparent paradox should be so. In practice, s_o might be considered identical to w_j, the common ground. In fact, this would be incorrect, although the common ground IS logically included in s_o. Moreover, since w_j is also a world, it too will consist of a triple of situation, time and location, as shown in Fig. 3.4.

$$w_o = (s_o, t_o, l_o)$$
$$\overbrace{(w_j = (s_j, t_j, l_j))}\; Included\text{-}in\; s_o$$

FIG. 3.4

This helps us to see in what way it makes sense to say that the state-of-affairs as a whole changes as soon as there is a change in one of its co-ordinates. If we consider an alternative reality in which you are reading this book now, but in a

[47]

Context

different location from where you actually are, then, from our Olympian standpoint, you would also be forced to revise your perception of s_o, since different locations are recognised as such by way of the different objects they contain, in different configurations, and so on. Similarly, if the time-coordinate is changed (so that you are now in next Wednesday, or December 20th 1830), then again s_o will be different — there will be different cars passing, or no cars, but horses and carriages, or there will be a different newspaper on the mat etc. The point is, then, that differences in time and location are perhaps only perceivable as differences in situation, even if this is only the position of the hands on the clock.

Viewed in this light, there is nothing particularly unusual or special about w_o, the actual world, except that it occupies a privileged position psychologically: it is always from this subjective basis of "reality" that we assess, and perhaps access too, other states-of-affairs[4]. Yet it is obvious that your w_o is not my w_o: they may be very close, particularly if you and I are very close, but they will never be identical. Indeed, much of the construction of the common ground in a conversation consists of a process of negotiation over what we may jointly agree is relevant in our individual versions of w_o. In addition, though, we may very well not be at all concerned to talk about what we both perceive as reality, but instead we might wish to discuss something remote from w_o — remote, that is, in time, in place, or in situation (including imaginary situations). Consider the following:

8. Who on earth is that strange man?
9. What is this dagger I see before me?
10. This chair was in the opposite corner last week
11. The winner of our super contest will receive an all-expenses-paid holiday for two in Pontefract
12. Myrtle is going to bake a cake
13. What would you do if you found £100?
14. What would you have done if Mrs. Thatcher had lost the election?
15. I dreamt I'd invented a whole new theory of grammar
16. The only interesting thing about the planet Trafalmadore was that you could find unicorn's eggs there

Context

We will confine our attention to the worlds evoked by each of (8-16), and the objects contained in each world. Each world necessarily (we will assume) has an observing speaker (S) and hearer (H); it also contains a number of objects actually referred to, each of which may activate a scene for subsequent modification.

In (8), $w_j = w_o$, at least to the extent that an image of <u>that strange man</u> is present in w_o. In such a case, though, we would say that the image (picture, film, whatever) is in w_o as a physical object, but that it also depicts a non-actual world w_i, the world of the image.

(9), in the context of Macbeth, refers to an imagined or remembered dagger, (we shall discuss the problem of **reference** in Ch. 8). For H in this case, consisting of the members of the audience "overhearing" Macbeth's soliloquy, S is referring to an object in a non-actual world w_m, a world of Macbeth's imagination.

(10) asks about an actual chair in an actual room in the w_o of the utterance, but compares the w_o state-of-affairs with a w_c, such that $w_c = s_c, t_c, l_o$ (i.e. the location remains the same, but both the time and the situation co-ordinates differ from w_o).

(11) sets up a stipulative world, a world of the near future, which is conditional upon somebody winning a particular contest. In a sense, this contest already exists in w_o: its terms and conditions, its entry-forms and its prizes have already been announced, we may surmise. In another sense, the real contest does not take place until the entries are assessed. This demonstrates that "objects" are not always finite and discrete entities. In w_w, however, the referent for the term <u>the winner</u> exists. Access between w_o and w_w is effected via a "Conditional 1" type of sentence (i.e. one with the simple present in the condition-clause, and simple future in the consequence-clause).

In (12), we have a kind of comparison between w_o and w_b, a world of Myrtle's intentions, similar to w_o except that it contains a cake, and no longer contains a number of disparate cake-ingredients.

(13) refers to a "purely conditional" world w_p, containing H, £100, and a relation between them of finding. S asks H to visualise his subsequent actions in w_p.

(14) refers to an "impossible" world w_t,

Context

similar to w_o in that it contains Mrs. Thatcher and an electorate, part of which e_1 voted for her party, and part of which e_2 voted for her rivals. However, in w_t, unlike w_o, $e_2 > e_1$. The impossibility of w_t, note, is contingent impossibility: in w_o, Mrs. Thatcher won the general election of 1983; but it could have been otherwise, and in w_t and countless other worlds it WAS otherwise! Again, H is being asked to compute his subsequent actions in w_t.

(15) introduces another kind of possible world, one much discussed in the linguistic literature, namely the world of one's dreams, w_d (to which we might compare, in terms of its accessibility, w_m in example (9) above). In such a world, the normal physical laws which apply in w_o may be suspended or modified: S may be capable of doing something completely outside his normal w_o abilities, such as flying, being another person, or inventing a new theory of grammar.

The world of example (16) is similar to that of (15) in that in a fictional world w_f, the normal laws of space and time may be suspended. Thus, w_f here (with acknowledgments to Kurt Vonnegut) contains the planet Trafalmadore and unicorn-eggs. By implication, it also contains unicorns, though apparently somewhat differently constituted from the unicorns of our mythology (i.e. the alternative fictional world w_u, in which unicorns exist and, moreover, are unmistakably mammalian).

All fiction, in fact, depicts non-actual worlds, although much mainstream fiction strives to keep its world as close to w_o as possible. Only science-fiction, perhaps, regularly exploits this trait of fictional writing, an exploitation which is carried to its extreme in the sub-genre known as science-fantasy. In science-fantasy, writers feel free to explore worlds which run on physical laws of magic rather than of science, worlds peopled by princes, demons, warlocks and goblins, and containing magic swords and potions, alongside starships and anti-gravity machines.

We wish to make the point, however, that it is not only fiction which sets up these elaborate non-actual worlds. We would claim that every discourse in fact refers to a complex world, and that for many discourses, perhaps the vast majority, it is a non-actual world, whose properties are specified gradually by the speakers as the discourse progresses. Even if the reference is strictly to w_o, the speakers are not working with w_o itself, but

[50]

Context

with a representation of it. In every case, therefore, it makes sense to talk about a **TEXT WORLD** or **WORLDS**, containing those scenes evoked by the speakers of the discourse. A text world is **the representation of the conceptual focus of the participants in a discourse.** For example, if S is discussing the contents of H's handbag, then the text world represents that physical space bounded by the fabric of H's handbag at t_o and in l_o, and containing an assortment of objects: a small mirror, a wrapped sweet, three coins, a wallet, a crowbar, a tin of Mace, etc.

Van Dijk 1977, discussing a James Hadley Chase story, describes how the text-world, the focus of attention, can change or evolve:

> 17. Clare Russell came into the Clarion office on the following morning, feeling tired and depressed. She went straight to her room, took off her hat, touched her face with a powder-puff, and sat down at her desk.
> Her mail was spread out neatly, her blotter was snowy and her inkwell was filled. But she didn't feel like work. She pushed the mail away and stared out of the window. The sun was already hot and the streets looked dusty. Fairview wanted rain badly. There was a burnt up, frowsy look about the small straggly town. (James Hadley Chase)
> (Quoted by Van Dijk 1977: 98sq.)

Van Dijk shows how the focus moves from the office-world to the desk-world to the town-world as seen through the window (an object in the office-world). He also makes the point (103) that accessibility between these worlds is effected by the text itself, as we have already suggested above. In fact, we may speculate that it is an important function of a text to keep track of all the worlds developed in it, and the relationships which hold between them. This is the function of **COHERENCE**, which we will discuss in Ch. 4.

An important spin-off of the notion of text world (suggested to me by Kitty Jacobs) is that it regulates the categories by which we group objects together into sets. The categories which are habitually recognised and discussed, even by upholders of fuzzy set theory, are rather objective

[51]

Context

constellations, certainly in their central membership (cf. Prototype Theory: Rosch 1973, 1975, 1977, 1978; Lakoff 1982). Thus, although the membership of the category <bird> may be somewhat indeterminate, and some members may be more representative than others, there is somehow no doubt as to the external viability of the category itself. Members of the category, even fuzzy ones, may be compared with each other, contrasted with each other, and the characteristics, necessary or contingent, of the category as a whole may be discussed:

18.(a) A parrot is bigger than a budgie
   (b) Birds are feathered bipeds which, typically, are capable of flight.

Such knowledge is presumably part of our conceptual system, and sentences like (18) need no contextual backup. In particular, they function well as generics. Contrast, however, the following:

19.(a) The parrot is smaller than the budgie
   (b) A parrot is smellier than a carrot
   (c) I've repainted the parrot, but the tree will last us another year.

In all of these cases, it is obvious that reference is being made not to the general category of <bird>, but to the constellation of objects in some particular text world. In (19a), the reference is presumably into the text world of a conversation between particular individuals, such that in the abnormal case of that S, the two birds are of different respective sizes than normally expected. In the text world of (19b), parrots and carrots are both members of some ad hoc set, perhaps defined from simple contiguity (since it is obvious that very few frames will contain both). In that text world, but not elsewhere, it is perfectly natural to compare carrots and parrots. The world of (19c) might be something like the props department of a pantomime company, preparing for the new season of Robinson Crusoe. In that world, parrots can not only be repainted, but they can also be congeners of such normally disparate items as trees, glass slippers, and golden eggs.

[52]

Context

3.5 The common ground

We have frequently referred in the foregoing sections to a concept which we have called the **COMMON GROUND**. Informally defined, this is the set of propositions which make up the contextual background of a particular utterance. The set includes all those propositions which have been expressed and accepted by all participants, together with the propositions composing the specific and general background knowledge which is necessary in order to participate in the discourse. A **text world,** as defined in the previous section, will obviously form part of this necessary background, while the notion of **scene,** characterised in section 3.3, helps to explain how the common ground propositions accumulate in a given discourse.

At the beginning of a discourse, we may suppose, parts of the common ground consist of rather bare patches which take shape only gradually as the discourse proceeds. In other cases, certain crucial propositions will undergo modification from the effect of fresh information added later; in extreme cases of persuasion, they may be modified into their opposites. We may expect, therefore, that there will be processes of common-ground accretion, deletion, or modification.

A crucial notion in the literature has been that of the pragmatic presupposition; the common ground is sometimes defined as the set of these operating in a particular discourse. Both of these concepts rely essentially upon the notion of context; consider for example, Karttunen 1977:

> Context X satisfies-the-presuppositions-of S, just in case the presuppositions of each of the constituent sentences in S are satisfied by the corresponding local context. (1977: 153)
> ...a conversational context, a set of logical forms, specifies what can be taken for granted in making the next speech act. What this common set of background assumptions contains depends on what has been said previously and other aspects of the communicative situation... At each step along the way... the current context satisfies the presuppositions of the next sentence that in turn increments it to a new context. (1977: 155-6)

[53]

Context

In a later paper, Karttunen and Peters 1979 are little more explicit about these "other aspects of the communicative system", and also about a process which they call "incrementation":

> Imagine a group of people in an exchange of talk. At each point in their conversation there is a set of propositions that any participant is rationally justified in taking for granted, for example, by virtue of what has been said in the conversation up to that point, what all the participants are in a position to perceive as true, whatever else they mutually know, assume and so on. This set of propositions is what we call the common ground...
> When a participant says something, thereby advancing the conversation to a new point, the new set of common presumptions reflects the change from the preceding set in terms of adjunction, replacement, or excision of propositions.
>   (1979:13-14)

Let us consider this account of contextual incrementation as suggested by Karttunen and Peters. If we regard the process of incrementation as the result of speaker and hearer negotiating for the acceptance of information (as is always claimed in ethnomethodological accounts), then there is no reason to assume that a given proposition must be either in the common ground or not. There is a third state possible, namely, "pending", in which an assertion or any entailments associated with it have been uttered – are being negotiated – but have not yet been entered into the common ground. McCawley 1979 also recognizes temporary incrementation as a device in the interpretation of both assertions containing definite descriptions and also the consequent clauses of conditionals.

We therefore regard discourses as co-operative ventures in which the participants seek to increment the commonly-accepted set of propositions by contributing further relevant propositions. The process, we suggest, goes something like this: the current speaker puts up some propositional information as a relevant contribution. The listener either accepts it (with a "back channel" feature signifying agreement, or at least compliance), or he

[54]

Context

rejects it (with a contrastive feature of contradiction, plus some propositional information justifying his rejection – if he is being co-operative, that is). The listener may go on to propose a further contribution, subject to the same constraints of relevance. We can diagrammatically represent this simplified account of a neat alternation between speakers, each one processing the successive contributions and constantly monitoring them for relevance: see Fig. 3.5.

In Fig. 3.5, A, B, C, and D are alternate speakers, each initiating a "message" of propositional information, which he has selected as being relevant to the common ground of the discourse. The hearers, in line with the Co-operative Principle, assume that the current contribution is intended to be relevant, and assess it for that property. If relevant, those propositions are incremented to (made to modify) the common ground appropriately.

Much has been written in recent years about the concept of "mutual knowledge" (cf. Kreckel 1981, Smith 1982). The common ground of a discourse consists of knowledge that is mutually known by the participants. However, it would be a mistake to equate common ground with mutual knowledge *tout court.* In fact, any pair of reasonably well-acquainted people will have mutual knowledge of a range of propositions extending well beyond the common ground of a single discourse (cf. Clark and Marshall 1981, Sperber and Wilson 1982). Even in the case of total strangers, there will be a vast mutual store of 'community knowledge' (Clark and Marshall 1981). The common ground will therefore in all cases be a subset of the mutual knowledge of the participants. To be more precise, the common ground of a discourse is that subset of the participants' mutual knowledge which is progressively activated by the propositional content of the discourse, as well as being incremented by it. The main check on this cumulative process is the requirement of **RELEVANCE,** to which we now turn.

[55]

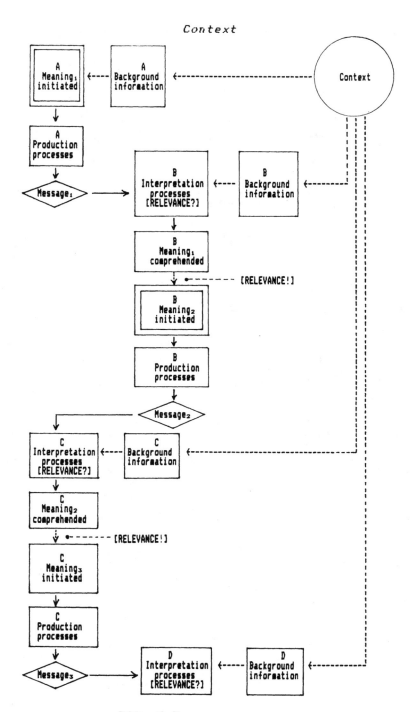

FIG. 3.5

Context

3.6 Relevance

We have come to see that the whole conception of the interrelationship between discourse and context, not to mention that between the individual utterance and its linguistic context, ultimately rests on the single criterion of **RELEVANCE**. We will now attempt to point the way forward to an understanding of this term (a fuller version of the argument appears in Werth 1981a). In its modern form, the study of the notion probably goes back to Grice 1975 (circulated 1967). Grice's "Maxim of Relation" is, succinctly enough, 'Be relevant'. However, he admitted that he found the notion "extremely difficult" to define.

Since 1967, when Grice's ideas on conversational logic were first made public, other scholars have taken up the concept of relevance and attempted to give it a more rigorous treatment within Grice's framework. We may cite in particular Wilson and Sperber 1981, who deal directly with the notion, seeing it as a relationship between the current proposition and the common ground:

> ...relevance is a relation between the proposition expressed by an utterance, on the one hand, and the set of propositions in the hearer's accessible memory on the other. (169)

In another paper, (Wilson and Sperber 1979), they describe the nature of this relationship in more detail. Given the current proposition P, there are a large number of other propositions related to P either because they entail P or because they are entailed by P; (there are also, of course, even more propositions which hold neither relation to P). Wilson and Sperber show that the P-entailed or P-entailing propositions can be ordered logically, and that the higher-ordered an entailment is, the more relevant to P it is. However, this ordering, though internally logical, is externally (pragmatically) determined by the context of utterance, i.e. the common ground. In particular, which of P's entailments are relevant to the exchange depends on which of them occur in the set of propositions in the common ground, i.e. which of them has been accepted by the interlocutors, having been asserted or entailed previously[5].

Assuming, therefore, Wilson and Sperber's

[57]

Context

definition of relevance as a relation between the current proposition and the common ground, we can begin to spell this out a little. In order to form a relationship, the two entities must be of the same order. As we have seen, this is indeed the case: both are propositional. Furthermore, the sets of propositions involved are made up of asserted propositions and entailed propositions. We will not take a stand on the question of whether these entailments are the classical logical entities, or some looser pragmatic consequence. However, judging from everything else in this area of study, the latter situation looks a lot more probable. Therefore, any relationship between the current proposition and the common ground must necessarily be a relationship based on (partial) equivalence, inclusion, implication, and perhaps a few other possible relations. But this is precisely the definition of **COHERENCE** which we shall be putting forward in Ch. 4. Relevant propositions, that is to say, are coherent propositions. Exactly what the ramifications of this view are, we shall go on to investigate in the following chapter.

NOTES TO CHAPTER THREE

1. Recent sentence-grammars, too, have been forced to consider non-deterministic rules, dialectal variations, assortments of queries and stars, etc., chiefly because of their insistence upon viewing sentences in isolation. Perhaps, though, only low-level "house-keeping" rules are fully deterministic, i.e. providing a clear distinction between "grammatical" and "ungrammatical". The higher level rules, e.g. those of the cycle, or in GB, major applications of 'Move-alpha', seem to apply unequally or spottily in different cases - cf.Ross's work on "squishes". This suggests that even they, like the rules of discourse, should be computed in terms of probability or contextualisability, rather than strict either/or grammaticality. Cf. further McCawley 1976.
2. This notion of "intermediate area" is somewhat hard to grasp. Since it appears in the context of a lack of fit between grammar and discourse, then presumably this is where Situation and Tactics have their domain. That

Context

the latter should be of concern to both grammar and discourse, and therefore in some sense intermediate between them, seems reasonable enough. However, a similar argument does not seem to apply to Situation at all, since if anything it surely ought to be subsumed under "Non-linguistic Organization".

3. Chomsky 1982a: 91 sqq. succinctly summarises the major arguments against the use of Possible World Theory as part of the semantics of natural language. We consider that the direction we take in the following pages will meet some of these objections, at least.

4. For the notion of *accessibility*, cf. the brief discussions below and in Ch. 8.2, and the useful analogy and discussion in Hughes and Cresswell 1968: 75sqq. We take Lewis's position (1973: 85sq.) that there is nothing LOGICALLY special about w_0. Rescher's (1975: 92) and Kripke's (1972: 267sqq.) objections to this position amount to the observation that there is nevertheless something PSYCHOLOGICALLY special about it, in that any w_1 is constructed from the vantage-point of w_0. Kripke holds that alternative worlds "come into being" as a function of our descriptions of them. This seems compatible with the notion of *text-world* as developed below.

5. For incisive criticisms of the Wilson-Sperber account of relevance, see Bossuyt 1981.

[59]

Connectivity

Chapter Four

CONNECTIVITY

4.1 Introduction

We have given ample evidence by now that what constitutes "well-formedness" for a discourse is not grammaticality, but **CONNECTIVITY**. This can be realised in four ways:

    (i) **COHESION** (formal connectivity)
    (ii) **COLLOCATION** (lexical connectivity)
    (iii)**CONNECTORS** (logical connectivity)
    (iv) **COHERENCE** (semantic connectivity)

We shall argue here, however, that all four of these are ultimately the same: that is, the first three are subsumed under the fourth. **Cohesion** is wholly to be accounted for by the exigences of identification and contrastivity in a discourse (for which, see Chs. 5-8), and both of these conditions are semantic. **Collocation** operates by means of semantic field links between lexical items. **Connectors** are lexical items (for example, sentence adverbials), having the function of expressing the logical relationship between successive sentences in a discourse, or between different parts of a discourse. **Coherence** therefore turns out to be an umbrella-term covering all discourse-connectivity. However, it does have its own content as a term also: an important type of coherence much discussed in the last decade is IMPLICATURE (cf. Grice 1975), the pragmatic connectivity between one utterance and another in a discourse.

4.2 Cohesion

Cohesion is usually regarded as a syntactic process of interconnecting sentences in a text, and sure enough, the effects of cohesion appear in the linguistic forms of sentences. (A typical, and classic, treatment along these lines is that of Halliday and Hasan 1976.) The linguistic forms

Connectivity

involved include pronouns, definite Noun Phrases, ellipsis and emphasis. However, when we come to examine such accounts closely, we find that they are crucially conditioned by the requirement of semantic connectivity (cf. for example, Halliday and Hasan 1976: 11sqq.). However, we should add an important proviso at this point. Semantic connectivity here, as elsewhere, is not merely a matter of a binary decision as to identity, but is much more often a question of partial identity, sloppy identity, implication, pragmatic connection, or free association between a cohesive item (an **ANAPHOR**) and an **ANTECEDENT.** Contrary to the traditional TG treatment (and even the current treatment within "Government-Binding Theory", cf. Chomsky 1981, 1982b), this antecedent is likely to be in a different sentence from the corresponding anaphor. We shall henceforth substitute for the term 'cohesion' the term **ANAPHORA,** thus overtly recognising that it is first and foremost a semantic process. We are nevertheless indebted to Halliday and Hasan 1976 for their many insights in this area which have now become commonly accepted by all working on textual semantics. We will continue now by touching on the phenomenon of anaphora, though a fuller treatment will follow in Ch. 8.

4.21 *Anaphora: a first glance*

In communicative terms, the general function of anaphora is to enable items, once mentioned, to be maintained in the active discourse. However, one of the most vexatious problems with the study of this phenomenon, is the multiplicity of subtly-different definitions of the term itself which exist in the literature. To bring some unity to our discussion, therefore, we will start with the broadest possible characterisation of the notion, moving down to more restrictive definitions favoured by this or that current school of thought.

By the broadest definition, then, anaphora is a semantic relationship between one entity (call it A), which may be linguistic or not, and another one (call it B), which has to be linguistic, such that in some text world B corresponds to A. For the notion of 'text worlds', see Ch. 3. The word correspond has been deliberately used in this broad definition for its neutrality. However, it could be taken as a shorthand equivalent of some such lengthy and complex locution as follows: "B relates to A by

[61]

Connectivity

virtue of either sense or reference (in cases where both A and B are linguistic items), or otherwise by virtue of identity between A and the reference of B". In either case, we shall see that anaphora is not a completely *sui generis* phenomenon, but rather a special case of coherence.

As is the case with broad definitions, of course, this lets in as anaphora certain arrangements which some scholars would reject. Nevertheless, we may take it as a useful starting-point from which to home in on a more workable definition. A very brief review of the literature at this point will enable us to put the matter in perspective. We may start by putting names to A and B, which in fact correspond to **antecedent** and **anaphor**, respectively.

Let us first examine, then, the varying status of A, the antecedent, from one approach to another. As it stands, our definition in its broadest form is probably subscribed to by rather few, but the work of Hankamer and Sag (e.g. 1976) perhaps comes closest. They allow for A to be either linguistic or non-linguistic, differentiating between the resulting varieties of anaphora as "syntactically-controlled" or "pragmatically-controlled", respectively. Most other current approaches, however, agree in restricting A to linguistic manifestations. For example, Lyons (1977: 659), in defining anaphora as "textual deixis", thereby limits A and B to co-occurrence in the same text: thus A is necessarily linguistic. For Halliday and Hasan (1976: 14 sqq.), there is a further restriction on the use of the term 'anaphora' itself (although as we will see immediately, this is in fact rather misleading). Like Lyons, they confine the A-B anaphoric link to the text, but in addition, in line with traditional rhetorical theory, they dub only the retrospective direction of relationship (i.e. when B follows A) "anaphora". Its prospective counterpart, they term "cataphora" (after Bühler 1934). Nevertheless, like Hankamer and Sag, they allow for an extralinguistic type of connection, where A is "out there" in the real world, and this they call "exophora", (anaphora and cataphora collectively being termed "endophora"). Their total system, therefore — which they somewhat oddly call "reference" (p.33) — is entirely compatible with our original broad definition of anaphora. (See Huddleston's (1978) review of Halliday and Hasan

[62]

Connectivity

1976 for incisive comments on some of the positions we have mentioned so far).

In mainstream generative theories, the current orthodoxy is to restrict the A-B relationship still further. All three approaches we have mentioned so far agree that A, when linguistic, may be in a different sentence from B: they countenance, that is, what is sometimes called "discourse-anaphora". Mainstream generative grammar, on the other hand, excludes discourse anaphora entirely. Not infrequently, this is claimed to be not for reasons of principle (though given the strict S-grammar orientation of most generative grammar, it is difficult to see how it could be anything else). Wasow (1979: 4), for example, remarks that intersentential anaphora is reasonably straightforward to account for, and he proposes to ignore it in the remainder of his monograph. This implies, of course, that, from the point of view of comparative complexity, discourse anaphora is considerably simpler than the sentental variety. As a consequence of this kind of view, many researchers urge a postponement of the study of discourse anaphora, arguing that it is a much more practical research strategy to take the approach of "solving" sentential anaphora first, and then letting discourse anaphora simply fall out in the final "mopping-up" operation.

In the cluster of approaches which call themselves the Revised Extended Standard Theory (REST) of generative grammar, the current stance of Chomsky 1981, 1982b, i.e. Government-Binding-Case Theory (GB), defines our A-B relationship even more restrictively. Indeed, we shall argue in Ch. 8 that it is almost defined away completely . For Chomsky, this is the relationship of "antecedent- (or A-) binding" (1981: 183 sq.), earlier "argument-binding" (1979: 12). By A-binding, B is bound to A by a syntactic condition known as "c-command" (the alphabetic progression is unintentional). Moreover, the two elements are co-indexed, i.e. they are marked as referring to the same entity. This is clearly a semantic condition similar in part to what we have distinguished as coherence. Nevertheless, Chomsky argues that co-indexation takes place either as a result of syntactic processes - notably his one remaining transformation, "Move-alpha", itself constrained by c-command too - or else is simply free. This latter possibility is to account for anaphoric elements in the wider sense, e.g.

[63]

Connectivity

pronouns, occurring in positions which are not c-commanded. Presumably, this should also include those not necessarily restricted to a single sentence, but such a possibility is hardly mentioned by Chomsky. (A partial exception to these generalisations about current work on anaphora in REST is Reinhart 1983).

The upshot of all this is that in GB the A-B relationship is necessarily sentential. "Free indexation" takes place either when A and B are in separate sentences, or else when, from a sentential point of view, B could be anaphoric to one of at least two possible A's. Thus, for Chomsky, there is no anaphora (his "binding") above the sentence. As for the term 'anaphora' itself, he restricts it still further to a small class of overtly-marked anaphors: the Reflexives, the Reciprocals, and a few idioms, such as *lose x's* way. Even in principle, therefore, he only attempts to account for a few of the possible A-B relationships. He excludes by definition several other types of referential anaphora (in particular, most pronouns and some types of zero-anaphora), as well as all non-referential anaphors. Nevertheless, we shall return to the GB account of anaphora in Ch. 8, if only because it illustrates the lower boundary of our broad definition.

This brings us to the consideration of the B element. B is universally defined as a linguistic item, but not all linguistic items, of course, are capable of being anaphors. Hinds (1978: x) lists five kinds of anaphora, depending on different manifestations of B:

(a)   pronouns
(b)   definite descriptions
(c)   epithets
(d)   zero-anaphora
(e)   repetitions

Pronouns include, presumably, not only personal pronouns, but also relative pronouns, possessive pronouns, reciprocals and reflexives, all of which display many different characteristics. Perhaps the only thing they have in common is some sort of semantic relationship with a NP. (Other pro-forms exist, of course, whose relationship is with VP or S). For (b), a **definite description** is a philosophical term meaning "NP containing a definite article in certain of its senses", and specifically,

[64]

Connectivity

its anaphoric senses (cf. Werth 1980c). **Epithets** too are definite, and they differ from definite descriptions at least on the pragmatic level, but it is not obvious that they are a fully-independent form of anaphor. **Zero-anaphors** are of several kinds: those corresponding to "gaps" left behind by various movement-rules, such as Gapping or Conjunction-Reduction; those "built-in" by Phrase Structure rules (these alternatives partly depending upon one's theoretical orientation); or in certain cases, part of the complementation selection of certain "verbs of control", (cf. Chomsky and Lasnik 1977). Recently, GB has added two new variants of zero, namely trace, though not all traces are anaphoric, (cf. Chomsky 1981: 184), and PRO. These are known collectively as "empty categories" (cf. Chomsky 1982b). **Repetitions** present no special conceptual problem. However, normally, as is also the case with epithets, their only overt anaphoric marking is reduced stress. We shall return to these varieties of anaphora in greater detail in Ch. 8. As for the question of stress — or more precisely, of **emphasis**, which underlies stress — it has not been recognised what an important role it plays both in anaphora and more generally in discourse-connectivity. The elaboration of this view of things will be the object of Ch. 6.

4.3 Collocation

Some observed facts about collocation have already been noted in Ch. 2.1. At this point, we will merely add a few general comments and demonstrate that the most important constraints on collocation are semantic in nature.

First, we must distinguish between two relevant traditions: the Firthian and the Chomskyan. The term **collocation** is itself due to Firth (see the references in Ch. 2.1), but the (neo-)Firthian tradition of study has confined itself almost exclusively to observation. The Chomskyan approach, on the other hand, examined similar data in terms of "selectional restrictions". At one time, these constituted a mechanism for marking mostly predicate items (verbs, adjectives) for their "privileges of occurrence" (to use Firth's ringing phrase). Presumably this mechanism still operates in REST, though current work on the lexicon rarely mentions

[65]

Connectivity

the phenomenon.

In ST and EST, selectional restrictions were imposed as constraints on combination (specifically, as constraints on the rule of lexical insertion), and on interpretation (by including them among the conditions governing projection rules). Chomsky himself at one time maintained, at least provisionally, (1965:75 sqq.) that these were syntactic features, but it was always perfectly clear that they were at least partly semantic, since they depended crucially upon the intensional specification of lexical items. McCawley (1971) in fact argues that they are completely semantic.

Our concern with collocation at this point is as a type of connectivity: lexical items in coherent discourse will form **"collocational chains"** which are not confined to syntactic constituents. Furthermore, the connections they evince are not necessarily semantic-logical, but frequently are pragmatic-ontological. On the whole, however, we will not attempt to maintain a distinction between semantic and pragmatic in this study. That said, nevertheless we would claim that certain basic notions of modern grammatical theory, such as constituency and anaphora, are in fact crucial in the study of collocation. Of course, as we have tried to show in the previous section, anaphora is not actually a syntactic phenomenon. Constituency, too, may turn out to be semantically-based, but we are content to continue to regard it as syntactic. We shall, however, attempt to show that many phenomena standardly regarded as syntactic are in fact based upon communicative requirements which are essentially discourse-semantic in nature (see particularly Chs. 8 and 9).

Let us consider example (2) of Ch. 2 once again. Even in such a short text, collocational chains build up: hungry, alligator, bite; bar, hotel, owner, business; alligator, dead, stuffed; alligator, tank, electric heater, warmed. These are clearly very short chains, and very restricted lexically. But even so, we can demonstrate several different directions of collocation, showing incidentally the poverty of the selectional restrictions (SRs) approach. Nevertheless, SRs constitute the only substantial theory of collocation around.

Let us take the progression alligator, dead, stuffed: for something to be stuffed (in the relevant sense) it must be dead; for something to be

Connectivity

dead, it must have been alive. SRs can at first blush handle this progression, since it involves relationships of predication:

1.(a) STUFFED   DEAD   ALLIGATOR

   +[NP BE ___]   +[NP BE ___]   ...

   [+ dead]   [+anim]   [+anim]

                                   ...

However, the syntactic connections are a little harder to make:

   (b) We're going to have him stuffed
   (c) Fred, the hungry alligator, ... is dead.

For interpretation based on S-grammar syntactic facts, and assuming that intensional meaning is handled in the lexicon, (1b) requires: (i) the embedded sequence him stuffed to be syntactically related to the S he be stuffed; (ii) the pronoun he to be anaphorically related to Fred, the hungry alligator; and (iii) the information contained in the whole S (1c) to be included syntactically in the subject of (be) stuffed (as displayed in (1a)). The first of these requirements is necessary in order to get a "readable" grammatical relationship between him and stuffed, thus enabling the SR [+dead] in (1a) to come into operation. Technically, though, there is no difficulty in relating the complement type 'have + OBJ + past participle' to a complex causative + copulative construction. The second requirement is to allow the link to be made that the entity which is going to be stuffed is the same entity which has been mentioned earlier. This enables the transfer of all information known about Fred to the pronoun anaphoric to it. The third requirement allows the selection of the information that Fred is reported to be dead, thus satisfying the SR on stuffed. It is not immediately obvious, however, that all of these processes can actually be effected in any current generative model of lexical relations. (1c) is perhaps less problematic, though even here the information carried by the appositive phrase the hungry alligator has somehow to be transferred to Fred, the actual grammatical subject of is dead. Otherwise, there is nothing to prevent "Fred" being the title of a novel or the name of a

Connectivity

house, for example, which would violate the SR. Nevertheless, (1) may in fact represent the most straightforward type of case, as far as SRs are concerned.

Consider further, however, the quite unexceptional progression: <u>bar</u>, <u>hotel</u>, <u>owner</u>, <u>business</u>. We can see the connections quite clearly: if something is a business, it has an owner; a hotel is a type of business: therefore it has an owner; hotels have bars. There are, however, at least two problems here, each of them fatal for the theory of SRs. First, these connections are of the contingent type, i.e. what we have called pragmatic-ontological. In particular, they are probabilistic, and therefore cannot be part of the intensional specification of the lexical items (bars are found elsewhere than in hotels; not all hotels have a bar). Second, the connections are not of the predicating type; even worse, they operate in syntactic constituents, but do not involve the small number of accredited grammatical relations which are posited as constraining SRs[1]. Let us look at the actual sequences:

> 2. (a) Fred...— bar attraction of the Mill Hotel...
> (b) Hotel owner Mrs June Hodson...
> (c) Fred was good for business.

(2a,b), as it happens, are again appositive (a structure found with much greater than normal frequency in journalistic prose). But notice in (2a) that <u>bar</u> is an epithet of the NP head <u>attraction</u>, while <u>hotel</u> occurs in a post-modifier phrase. In (2b), <u>hotel</u> and <u>owner</u> do co-occur in a close construction, but one cannot stipulate any SR on either, since their syntactic relationship is not predicating, nor really one of modification. The connection between <u>hotel</u> and <u>business</u> is not made in (2c), but is in fact highly contingent: we have to be able to piece together somehow that Fred was good for business because he was the bar attraction of the Mill Hotel; a hotel is a business: therefore Fred was the bar attraction of a business. The existence of a bar attraction means that lots of people get attracted to the bar; if a good many people come to the bar (in the hotel, which is a business) they spend lots of money. Customers spending lots of money is good for business: therefore Fred, by attracting spenders, was good for

[68]

Connectivity

business. Of course, the human brain can make such inferential connections in a split second; but no theory of language or thinking has yet been able to replicate this. We make no claims about presenting a fully explanatory account of collocation here; but we do suggest that an essential requirement is an intensional discourse-semantics articulated for both precise semantic (perhaps truth-conditional) specifications, and open-ended, perhaps fuzzy, pragmatic entailments of a probabilistic kind.

4.4 Connectors

There is yet a third aspect of coherence which we have hardly mentioned, namely **CONNECTION**. By this term, we mean the employment of connectors used to show intersentential relationships, i.e. in essence, propositional relationships. The logical connectors & *(and)*, *Or*, *If...Then*, *Not* and *Entails* etc. (collectively, '+' : cf. Ch. 2.4) have been extensively studied for about a century now, but nevertheless there seems to be a consensus that they are only partially relevant to natural language. The natural language connectors <u>and</u>, <u>or</u>, <u>if... then</u>, <u>not</u>, <u>only if</u>, <u>but</u>, <u>however</u>, <u>moreover</u>, <u>so</u>, <u>therefore</u>, <u>not only... but also</u>, <u>on the one hand... on the other</u>, <u>alternatively</u>, <u>nevertheless</u>, <u>despite...</u>, <u>although...</u>, and many others, appear to "contain" the logical connectors (sometimes more than one), together with other types of relator, such as causality, temporality, or concession. The last of these, in particular, would appear to involve modality, but all of them evidently require pragmatic as well as semantic specification.

Linguistic connectors such as those exemplified above fall into several broad functional categories (cf. Greenbaum 1969). As it happens, we shall have little recourse to connectors generally in what follows, but we may nevertheless note some of these categories which are more relevant to our present purposes.

A. S-connectors, such as <u>however</u>, <u>therefore</u>, <u>moreover</u>, and <u>for example</u>. These have the function of explicating the conceptual connection between different propositions, normally occurring in separate sentences.

[69]

Connectivity

3.(a) No fully-descriptive theory of language yet exists. However, we are optimistic that the present study may make some small contribution to this goal.

(b) We do not yet understand the neurological processes which underlie language. We do not even know, moreover, where in the brain these processes are located.

The pragmatic load borne by the S-connectors is considerable: however, for example, opposes some inference of the preceding proposition. In (3a), this is perhaps the implication that only fully-descriptive theories are adequate, and that nothing less should be attempted.

B. Conjunctions, such as but, and, or (co-ordinating), and although, after, and because (subordinating). Semantically, these correspond closely to the S-connectors, and most of them pair up with an equivalent from group A. The chief difference between them is syntactic: group B operates within sentences. They rarely operate between text Ss, and when they do, they are rather marked rhetorically.

4.(a) The goal may be remote, but it is as well to keep it in mind as we develop intricate specific theories and try to refine and sharpen them in detailed empirical inquiry. (Chomsky 1977a: 207)

(b) The engineer was unable to complete the repair because he had run out of the essential spare parts.

C. "Attitudinal disjuncts", such as unfortunately, of course, in fact, actually. These have a function analogous to that of performatives (cf. Ch. 6.23), in that they modify the truth-value of the proposition to which they are attached, so that it is to be interpreted relative to the speaker-attitude expressed. This implies, therefore, a multivalent ("fuzzy") logic of the kind proposed in Lakoff 1972. To group C, we should probably add "hedges" (Lakoff 1972), such as strictly speaking, technically, kind of, and broadly; "performatives" (Austin 1962), such as I

Connectivity

think, I assume, I realise, and I doubt; **"style disjuncts"** (Greenbaum 1969), such as personally, and in my opinion; and **"aspectual adjuncts"** (Greenbaum 1969), such as historically, politically speaking, and results-wise.

5.(a) Traditionally, language has always been described as the use of words in grammatical patterns. In fact, we now know that it also partakes of its social context in a very complex way.

(b) Hopefully, the next round of SALT negotiations will achieve some limited success as far as European involvement is concerned. Unfortunately, the recent action of President Reagan has done little for his credibility as a bearer of peace.

So, in (5a), the aspectual adjunct traditionally places its proposition relative to the relevant tradition. Pragmatic knowledge, including beliefs, prejudices, etc., will contribute towards the calculation of the truth-value of the stated proposition. Another factor in the calculation is the linguistic context, particularly the clues it offers about the speaker's position on the proposition he has uttered. In this case, the attitudinal disjunct in fact tells us that in the speaker's view, the traditional claim is not the complete truth.

D. D-connectors, such as firstly, in conclusion, the latter, above, on the one hand... on the other hand, to digress, etc. These have a metalinguistic function, in that they direct the reader (especially, though they also occur in spoken discourse), to the structure of the text itself.

6.(a) There are three tests for the rule of Hedge-clipping. First, the LEAF-drop parameter is a reliable indication of viability. Second, branching constraints offer some measure of control over the complexity and density of the structure. Finally, if pruning has not taken place at this level, a root transformation will provide fairly

[71]

Connectivity

> decisive evidence on the previous
> application of chopping procedures.
> (b) In conclusion, it should be pointed out
> that, as the above remarks make
> abundantly clear, Hedge-clipping is
> not something that should be
> undertaken lightly by secateurs.

To sum up this classification of connectors, therefore, we may say that groups A and B are propositional connectors, linking the content of pairs (or n-tuples) of propositions. Group C are pragmatic connectors, linking the content of a proposition or group of propositions with some aspect of the common ground or potential common ground (the "pending file", cf. Ch. 3.5). Group D are textual deictics (Lyons 1977), metalinguistically linking one part of the text structure with another or others.

4.5 Coherence

COHERENCE thus emerges as a superordinate term to which cohesion, collocation, and connection are subordinate. Collocation, as we have just seen, is essentially semantic-pragmatic in nature, rather than merely an observable idiosyncracy of lexical items, which is the Firthian view. Furthermore, not only do lexical items collocate in texts, but this is also an essential characteristic of words in any use of language, and not only in isolated linguistic booksentences (which is basically what SRs were designed to account for). So essential, indeed, is this lexical characteristic, that we represent it in terms of a constraint upon texts: all texts of more than minimal length must contain chains of lexical items bound by (partial) semantic or pragmatic similarity. But this, of course, is precisely what is covered by a coherence constraint, thus enabling us to discard the notion of collocation in favour of the wider notion of coherence.

It is also our contention, moreover, that cohesion is a semantic-pragmatic process too, albeit with syntactic effects. In this view, the function of cohesion is to link together items which share meaning (at least partially) or reference. If this is the case, then all such operations are semantic-pragmatic ones, since "sharing" in this sense is a condition on sameness of reference for

[72]

Connectivity

referring items, and complete or partial sameness of meaning otherwise. We shall be arguing, therefore, that cohesion may be handled with the rules for coherence, and specifically that the partial repetition which characterises cohesion may be handled without modification by such rules as the global coherence constraint (see next section and Ch. 5). We can therefore abandon the notion of cohesion, too, viewed as a phenomenon distinct from coherence.

Connectors, as reviewed in the previous section, are arguably manifestations of coherence too. The linking of propositional content, involved as we have argued both in textual propositions and in common ground assumptions, clearly requires connections of equivalence, implication, inclusion, temporality, causation, etc., as provided for in the notion of coherence. Accordingly, it is to this global phenomenon that we now turn.

Coherence, therefore, includes both formal and semantic connectedness. It is perhaps most obviously seen in the lexical deployment of a text, i.e. its collocation. In terms of production, successive semantic configurations will connect up with preceding ones as the discourse proceeds. In terms of reception, semantic configurations have to be inferred, and coherence may be postulated to result from scrutinising these same configurations for similarity and other kinds of relatedness. In literary studies, the coherence of a work is usually called its 'theme', and it is this which van Dijk is trying to capture by the notion of 'macro-structure' (Van Dijk 1972, 1980).

4.51 *An informal analysis*

Let us now return to the "alligator" passage (example (2) of Ch. 2), to take an informal look at its coherence. The intensional meaning of <u>alligator</u> contains the predicates LARGE, PREDATORY, SEMI-TROPICAL, AQUATIC, and REPTILE. The extension of this particular instance of the class provides further characteristics which contribute to the common ground information which we may build up and add to our cultural knowledge about alligators, and so on. Thus, at the point in the text where the word <u>alligator</u> is mentioned, we may postulate that something like the following set of propositions is available to the reader:

[73]

Connectivity

7. (a) Alligators are large (compared to newts or lizards)
   (b) Alligators are predatory
   (c) Alligators are semi-tropical
   (d) Alligators are aquatic
   (e) Alligators are reptiles
   (f) Alligators are similar to crocodiles
   (g) Alligators are found in Florida, South America...etc.
   (h) Alligators have powerful jaws, sharp teeth, etc.
   (i) Alligators may sometimes be found in captivity
   (j) This alligator was called Fred
   (k) This alligator was (chronically or especially) hungry.

Also in the common ground will be certain probabilistic inferences that can be drawn from these propositions:

7. (l) Alligators are dangerous
   (m) Alligators eat animals
   (n) Alligators kill with their teeth
   (o) Alligators need water and heat
   (p) This alligator, having a name, is probably in captivity.

Many of these propositions will subsequently be confirmed or disconfirmed as the text proceeds; others will remain unchallenged. This process (of **incrementation**, cf. Ch. 3.5) crucially depends on coherence. Let us follow some instances of this in practice.

Many of the characteristics predicated in (7) cohere with something in the subsequent context of the passage. Thus, PREDATORY coheres with <u>hungry</u>, <u>hungry</u> and SHARP TEETH with <u>bite</u>; SEMI-TROPICAL coheres with <u>heater</u>, <u>warmed</u>; AQUATIC coheres with <u>tank</u>; LARGE coheres with a measure of size, <u>six-foot</u>; REPTILE (an animal, hence living) coheres with <u>dead</u>, and <u>dead</u> coheres with <u>deep freeze</u>, <u>stuffed</u>.

This perhaps enables us to refine the notion of coherence slightly: we suggest that it refers to a complex set of semantic relationships between concepts, including (partial) synonymy, hyponymy (inclusion), and implication. Take, for example, the set of terms initiated by PREDATORY: if x is

[74]

Connectivity

predatory, then x hunts for its food; if x hunts for food, then x wants food; if x wants food, then x is hungry and wants to eat; if x wants to eat and x has food, then x will use its eating mechanism; if the eating mechanism which x has includes teeth, then x is likely to bite the food; and so on. Most of these 'if...then' pairs are, it should be noted, pragmatic assumptions which actual events might disprove (i.e. many of them are essentially probability statements). In particular, one must be wary of the switch from generic to specific, e.g. from the general definition of predator 'an x which hunts for its food', down to the specific 'if x wants food, then x is hungry'. We have handled this problem in a fuller account by generating only generic expressions and subsequently specifying them further by way of the context (cf. Werth 1980c). In the present work, however, we will on the whole have little more to say about this problem.

We have already looked at the cohesive variety of coherence (i.e. the anaphora) in this passage in Ch. 2. Just as lexical coherence (collocation) sets up collocation-chains in a text, linked as we have seen by logical and pragmatic inferences, so does similarity-coherence (anaphora) set up **reference-chains**, linking together items by inferences about probable identity.

We take coherence, therefore, to be essentially a matter of logical or pragmatic relationships between semantic-pragmatic configurations (including both semantic and pragmatic inferences). In certain circumstances of complete repetition, i.e. semantic and lexical equivalence (involving stress reduction), certain kinds of deletion and substitution take place which collectively have been studied as cohesion or anaphora. The general operation of coherence, however, (including cohesion and anaphora) is, we would suggest, rather rarely a matter of complete equivalence. Normally, it operates through inference, i.e. partial or implied semantic-pragmatic relationships. The notion of coherence was formalised to some extent in Werth 1976: section 5.2, though the model used there was essentially generative-semantic. The account which follows immediately represents our latest views on the subject.

[75]

Connectivity

4.52 *The coherence constraint*

We emerge, therefore, with a picture of coherence as a global condition on the well-formedness of texts, a picture which we will attempt to colour in later, in Ch. 5. Conditions of the type discussed by Chomsky in recent work (e.g. Specified-Subject Constraint etc.) are syntactic conditions on sentences. The constraint on coherence, however, is a semantic-pragmatic condition on texts. As we saw at the beginning of this book, it makes no sense to talk of text-grammar in the narrow sense of autonomous syntax. Instead, we should concern ourselves with the task of extending S-grammar in order to be able to adequately deal with texts. To do this, we suggest, what we need is a constraint on the possible combination of sentences, ensuring that a given sequence of Ss is not merely a randomly-generated list, but constitutes a connected succession. This is precisely the function of the coherence constraint we have been discussing. At this point, we may briefly consider what should be included in the coherence constraint, i.e. what its terms and scope should be.

Since we have argued that it scans propositional material, or rather, the semantic structures underlying propositions, for connectedness of various kinds, it must include a means of representing both the semantic structures it encounters and the connective relationships it stipulates. Secondly, since the propositional material we have spoken of derives both from utterances and from the common ground, the constraint must be able to refer to both. Thirdly, since connected PFs may be linked in a number of ways, including partial identity, implication and antonymy, the constraint must be capable of specifying positive, negative and implicit connections, and distinguishing between negative and non-existent connections. We shall present all these aspects in much greater detail in Ch. 5, and also present there our specific proposals for a constraint of the kind we have outlined.

NOTE TO CHAPTER FOUR

1. Selectional restrictions were developed out of

[76]

Connectivity

the work of J. J. Katz (Katz and Fodor 1963, Katz and Postal 1964, Katz 1966, 1972 etc.), and took their "classical" form in Chomsky 1965. They were further developed by Jackendoff 1972, as conditions on well-formedness of semantic interpretations, i.e. as properties of semantic rather than syntactic representation. McCawley 1971 presented cogent arguments in favour of a semantic origin for SRs, too. Further criticisms, in the context of a theory of metaphor, were made in Werth 1977. By this time, however, it seems that the theory of SRs had been quietly dropped, or at least shelved, since little or no work using the concept has appeared in the last decade.

[77]

Chapter Five

THEORETICAL CONSIDERATIONS: SHARPENING THE FOCUS

5.1 Constraints in general

5.11 *Review section*

The recent history of theoretical linguistics is characterised by a change in direction from rules to rule-constraints. Nevertheless, to get a generalised metatheoretical view of what this entails, we will go back to some papers written in the early seventies. G.Lakoff (1971a,1973) distinguished the following types of constraint:

- local derivational constraint
- global derivational constraint
- transderivational constraint

Given that a derivation consists of a series of labelled diagrams (trees, bracketings):

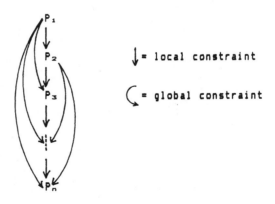

FIG. 5.1

in which P_1 represents the first or "deepest" tree, and P_n surface-structure, then each tree is related

Theoretical considerations

to its successor by means of a local derivational constraint. Global constraints,according to Lakoff, imposed on trees restrictions governed by conditions which perhaps obtained in preceding trees, other than the immediately-preceding one. These conditions were not necessarily still present at that particular point in the derivation. Local derivational constraints were simply transformational rules in a different guise: from this point of view, a transformation is a condition linking two contiguous trees in a derivation. Global constraints were always extremely controversial (cf. Brame 1977), were never really developed very far, and in any case are not relevant to our present concerns. We shall say no more about them.

Transderivational constraints, on the other hand, deserve some attention, even if only because Van Dijk 1973 regards his coherence constraint (of which ours is a descendent) as being transderivational in nature. We shall argue that this is the case only with a somewhat different definition of "transderivational" than that given by Lakoff.

According to Lakoff, transderivational constraints were

rules that apply not to individual derivations, but to classes of derivations... [for example], there are cases where the well-formedness of one derivation depends on certain properties of other related derivations (1973: 442)

The derivation-pairs which he then went on to investigate were all, however, what one might call paradigmatically-related. Their outputs, that is to say, would never co-occur, but would in fact be alternative forms. For example, he suggested that the interpretation of certain types of pronoun and zero-anaphora seemed to depend upon a condition that there would be no ambiguity in their eventual output. However, Lakoff made no real analysis of his examples, and offered no machinery or formalisation for the notion of transderivational constraint. Furthermore, as constraints they leave a great deal to be desired, since they actually release an uncalculable amount of extra power into grammatical theory, in return for benefits which remain vague and unspecific. They really represent mere further tinkering with S-grammar, when what we actually need to account for anaphora, ambiguity, presupposition

[79]

Theoretical considerations

etc. is a full theory of context[1].

Mainstream generative grammar, however, in the form of REST/GB, has made enormous strides in the ten years since Lakoff's work appeared, not all of them in the same direction. Constraints in REST/GB are "conditions upon grammars" rather than "conditions upon rules". They are concerned, that is to say, with properties of the grammar itself, rather than confining themselves to the progress of a single derivation, as before. Lakoff was talking about the process of derivation itself, and specifically the interaction of the trees resulting from the various stages of that process: he was concerned to monitor, as it were, the progression from P_1 to P_n. REST/GB, on the other hand, concerns itself with constraints on classes of rules, whose latest manifestation (Chomsky 1981: 5, 1982b) is as "subsystems of principles", such as government theory, binding theory, control theory etc. These pose conditions upon certain relationships in grammatical structure, such as head-modifier (government theory) and antecedent-anaphor (binding theory). Crucially, they are not at all concerned with successive trees, but with structural relationships in any tree. A "super-principle", invoked in many contexts (cf. Chomsky 1981: 6) is that of "c-command", w'iich we will discuss further in Ch. 8.

The coherence constraint, as we informally specified it earlier, is, unlike any of those discussed above, textual in nature: its domain of application goes beyond the single sentence. In this sense, a very different one from Lakoff's, it is transderivational. GB constraints, as we have seen, are constraints on possible structural relationships – normally syntactic, but according to Chomsky, also applying in semantic interpretation. The coherence constraint is a condition upon the semantic structure of sentence-sequences. It therefore seems to represent a third type of constraint from those discussed by Lakoff and by Chomsky. Another constraint of the same general type will be discussed in Ch. 9.

5.12 *Coherence constraints: general considerations*

A single derivation ends up, more or less, as a single sentence (including such elliptical types as short-form responses). But a text-grammar

[80]

generates not structures underlying sentences, primarily, but structures underlying sequences of sentences: see Fig. 5.2.

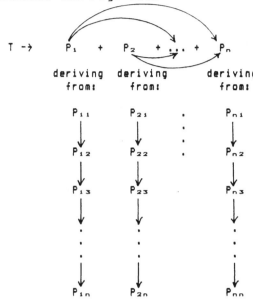

FIG. 5.2

A coherence constraint, therefore, (indicated by the plus-signs and curving arrows in Fig. 5.2), is one which imposes restrictions on a (tree in a) derivation P_k, which are governed by conditions obtaining in some previous derivation P_{k-j} (where j ⩾ 1). Depending upon the proximity of P_k and P_{k-j}, we might expect both local coherence constraints and global coherence constraints, the former (+) applying only to immediately contiguous derivations, the latter (⌢) referring a tree back to any preceding derivation. Thus the constraint on responses, which presumably normally cites only the immediately-preceding P, would be a local coherence constraint, while such processes as anaphora, sequence of tenses and semantic coherence, which are relevant both to the wider text and to the situation, would be covered by global coherence constraints. (As we have suggested in Ch.3, it seems reasonable, at least in the present state of knowledge, to take verbal and situational context to be semiotically equivalent).

Theoretical considerations

Basically, then, the principle of the coherence constraint is that preceding discourse informs subsequent discourse. Furthermore, this would apply not only in terms of antecedents for pronouns and deictics, but more crucially in terms of semantic coherence, (which includes anaphoric reference). This, we would argue, is a natural extension of the early principle in generative grammar that preceding P-markers in a single derivation should be recoverable from later P-markers, together with their derivational history (the Recoverability Principle). While the Recoverability Principle in this form is no longer applicable in current generative models (nor was it ever precisely formulated), it seems clear that Trace Theory and certain of the subsystems of principles in GB, such as binding theory, are intended to perform much the same function.

The important distinction between coherence constraints, as diagrammed in Fig. 5.2, and transderivational constraints, as proposed in Lakoff 1973, should be stated again. Lakoff's constraints are paradigmatic, i.e. they operate across alternative derivations having (for example) the same surface structure, or same phonetic realisation. Coherence constraints are necessarily syntagmatic, applying to derivations in a connected sequence. An example of the latter is given in Van Dijk (1972:128 sq.) as a "global coherence constraint on the derivation of sequences", imposing a condition for "partial identity (e.g. by inclusion, membership, equivalence) of subtrees", quoted here (but substituting different letter-symbols). In Fig. 5.3, a,b,c are "abstract semantic terminal subtrees", at least one of which bears one of the contextual relations (equivalence, inclusion, membership — though there are certainly others) to d, which is a subtree of P_i, which precedes P in the discourse.

P → ...

X → a

                        (R 'Equivalent-to')

Y → b   (R 'Included-in')   ⟨d ⟨Included-in

                        (R 'Member-of') P_i⟩, __⟩

Z → c

FIG. 5.3

Theoretical considerations

This guarantees, then, that every sentence in a discourse will bear some sort of logical implicational relationship with some other sentence in the discourse. Coherence, in other words, is a function of recurrent semantic relationships across a connected sequence (though as we have already shown, such relationships are not only those of standard logical inference, but are also encyclopaedic and pragmatic).

Essentially, then, such constraints work across sequences of connected derivations, and are not of the type investigated by Lakoff, which scan alternative derivations at the "same" point for possible ambiguities. Nevertheless, in a later paper, Van Dijk 1973 accepts Lakoff's term as appropriate to his coherence constraint. We would argue, though, that coherence constraints are not transderivational in the narrow sense investigated by Lakoff, but are transderivational in a wider sense which his informal definition seems to allow, and constitute, in fact, a more useful application of the term[2].

It will be our contention, in the following sections, that the operative mechanism of Fig. 5.3 (or something very like it) is actually the process of **emphasis**, which we will characterise in greater detail in Chapter 6. Thus, approximately speaking, where Fig. 5.3 applies only in certain ways (excluding identity), those subtrees will remain A; where Fig. 5.13 applies to mark complete or partial identity, the subtree will be marked R; and where Fig. 5.3 applies as for R, but in the area of a self-negation, the subtree will be marked C. Most anaphors will end up as R, though it is possible for them to be stressed under the conditions for C. This is, of course, a very rough approximation of the application of this constraint, but both the constraint and its application will be sharpened up in the subsequent sections.

5.2 Positive coherence and synonymy

As we suggested in Ch.1 above, Reduction is governed by what we may loosely call "repetition". In actual fact, this is synonymy of varying degrees and domains. In Chomsky 1975, there appears the suggestion that synonymy may be, at least for the sake of argument, considered as a semantic primitive term, though no definite proposals to this effect

[83]

Theoretical considerations

are made there. The career of the notion of synonymy in recent linguistics has been somewhat chequered, but we can perhaps summarise it by saying that the use of synonymy as a heuristic for linguistic relatedness has steadily been increasing over the quarter-century of generative grammar (see Werth 1976 for detailed arguments). In fact, judgments of synonymy seem to be challenging judgments of grammaticality as the major heuristic device of linguistic research (but see Bolinger 1977, and Soames and Perlmutter 1979: 533sq., for caveats on this trend). It would, therefore, seem rather important to arrive at some sort of characterisation of the notion.

If Chomsky's tentative inclusion of synonymy among the primitives of semantics is correct, this would remove its definition and characterisation from linguistic theory into linguistic metatheory (although this is seemingly often an excuse to postpone such definitions, perhaps indefinitely). Nevertheless, some sort of definition of the term would appear to be not only desirable, but also feasible, at least for our present purposes.

But first, let us remove a traditional red herring of great venerability: the denial that full synonymy exists at all. This argument takes such pairs as <u>freedom</u> and <u>liberty</u> and points out (i) that they differ in connotation (the former being perhaps more "homely", the latter more "formal"), and (ii) that they differ in use (there are no such phrases as *<u>freedom bodice</u>, or *<u>liberty fighter</u>, for example).

There are two points that need to be made about such arguments. First, they are always confined to lexical, non-syntactic, synonymy, i.e. synonymous lexical items, rather than synonymous sentences. Yet accepting synonymy in sentences is surely much less problematical (but see Bolinger 1977: 17):

1. (a) John picked up a pound
   (b) John picked a pound up

There seems to be no argument from connotation, and the argument from use is confined to questions of emphasis (which we will examine in Chapter 9). Furthermore, from a semantic point of view, lexical items, as is argued in Werth 1976: 219sqq., are fairly superficial labels for complexes of semantic material.

[84]

Theoretical considerations

Therefore, the question of synonymy of lexical items reduces to that of the synonymy of the semantic complexes underlying them; and since these are complex items, with internal structure, the possibility of partial synonymy arises — a possibility difficult to account for with unanalysable lexical items. Much the same is true of compounds such as <u>liberty bodice</u>: which of a set of putative synonyms is used in a compound seems purely fortuitous, a product of cultural rather than linguistic processes. Thus there seems to be no reason why <u>liberty</u> should have been chosen in <u>liberty bodice</u> and <u>freedom</u> in <u>freedom fighter</u>: they are merely the traditional locutions. But it is also this very fortuitousness which lends weight to the claim that lexical items are mere labels.

The second point is a generalisation of some arguments made by Lakoff in his 1975 paper regarding the domain of satisfaction (i.e. truth or felicity) in a model. He makes the point that satisfaction is statable only at the underlying level of semantic structure. This argument would appear to extend without difficulty to the relation of synonymy (and perhaps to all other semantic relations too). Thus, if synonymy applies only at the underlying semantic structure level, then it makes no sense to ask whether surface items (whether lexical or sentential) are synonymous. Furthermore, a point we have already made, this allows the possibility of partial synonymy (e.g. semantic field, or set, relationships), and synonymy of entailments. It is not indeed even clear that lexical items can claim to have entailments, whereas in the case of full semantic structures there is no dispute on this question.

We will define synonymy, then, in terms of PFs. To the extent that the semantic specifications of two items in a discourse context contain identical PFs, then to that extent the two items are synonymous. Remember that the semantic specification of a linguistic item may be a complex of many propositions, both asserted and entailed. Thus the sharing of only one underlying PF may give only a very low degree of synonymity. Conversely, if the discourse context, and specifically the common ground, shows that two occurrences of the "same" item, (i.e. two items having almost all their PFs in common) in fact refer to different entities, or use different "levels" of reference, then no amount of PF identity will make such items synonymous.

[85]

Theoretical considerations

2. (a) The Inspector of Taxes wrote, threatening me with legal action. I received an official letter only yesterday
   (b) There were two cops by the exit, two cops patrolling the front lobby, and two cops outside the main entrance. They must have been expecting trouble
   (c) The ox fell into a well. The bubble burst as soon as it was pricked. We sought for him in vain. I felt very sorry when I heard that. He meant everything that he said. (Nesfield 1918: 74)
   (d) He's so obliging. You ask him for a chair, he brings you a chair. You tell him you fancy a pizza, he goes and gets you a pizza.

In the brief text (2a), the two sentences presumably contain shared PFs at some level, assuming that the common ground allows us to infer that the official letter was the object written by the Inspector of Taxes. In that case, there is some common entailment structure to the effect that the set of written things includes letters, and that Inspectors of Taxes are official people. Along with these, of course, there are a good many more which are not shared. However, to the extent that these two sentences in this discourse share PFs (let us say two PFs out of twenty), then to that extent the two sentences are synonymous (i.e. 10% – though the quantities are, of course, entirely spurious). In practice, we shall not refer to this low level of synonymy much. It may have a surface effect in the form of Reduction on <u>official letter</u>, but the degree of synonymity in this case is perhaps too low to compel such marking.

(2b) shows the obvious case where complete intensional identity nevertheless fails to provide synonymy. We may assume that each constabular duo lacks any referential link with the others. This information is provided contextually, by locating the three pairs in different places at the same time. Nevertheless, the identity of sense apparently provides enough synonymy to allow, though not compel, Reduction on [cops].

(2c) is in fact rather similar in a way to (2b), except that there is no embracing common ground within which identical forms could be judged as referentially identical or not. It is therefore

Theoretical considerations

precisely equivalent to example (1) in Ch. 2, and also to similar examples in the literature, showing that coherence is not a matter of mere sameness of sense (cf. Enkvist 1978: 110sq., Dascal and Katriel 1979: 205, Hobbs 1979: 67). Thus the difference between (2c) and (2b) is in fact crucial: it is in the text-world(s) created by a coherent discourse that an act of reference takes place. Synonymy is therefore intimately bound up with textual coherence, and particularly the text-world(s) created in the common ground.

(2d), finally, shows another case of partial synonymy. The first occurrence of a chair is non-referential: it means 'any member of the set {chair}'. However, for the object of verbs like want, ask for and fancy, there is no necessary entailment of existence. The second occurrence may refer to a specific chair (particularly in the past tense, cf. Werth 1980c: 278sqq.), or it may itself be non-referential too, since the present tense often gives a habitual meaning. However, even when non-referential, it has an entailment of existence: that is to say, we are guaranteed that on any occasion when the bringing of a chair or of a pizza take place, there will be an existing chair or pizza. Thus the two occurrences of a chair can never be fully synonymous; yet these various non-referential uses apparently share enough meaning to compel Reduction most of the time, and even to allow pronominal forms occasionally:

> (e) ... and he brings me it. ... and he goes and gets me it.

5.3 Negative coherence and antonymy

We have already suggested that the semantic relation of antonymy is founded on that of synonymy, though the former is more complex at least to the extent of containing an extra negative operator. Lyons 1977: 286 makes a similar point: "Oppositions are drawn along some dimension of similarity" — within which, one or more properties are converse. Here, in a nutshell, we find the basic properties of antonymy which give **Contrastive** coherence its special character: similarity and negativity.

Lyons' account (1977: Ch. 9.1-3) is one of the fullest in the literature[3]. He draws a large number of distinctions within what is normally covered by

[87]

Theoretical considerations

the term 'antonymy':

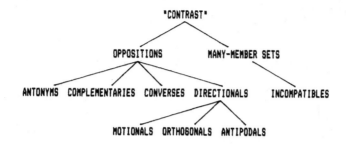

FIG. 5.4

Of these, it should be mentioned that Lyons does not use 'many-member set' as a technical term, and that he does not use the term 'motional', though this is an important property of the type that appears at this point (pp. 281-2). Note, too, that the term 'antonym' itself is not used as superordinate (instead, he uses 'contrast'), but is reserved for a hyponymic sense[4] corresponding to the more widely-used expression 'gradable opposition' (cf.Kempson 1977: 84-85). Leech (1974:108 sqq.) uses the term 'polar opposition'.

We shall confine ourselves here to a brief description and exemplification of Lyons' terminal terms: for full discussion, the reader is, of course, referred to Lyons' own account. **Antonyms**, as noted, are gradable oppositions, where negation of one term does not necessarily imply the assertion of its opposite: somebody who is not old is not necessarily young. **Complementaries** (called 'binary' oppositions by Kempson and Leech), are ungradable oppositions, such that the negation of one term does necessarily imply the assertion of its opposite[5]: if somebody is not dead, then he must be alive. **Converses** are two-place relations, which are systematically equivalent to each other if their pairs of variables are inverted: R is the converse of R' *iff* R <x,y> *Entails* R' <y,x>. So if Matilda is Monty's wife, then Monty is Matilda's husband. **Motional oppositions** are directional oppositions[6] which impute motion with respect to some given location, which may coincide with the speaker's position as in the case of come *vs.* go , but need not, as in arrive *vs.* depart. **Orthogonals** are

[88]

Theoretical considerations

oppositions between pairs of members of sets, which may be regarded as "oblique". The most typical examples given are those between, say, north and east , or north and west , but others given by Lyons include man and woman , and man and boy . **Antipodals** occur within the same sets as orthogonals, but involve the diametrical oppositions (north *vs.* south , man *vs.* girl). **Incompatibles,** finally, like the binary complementaries, are mutually exclusive items, occurring, however, in multiple rather than binary sets. Examples are Saturday , Sunday ,...Friday , or red , blue , yellow ... They may be ordered, either serially (e.g. examination results) or cyclically (e.g. days of the week), or unordered (e.g.hand-tools, items of furniture, or containers).

The common notion of antonymy, or oppositeness, then, covers a large number of different relationships. "Full" antonymy, however, is not a useful, or even feasible, relation. It is not, for instance, the counterpart of full synonymy, since complete dissimilarity of meaning is, needless to say, no relationship at all. All antonymy, then, involves only the partial contrast of semantic structure, and by the same token, it involves partial synonymy also.

5.4 The coherence constraint: precise formulation

We take coherence, then, to be essentially a matter of a relationship between semantic-pragmatic configurations (including both semantic and pragmatic entailments). In certain circumstances of complete repetition (involving stress reduction), certain kinds of deletion and substitution take place. The general operation of coherence, however, is often, as we have suggested, a matter of partial rather than complete repetition, i.e. repetition of partial rather than entire semantic-pragmatic specifications (although the distinction is not always easy to maintain). Moreover, other semantic relationships than repetition (equivalence) are frequent.

As we said in Ch. 5.21, Van Dijk's 1972 global coherence constraint provides a valuable formulation of the kind of approach we want to make. Nevertheless, it will be necessary to reformulate the constraint for three reasons: (i) in order to accommodate more possible textual relationships than

[89]

Theoretical considerations

the three included by van Dijk; (ii) in order to be able to state the constraint in both a positive and a negative form, so as to include both synonymy (Reduction) and antonymy (Contrast); and (iii) in order to include some specific reference to the common ground as a condition of coherence.

What van Dijk's constraint stipulated, in effect, was that every P in a text must relate part of its semantic-pragmatic specification to that of some previous P in the text. In order to allow a large, possibly open-ended, set of such relationships, van Dijk's constraint (Fig. 5.3) can be recouched in the form of a postulate:

> 3.(a) *All* P: *Exists* a <a *Included-in* P>, *If* <*Exists* P_1 <<P_1 *Precedes* P> & < Exists d <d *Included-in* P_1 >>>> *Then* F <a, d>
>
> "For all P, having some a as a proper part, and with some preceding P_1, having some d as a proper part, then a bears a semantic or pragmatic relationship to d, (where P and P_1 are text-propositions and their entailments)".

(3a) is more or less the same as Van Dijk's constraint, except that the meaning relationships between a and d are generalised here. However, in line with our previous discussion, we can probably simplify this without loss of power, while still managing to include the features which we felt were lacking in the original:

> (b) *All* a: *Exists* d <D <d, a> & F <a, d>>

Here, a is a PF, d is the common ground, made up of PFs deriving from both previous discourse and situational context, and again F is any semantic or pragmatic function. The function D ("same discourse") replaces the expression (P_1 *Precedes* P) in (3a). (3b) stipulates, then, that for any PF there is a PF in the common ground to which it is related semantically or pragmatically[7].

In this form, we can now see that our previous remarks on synonymy and antonymy, bearing respectively on Reduction and Contrast, boil down to special cases of the coherence postulate (3b). The Reduction constraint, which requires repetition of semantic-pragmatic structure, or what may be called

[90]

Theoretical considerations

'positive identity coherence', is straightforwardly a case of (3b):

>   4. *All   x,y: If   R   <x, y>, Then   D <x, y> & <<Exists   z <z Included-in   x>   &   <z Included-in   y>> Or If   F <x> Then   F <y>*
>
>   "If   x Reduces y, then they are in the same discourse and either there is an element   z common   to   both   of   them,   or   there is a function   F   which   they   share implicationally".

D here is identical to the function D in (3b). The stipulations on x, y, and z are equivalent to the expression F (a,d) in (3).

The Contrast constraint requires denial of some previous semantic-pragmatic element: we may therefore call it "negative coherence":

>   5. *All   x,y: If   C   <x,   y> Then   D <x, y> & <Exists   z <z Included-in   x>   &   <z Included-in   y>> & Exists   w, If F<x> Then F<w> & If F<y> Then   -F<w>*
>
>   "If   x   contrasts   with y, then they are in the same discourse, and there is an element z common to both of them, and an element w, such   that   x   shares   an   implicational function with w, but y denies it".

Again, the function D is the "same discourse" function of (3), while the stipulations involving w, x, y, and z are covered by F (a,d) in (3), assuming that a negative F is also an F.

The notion of "same discourse" includes not only the verbal discourse which has gone before, but also the common ground, as defined in Ch. 3.5. Furthermore, as we saw in Ch. 3.4, this will also include worlds accessible to each other, to allow for the frequent possibility of displaced or speculative subject-matter.

(4) and (5) as they stand are **interpretive constraints**, i.e. they allow the hearer to infer contextual connections from the observed fact of Reduction or Contrast. It should be said, however, that neither Reduction nor Contrast are necessarily ever clearly observable facts (see Ch. 6.2). The actual behaviour of hearers in these cases involves not   identification   (a   binary   activity),   but

[91]

Theoretical considerations

hypothesis-testing (a multivalent activity). The actual application of (4) and (5) we may postulate, therefore, involves the formation of a hypothesis that y is Reduced or Contrastive, the testing of constraints (4) or (5) in context, to see if such a hypothesis makes sense or not, and the eventual acceptance or rejection of the various possible relationships.

If, though, we move the notation 'R <x, y> Then' or 'C <x, y> Then' to the end of (4) and (5), respectively, and invert *'Then'* with the PF in both cases, what we now have is a **production constraint.** (4'), the complementary of (4), will now read:

> 4'. "for any pair of semantic constituents in the same common ground, if they have either some PF in common, or share some implication, then one Reduces the other".

Thus (4') also is a version of (3), and assuming the nondirectionality of the latter, there is no formal distinction between (4) and (4'), though there may well be important processing differences. By the same token, there is no formal distinction between (5) and its reverse (5'). However, (5) and (5') seem to be antonyms (in the narrow sense, cf. section 5.3), in that they do not have an excluded middle. It is not necessarily the case that anything fulfilling the condition for Contrast will necessarily be Contrastive. However, given our earlier speculation that the actual application of these Contrasts is in terms of hypothesis-testing, the production constraint will simply initiate the hypothesis-testing procedure but in this case in respect of the intentions (plans, goals) of the speaker.

At this point, by way of summary, let us give concise ordinary-language definitions of our important terms:

COMMON GROUND: That world, or series of worlds, which includes all objects, events, states, and relationships necessary to comprehend a given discourse.

WORLD: A state-of-affairs, real, imaginary, or stipulated, consisting of a triple of situation, time, and location. The situation includes objects, events, states, and relationships which may themselves be complex combinations of the same

[92]

Theoretical considerations

elements.

COHERENCE: For any proposition in a given discourse, there is a proposition, or set of propositions, in the common ground, to which it is related by way of equivalence, implication, inclusion, entailment. These relationships may be logical or pragmatic.

ANAPHORA: Two elements, A (the antecedent) and B (the anaphor), are anaphorically linked if (i) they occur in the same common ground, and (ii) in the world defined by that common ground, they are either fully identical, or else partially identical in terms specified by either synecdoche, set-theoretical relationships (set, subset, member), or pragmatic implications.

IDENTITY: Two elements, A and B, are fully identical in some world if in that world they pragmatically entail each other.
Two elements, A and B, are partially identical in some world if in that world at least some of the pragmatic entailments of B are also entailments of A.

Assuming that all of this is correct and that it actually works, where are we? We have a way of relating the semantic-pragmatic level of discourse to surface-level facts of stress and intonation in a connected text. But we still need to know exactly how this machinery operates. This we will now go on to discover in the next chapter.

NOTES TO CHAPTER FIVE

1. See Kuno 1976, 1978, suggesting that a transderivational constraint on Gapping, proposed by Hankamer 1973, is in fact better handled by discourse constraints. Cf., however, the extensive discussion in Neijt 1980.
2. In a later paper, in fact, Lakoff seems to assume that transderivational constraints are essentially contextual rather than selectional:

   "Transderivational rules are constraints that specify which derivations are well-formed with respect to which contexts

Theoretical considerations

and which conveyed meanings". (1975: 274)

However, he still provides no analysed examples.

3. But cf. also Leech 1974: Ch. 6, Cruse 1976, Kempson 1977: 84-7, Lehrer and Lehrer 1982.

4. Cruse 1976 uses 'antonym' in this sense without further discussion.

5. Saving a certain fuzziness in the real world, which both Lyons 1977: 278-9, and Leech 1974: 106-7 note. However, they contend that the language system behaves AS IF these terms were mutually exclusive.

6. Lyons' 'directional oppositions' seem largely, if not completely, to correspond to Leech's 'relative hierarchy' oppositions (Leech 1974: 110 sqq.).

7. The coherence constraint as represented in (3b), then, is neutral on the question of Forwards-Only pronominalisation vs. Backwards pronominalisation (Kuno 1972, Carden 1982). Nevertheless, we feel that Kuno is essentially correct in his support of the discourse-reference explanation for apparent cases of Backwards anaphora in sentences – though neither his arguments nor Carden's counter-arguments (which are powerful ones) take account of the notion of common ground. (Bolinger 1979 is, as always, particularly insightful on the effect of previous knowledge upon the interpretation of pronouns). Carden, however, looks only for ACTUAL previous mention, but not previous implication. He accepts the marked stylistic use of "Withheld antecedent" as a special case, but finds other uses which from his viewpoint cannot be explained away. Notice that our TCA constraint (Ch. 9), in conjunction with the coherence constraint, predicts apparent Backwards anaphora, given (a) occurrence of an antecedent in the common ground, i.e. including not only the verbal, but also the conceptual context, and (b) the occurrence of the anaphor in an otherwise wholly anaphoric constituent, with the apparent Forwards antecedent occurring in a (mainly) non-anaphoric constituent.

[94]

Emphasis

Chapter Six

EMPHASIS

6.1 Emphasis-placement: an illustration

We shall argue that the role of discourse in syntax is much more intimate than current approaches (even those that utilise the notion) suggest.
As we have argued elsewhere, (Werth 1976, 1977, 1979, 1980a, 1981a), text-function motivates and relates many rules which in an S-grammar insensitive to it have to be regarded as separate and ad hoc. The machinery which we propose to carry out this function allocates **ACCENT, CONTRAST** and **REDUCTION** (collectively **EMPHASIS**) in response to the cumulative exigencies of the discourse. By this means, the progression of information and repetition is able to be presented to (cf. Hetzron 1975) and decoded by the listener in a comprehensible form. Accent (**A**) marks new or revived information[1] as prominent; Contrast (**C**) on an item implicitly makes it deny some other item in the discourse (which must be semantically or pragmatically linked with it); while Reduction (**R**) occurs on repeated semantic material. In their most straightforward form, these emerge into surface as variations in stress (not necessarily distinct from each other):

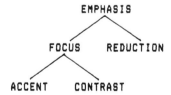

FIG. 6.1

However, R and C are often bound up with pronominalisation and other forms of anaphora, which as we will see will turn out to be rather important.

Emphasis

These distinctions can be illustrated quite briefly: the following is from a recorded conversation (for notation conventions, notes on intonation etc., see fn. 2):

1. A: This (1) *whole* (2) *topic* of a (3) *day* in the (4) *country*, or (5) LIFE in the (6) [country] I should say, is (7) *perhaps* a very (8) ENGLISH thing to (9) *talk* about because we are (10) *such* an (11) *urban* (12) *community* that we (13) *think* of it as (14) *important* and an (15) *event* when we (16) *go* to the (17) [country]. This might (18) NOT be so in (19) AUSTRALIA, for (20) *example*?
   B: (21) [No], I think (22) WE (23) *tend* to (24) [go] to the (25) [country] just to (26) [go] (27) SOMEWHERE. We don't (28) [go] (29) *out* just to (30) *look* at the (31) *birds* or anything like (32) *this*, unless it's in a (33) NATIONAL PARK (34) [district].
   A: You (35) *pass* (36) THROUGH the (37) [country].
   B: (38) *Yes*, and we have a (39) *place* to (40) *go* and we don't sort of (41) STOP, 'cos (42) *all* the (43) *trees* are the (44) *same.*
   (Dickinson and Mackin 1969: 90)[2]

The constituent-sentences of (1) tend to be rather simple in structure, and by and large show few of the syntactic ("movement") variations in which we shall subsequently be interested. The emphasis-marking is therefore of a rather straightforward kind.

Accent (italics) normally marks new material (e.g. (2) *topic,* (3) *day,* (4) *country*), or old material re-introduced[3] (e.g. (40) *go*). Contrast (capitals) marks the denial of another item in the common ground, i.e. either in the linguistic context: LIFE (as opposed to <u>day</u>), STOP (as opposed to <u>go</u>); or else in the extralinguistic context: ENGLISH (as opposed to Australian, American, Norwegian, the nationalities of the other speakers). Reduction (square brackets) marks material repeated to keep it current in the discourse, but then destressed to prevent it from assuming the prominence of new information (e.g. [country] and [go]).

[96]

Emphasis

6.2 Is emphasis a surface-structure phenomenon?

6.21 *What a phonological account must do*

In exemplifying these terms, however, we have allowed certain assumptions to be taken for granted. In particular, we have assumed, without yet arguing for it, that A and C are distinct. But a transcription of surface structure will almost certainly deny that this is so. We should therefore like to briefly consider how far one can get with a surface structure analysis of emphasis (while at the same time providing some details of the stress variations we have mentioned as representing the 'straightforward case' of emphasis-realisation).

Let us start by asking what any account of a phenomenon must do, before considering the specific case of a phonological account. In Werth 1979, the concept of 'theoretical adequacy' was expressed in informal terms as follows:

As is well-known, linguistic argument may be assessed at three levels, which, informally stated, are:

(i) it must correctly predict the observable facts; or, rather more rigorously, it must exactly specify surface structures;

(ii) it must conform to certain general requirements on formal systems, including economy, viability, and explicitness;

(iii) it should be compatible with the known (and, indeed, the unknown) facts about the human organism, and especially, perhaps, psychological and sociological systems.

(p.188)

A phonological account of emphasis — that is to say, a surface-structure account which assumes that emphasis is the same as stress, and is therefore phonological — must use surface-structure categories. From the speaker's point of view, these are of two kinds: **observables** and **inferrables.** Observables relate to phonetic elements such as voicing or fall-rise intonation. Inferrables (in the sense we are using the term here) are secondary linguistic phenomena which the speaker deduces about surface structure elements; they include such things as syllabification, phonotactics, and word-shape. However, a phonological account must not rely upon any unobservable categories or information not derived from surface structure, such as semantic entailments. Finally, all surface categories must be

[97]

Emphasis

unambiguously distinguishable from each other.

6.22 *A possible phonological account of emphasis*

We may start with the suggestion that the observable face of emphasis is "prominence" (cf. Ch. 1.3). We then have to recognise that prominence takes three forms or aspects:

(i)   phonetic prominence (carried by stress, intonation etc);
(ii) syntactic prominence (carried by word-order, constituent-order etc);
(iii) semantic prominence (carried by "content" words as opposed to "form" words)

Then the superficial type that we are examining here is primarily phonetic. Let us at this point, therefore, make a brief digression on the nature of **stress**.

Stress is of two types, or domains: **word-stress** and **sentence-stress**. Word-stress has to do with differential prominence on the syllables of words with more than one syllable. It seems to be agreed (Hyman 1977) that not all languages have stress in this sense: in particular, so-called "syllable-timed" languages (cf. Pike 1945, Abercrombie 1967, Adams 1979) evidently lack word-stress as a distinctive, that is, phonological, property. Other languages, such as Czech, lack word-stress as a phonological property because, though they have it as a phonetic property, it is completely predictable. We shall have nothing more to say about word-stress, since whatever else it may be, it seems quite uncontroversially to be a word-level phenomenon bearing no implications for textual processes (but cf. Bolinger 1978 for a possibly contrary view). Sentence-stress is the process whereby a particular word or constituent in a sentence is given prominence for one reason or another. Informal accounts of the phenomenon (such as Schubiger 1935 or Kingdon 1958) usually talk about "the most important word in the sentence" (cf. the quote from Coleman 1914 below). Such views seem to relate to speaker-intentionality, which is clearly not a phonological assumption. However, since sentence-stress appears as a pitch-intensity phenomenon, it might be (and indeed has been) argued that it should be accounted for at the phonological

[98]

Emphasis

level. We shall presently attempt an analysis based on this assumption.

Analysis of any kind, however, must necessarily be conducted according to some fairly general principles of organisation, pattern-recognition, and so on. In the case of surface-structure emphasis, we can, perhaps, make some reasonably minimal assumptions about the ability of speakers to impose or detect structural patterns in utterances:

(i)   that lexical (content) words can be distinguished from grammatical (form) words[4]

(ii) that relatively heavy stress (however achieved, phonetically) can be distinguished from relatively weak stress.

The first of these principles is semantic, the second phonetic. The first represents an organising principle of language as a model of the world expressed by way of a functional system of a different order (i.e. a system of signs and connectives) and is perhaps an inferrable, in our earlier distinction. The second represents the ability to produce and recognise regularly and correctly suprasegmental differences in articulation, whatever the origin and import of these differences may be. It is an observable, in the terms described above.

The remaining form of prominence mentioned above, the syntactic kind, also interacts with the others, but since its production and recognition is presumably more complex than surface stress, and since its description and derivation is part of the basic intention of this study, it would obviously be circular, and more than somewhat previous, to argue for it as a pre-analytical assumption. In fact, this type constitutes the "non-straightforward case" of emphasis, and we will return to it in Ch. 8.

Putting together the two minimal assumptions above, we may classify four possible categories of emphatic item, two of them lexical, L(exical) *vs.* G(rammatical) and two accentual, H(eavy) *vs.* W(eak):

2. (a)   LH
   (b)   LW
   (c)   GH
   (d)   GW

We may now take another look at passage (1). We

Emphasis

should remember, however, that items in italics may be no different suprasegmentally from items in capitals, and that items in square brackets may not differ suprasegmentally from unmarked items. Then it seems to be possible to arrive at some of the emphatic distinctions we have already made, without having to rely upon unobservable semantic criteria. So, (2d) must occur as an unAccented (-A) item (i.e. an unmarked or "inert" one); it cannot be Reduced since, as we shall see only L can be Reduced. (2c) must be Contrastive (C): that is the only possibility for stressed G words. (2b) is most likely to be a Reduced (R) item, though there is another possibility which we will return to. (2a), however, is ambiguous as to emphatic possibilities — not marginally, like (2b), but irretrievably so. Thus a stressed L item may equally (from the viewpoint of surface-structure) be either A or C, and there is no surface analysis which permits the distinction to be drawn accurately.

From assumptions (i) and (ii), therefore, we can distinguish all and only -A items (e.g. in passage (1), <u>might</u>, <u>be</u> and <u>in</u> between (17) and (19))[5]. We can also distinguish all, but not only, R items, e.g. [country] in (6,17,25,37), and [go] in (24,28); but not <u>think</u>, between (21) and (22), or <u>anything</u>, between (31) and (32). We cannot distinguish all C items, though anything which is GH must be C, e.g. WE (22) and THROUGH (36). An interesting example, which we will return to, is SOMEWHERE (27).

As for A items, we cannot distinguish for sure ANY of them: Accent always falls on LH items, but then LH items are not always Accented — they can be Contrastive.

6.23 *Some counterexamples*

We have already mentioned that destressed L items are likely to be R, but not necessarily. There are two classes of L items which are likely to be weak in stress, though not R; these are:

(a) the so-called 'weak impersonal' nominals, e.g. <u>someone</u>, <u>people</u>, <u>anything</u> etc.
(b) verbs used performatively[6], e.g. <u>I</u> (don't) <u>think</u>, <u>I wonder</u>, <u>I feel</u>, <u>I suppose</u> etc.

[100]

Emphasis

These behave like G items in all respects except for the definitional criterion : they appear to have semantic content. otherwise, they conform to G behaviour in its two most important respects:

- they are normally weakly stressed;
- if they receive heavy stress, this must be interpreted (just as with GH items) as Contrastive; it cannot be simple Accent. An example of this, already referred to, is SOMEWHERE (27), which contrasts with the implied 'nowhere in particular' of (29)-(32).

Could it be, then, that we are wrong in classifying these as L ? Perhaps we should ignore the semantic precondition, and count them as G on behaviour alone? But if we do this, we destroy any external justification there might have been for the surface-structure analysis of emphasis (and as we have seen, there is little enough of this, anyway). There is, though, an alternative to classifying them as GW, and that is to classify them along with other reduced items as LW. This would make these two sets "permanently Reduced". If this were the case, reduction as a process could not be said to take place there, and in particular, the condition of repetition could not be said to have been fulfilled. Nevertheless, it may be argued that both sets have special relationships with lexical items. Set (a) is very much like the set of pronouns in English: if we regard a pronoun like he as anaphorically related to a nominal such as the man, necessarily unstressed unless contrastive, and a pronoun like one similarly related to a nominal like a man, then a form like someone might be said to bear similar affinity with the nominal some man, everyone with every man and so on. Thus, we might relate all these forms under some such formula or construal rule (cf. Chomsky 1980: 6) as:

4. (a) Qx, x is human...

where Q = any quantifier. (This is assuming that (in)definiteness in nominals is a type of quantification). Then other forms in set (a) such as people, things, having no obvious pronominal character, might be related perhaps by analogy, or maybe more directly, though abstractly, via their semantic structure. For example, people might be a

Emphasis

special case of the above formula, such as:

(b) {   *All* x   } :   x is human ...
     {*Exists* x (>1)}

   Attractive though it seems, however, this solution simply does not work: it is in fact observationally inadequate. Thus, while it is quite easy to demonstrate the relationship between <u>he</u> and <u>one</u> and definite and indefinite NPs, respectively, it is impossible to do the same for weak impersonals. Consider the sentences of (5):

5. (a)   <The man who lives next door to George>$_i$ was in an accident. He$_i$ received multiple injuries.
   (b)   <The man who gets the job>$_i$ will be a career-grade executive. He$_i$ will take up his appointment on January 1st.
   (c)   <A <man from the Housing Department>$_i$ >$_j$ came round yesterday. <Another <one>$_i$ >$_k$ came today.
   (d)   There were <some <men>$_i$ >$_j$ on the street corner. <One$_i$ >$_k$ $_{Included-in\ j}$ shook his fist at the demonstrators.
   (e)   <Some <man from the Housing Department>$_i$ >$_j$ came round yesterday. *<<Someone>$_i$ else>$_k$ came today.
   (f)   There were <some <men>$_i$ >$_j$ on the street corner. *<Someone$_i$ >$_k$ $_{Included-in}$ $_j$ shook his fist at the demonstrators.
   (g)   <Some man>$_i$ was in an accident in the High Street. *<Someone>$_i$ received multiple injuries.

Note that (5e-g) are unacceptable with the stipulated anaphoric relationship. For example, (5e) cannot mean specifically 'Some other man from the Housing Department came today'. The weak impersonals are thus necessarily **non-anaphoric**: they can repeat neither reference nor sense[7]. As for true pronouns and related items, which must obviously be kept distinct from the weak impersonals, we shall return to their treatment in Chs. 7 and 8 (but cf. also Ch. 4.2).
   Set (b), the performative-type verbs, obviously requires different arguments. Our claim is that the constraints on textual coherence apply only to the PROPOSITIONAL components of utterances. Specifically, they do not apply to the modulatory

[102]

Emphasis

component, i.e. that part which relates a speaker to his own utterance, including performatives, attitudinal disjuncts, and the like, (cf. Ch. 4.4).

The exclusion of such elements from truth-conditional assessment is well-known. In sentences like:

$$
6. \quad I \quad
\begin{Bmatrix}
\text{know} \\
\text{believe} \\
\text{think} \\
\text{understand} \\
\text{realise} \\
\ldots
\end{Bmatrix}
\quad \text{that Ken passed his driving-test}
$$

it seems perverse to assess the truth-values in terms of whether the speaker actually does know, believe, think etc., that X — particularly in the case of factives such as <u>know</u>, <u>understand</u> and <u>realise</u>[8]. In these cases, truth is normally assessed on the embedded proposition, (cf. G.Lakoff's comment (1975: 256 sqq.) on the contrary view of Lewis 1972: "Lewis is simply wrong — natural language does not work that way"). In the communication of meaning (as opposed to truth), that is to say, (6) will be taken to convey that there is a certain probability that John passed his driving-test, this information being passed on with varying degrees of certitude. The meaning is carried by the embedded proposition; the performative (in our expanded sense, cf. fn. 6) carries the degree of certitude, or speaker-involvement. Since the performative does not advance the information-content of the discourse, we may argue, it therefore does not enter into the semantic ebb-and-flow of coherence. Consequently, it does not take part in the placement of emphasis — and this would suggest that performatives are indeed GW, as originally suggested, and not LW after all. (Cf. also, on performatives, G.Lakoff 1975: Appdx.3).

6.24 *Summary: emphasis-interpretation from surface-structure*

Attempting to assess the possibility of surface-structure analysis of emphasis, then, we can see that there are two major drawbacks:

(i) LH items may be either A or C;

[103]

Emphasis

(ii) W items are also ambiguous, depending upon the allocation of weak impersonals and performatives to L or G. If the former, then LW may be either R or "permanent R"; if the latter, then GW may be either —A without content, or —A with content. There is a worse — and real — further possibility, and that is that impersonals are LW and that performatives are GW, giving the worst possible case of intractable ambiguity for a surface-structure interpretation of emphasis.

Either of these problem-areas is sufficient to show that surface-structure analysis of emphasis is out of the question. We shall now turn to the alternative possibility, which is that emphasis is semantic/pragmatic in nature.

6.3. Is emphasis semantic/pragmatic in nature?

6.31 *What a semantic/pragmatic account must do*

The other basic facet of emphasis that we distinguished above is that it contains implications for meaning. We must therefore now explore the possibility of an approach whereby the facts of emphasis may hook on to the semantic/pragmatic analysis of the language, (having demonstrated that a phonological account is insufficient). But what must such an account achieve? First, it must obviously be capable of accounting not only for the facts which were also susceptible to a phonological explanation, but also for the counterexamples to that account, namely, the weak impersonals and the performative-type verbs. Secondly, it must be capable of distinguishing between the patterns of emphasis described in section 6.1. Thirdly, it must provide a principled basis for these distinctions. Fourthly, any such account must be compatible with both the requirements on formal systems, and the properties of the human organism (cf. our remarks in section 6.21 above). We begin this attempted account, then, by postulating a set of rules for the placement and differentiation of Emphasis. We shall then scrutinise these rules for their conformity to the above requirements.

[104]

Emphasis

6.32 *Rules for emphasis*

In order to examine whether these phenomena could be semantic/pragmatic in origin, we must first relate them to a semantic/pragmatic analysis of the material under observation. Let us assume an underlying sequence of the form suggested in Ch. 2.4:

7. $P_1 + P_2 + ... + P_n$

in which each P(roposition) coheres by virtue of constraints, both on P and on +, whose nature has been discussed in Ch.5. Furthermore, each P consists of a complex semantic structure at whose terminal nodes are semantic primitives, grouped in propositional functions (PFs). Any PF, or set of PFs dominated by a single node, may correspond, or be associated with, a lexical item of the language (cf. our discussion in Ch. 2.3).

The coherence constraint (cf. Ch. 5.4 above) operates essentially by marking PFs as "predictable from known information" (i.e. in the common ground). The mechanism of this operation, we postulate, is emphasis-placement. Making the sole assumption that the meaning-bearing element in a (terminal) PF is its predicate, we now propose the following set of rules for emphasis-placement:

8. (a) Mark as Accented each terminal predicate in a tree P_1:

$$<...Pred...> \rightarrow <...Pred\ A...>$$

(b) If a predicate is predictable within the common ground, i.e. if it positively coheres:

$$A \rightarrow R$$

(c) Under the semantic condition for contrast, i.e. negative coherence:

$$R \rightarrow C$$

The conditions referred to in (8b) and (8c) were discussed in Ch. 5.4. We shall apply them more explicitly below. Before explaining how this set of rules accords with the "facts" of emphasis as described in Section 6.1, we will exemplify their operation from passage (1).

A's second contribution is as follows:

[105]

Emphasis

9.(a) You *pass* THROUGH the [country].

The underlying structure of (9a), as broadly specified at the beginning of this section and in Ch. 2.3, is (in simplified form) shown in Fig. 6.2.

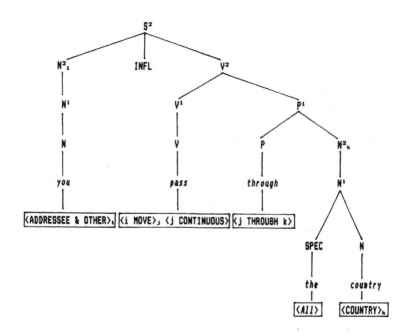

FIG. 6.2

Fig. 6.2 shows the structure in the reasonably familiar terms of X-bar notation, with the semantic specification somewhat more detailed than usual. The capitalised words here represent PFs, in line with the intensional semantic specifications of Jackendoff 1976. All PFs contain predicates; however, the difference between Argument PFs and Predicate PFs is that the latter contain variables, not all shown here. Where they are shown, they are indicated by subscripts corresponding to some portion of the tree marked by the same subscript (cf. Ch. 2.3). We give this tree at this point simply to display the relationship between our proposed system and the more familiar notations of

Emphasis

current grammars. However, in what follows, the X-bar superstructure will be omitted, leaving only extra bracketing, as appropriate, to show the constituent structure and variable-links. We should also make the point that the precise accuracy of such structures and their primitive terms are not actually at issue here: our present concern is simply to suggest a possible vehicle for the semantic/pragmatic placement of emphasis.

The tree in Fig. 6.2, then, can alternatively be represented as a bracketing:

9.(b)   <ADDRESSEE+OTHER>$_i$ <i MOVE>$_j$ & <j CONTINUOUS> <j THROUGH k> <COUNTRY>$_k$

The rules in (8) apply as follows to the predicates of (9b):

<ADDRESSEE+OTHER><MOVE><CONTINUOUS><THROUGH><COUNTRY>

By (8a):	A	A	A	A	A	A
By (8b):	R	R	R		R	R
By (8c):					C	
Result:	R	R	R	A	C	R

TABLE 6.1

(8a) marks all predicates (shown in capitals) as A. Rule (8a) is broadly equivalent in intention and result to the Chomsky and Halle (1968: 90 sqq) Nuclear Stress Rule, and its antecedents (Chomsky and Halle 1968: 16 sqq; Chomsky, Halle and Lukoff 1956: 75). The differences are obvious: the Chomsky/Halle rule is a rule of phonology, applying to surface structure — (8a) applies to semantic structure; NSR applies to lexical items — (8a) to semantic predicates; NSR applies to the results of syntactic transformations; (8a,b,c), as will subsequently be revealed, help to determine and motivate syntactic variation.

(8b) Reduces all items which are "predictable from the common ground". "Predictable" as used here is simply a shorthand form for the positive coherence constraint discussed in Ch. 5.4. <ADDRESSEE+OTHER> is predictable because the addressee, like the speaker, is always predictable (though not necessarily specifically) in any conversational exchange. It is among that group of items which we have elsewhere called "conventionally recessive" (cf. Werth 1981a). The <OTHER> component is here predictable as a recurrence of the parallel

[107]

Emphasis

component in <u>we</u> (= <SPEAKER+OTHER>). In our terms it is repeated, hence Reduced. <MOVE> is Reduced since it is repeated as the underlying predicate of <u>go</u> [9]. <CONTINUOUS>, however, is left as A, since it is not predictable. We are assuming that <MOVE <CONTINUOUS>> is the semantic specification of <u>pass</u>, which remains A by virtue of containing an unReduced component. The predicate <THROUGH>, like most surface prepositions, is really a complex semantic item and not a simple primitive term as represented here. It is a "change-of-position" term, charting movement past a location in two or three dimensions. It gets Reduced here because it shares much of this semantic structure with the predicate <TO>, also a change-of-position term, though one which charts movement terminating in a location. This predicate occurs between (16) and (17) in passage (1):

    10.(a) ...(when) we *go* to the [country]

The semantic representation of (10a) is something like (10b):

      (b) <SPEAKER+OTHER>$_A$ <<A MOVE>$_B$ <<B TO C> <COUNTRY>$_C$>>

(again omitting the labelling of brackets). Presumably, the semantic relationship between <THROUGH> and <TO> is one of implication: ′ if x goes through y, then x goes to y′ _ and beyond, of course. The semantic structure of <u>through</u>, that is to say, contains that of <u>to</u>. There is also a significant relationship between these items and <MOVE>. Finally, the predicate <COUNTRY> is Reduced because it is absolutely predictable at this point, being a straight repetition.

    (8c) operates only on the predicate <THROUGH> here. We have already seen that the reduction of this item depends on the context (10), whose own emphatic structure is derived as follows:

    <SPEAKER+OTHER> <MOVE> <TO> <COUNTRY>

	<SPEAKER+OTHER>	<MOVE>	<TO>	<COUNTRY>
By (8a):	A	A	A	A	A
By (8b):	R	R		R	R
By (8c):		(no change)			
Result:	R	R	A	R	R

TABLE 6.2

The structure of <TO>[10] is something like:

[108]

11.(a) <START<Loc^1>> & <FINISH<Loc^2>>

with Loc^1 unspecified and Loc^2 being country, then we might represent the structure of <THROUGH> as:

11.(b) <START<Loc^1>> & <-FINISH<Loc^2>> & <FINISH<Loc^3>>

In this case, Loc^1 and Loc^3 will be unspecified, and Loc^2 will be repeated from before. Rule (8c) to operate requires the previous imputation of negation upon the item, in line with negative coherence, as discussed in Ch. 5. (We will specify this further in Ch. 7). This is fulfilled in (10) and (11) by the PFs <FINISH<Loc^2>> versus <-FINISH<Loc^2>>, since in this case, there is an explicit denial.

Incidentally, the Reduction of <TO> in (10b) is explained by its repetition of the <MOVE> PF, which has an analysis identical to (11a)[11]. We assume that the sharing of this PF is responsible for the fact that there cannot be focus on both of these items in a single context:

11.(c) ...(when) we *go* to the [country]
   (d) ...(when) we [go] TO the [country]
   (e) *...(when) we *go* TO the [country]

It should at this point be noticed that R and C share an important property: both refer back to the common ground. That is, they are both **anaphoric**: R positively (since it requires at least partial synonymy) and C negatively (since it requires at least the imputation of antonymy)[12]. This means that semantically, the relationship between these phenomena is somewhat different from the phonetic relationship shown in Figs. 1.2 and 6.1:

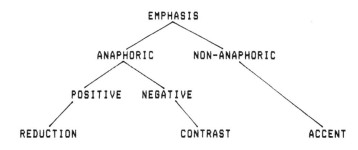

FIG. 6.3

Emphasis

This fact is represented in the rule-order — C is partly dependent upon the previous application of R. This is because the sense relation of antonymy is necessarily more complex than that of synonymy: an expression y which is antonymous to an expression x must contain the negative of some PF of x. Thus, in approximate terms, (8b) scans the text for synonymous PFs, and then (8c) scans the context for negation of at least one of those PFs.

6.33 *Arguments for the semantic/pragmatic nature of emphasis*

It will have been noticed that the category —A did not reappear in the previous section. In fact, items which in a surface analysis are unmarked (i.e.—A) do not correspond to any clear set or category in the analysis implied by section 6.32. Some of them are actually content-items, and must therefore be represented in underlying structure with predicates. These may then be reduced, according to context, and some (e.g. prepositions) may have undergone other processes, resulting in surface items which are R rather than —A. Others are perhaps 'empty' items (i.e. content-free) introduced at later stages (e.g. by *There*-insertion), and therefore not entering into the emphatic structure at all. We will see in Ch. 7.1 that it is nevertheless possible to distinguish quite clearly between these two groups, and moreover to account for the distinction in a principled way.

A semantic/pragmatic account also has to handle differently the two classes of superficially weakly-stressed items, discussed in section 6.23. The weak impersonals have PFs underlying them, like any other lexical element, and so their predicates will receive As by rule (8a) as usual.

Rules (8b) and (8c) will not usually apply, though exceptionally they may, as in the case of SOMEWHERE in (27) of (1), already discussed. This leaves these items marked as A — contrary to the superficial facts of stress, but as we shall see later, very significantly for certain movement rules, notably the passive. The performatives, on the other hand, are unaffected by the difference, since, as we have suggested, they are not part of the propositional content of sentences, but belong rather to the modulatory function.

It seems that the facts of emphasis can indeed

[110]

Emphasis

be captured by a semantic/pragmatic account, given the existence of certain constraints on coherence (synonymy and antonymy). Such an account also predicts that weak impersonals will behave like Accented items, contrary to their superficial phonetic properties. This prediction, among others, will be seen to be borne out presently.

6.5 Nature and behaviour of Reduction

The semantic notion of "absolute synonymy" is evidently closely related, if not identical, to the discourse-notion of "absolutely given". Let us look at another connected passage of speech, given here as (12), annotated for emphasis[13]:

> 12. A: (1) I wonder whether when it was FIRST [published] in nineteen-twenty-*seven*, / (2) that was, after all, AFTER *Freud*, wasn't it, / (3) the [average reader] *recognised* the *very strong sexual symbolism* throughout the *book* — / (4) because, of course, the *lighthouse* is a *phallic* [emblem], / (5) and *James*, the [son], the [little boy] *James*, who wants so *badly* to *go* to the [lighthouse] and is *frustrated* all the time, / (6) *explicitly hates* his [father] and *wants* to *stab* him to *death*, / (7) which [occurs] both [early] AND [late] in the [book]./
> B: (8) But just at the *end* there's a RECONCILIATION. /
> A: (9) It's this *Oedipus* [thing] really./
> C: (10) The [lighthouse] DOES [raise] all *sorts* of [questions] about *what exactly* the [symbols] ARE, / (11) whether in *fact* you *invent* your OWN, [rather], and [put] them IN. / (12) Certainly ONE of them is the [little boy] who, *now* in ADOLESCENCE, *steps* ON to the *lighthouse* / (13) and *that* is his *coming* to *manhood*, presumably. /
> A: (14) Well, *quite, yes.* /
> B: (15) Isn't it terrible, I just don't *see* ANY of these [sexual symbols], / (16) I never am *aware* of them, / (17) I just don't *see* them, / (18) I just don't CARE about these [phallic symbols]. /

[111]

Emphasis

C: (19) I think they're *meant* to *operate* on an – NOT on a [conscious level]. /
B: (20) *Good.* /
C: (21) And I don't think they're MEANT to be OBTRUSIVE. /
   B (22) Well they're *not* [obtrusive] to ME. /

Presumably, the least controversial candidates for absolute synonymy would be the same item repeated. The function of such **repetition** is the deictic one of keeping semantic material in the common ground. Therefore, its semantic structure must be identical from mention to mention. Examples from (12) are <u>lighthouse</u> lns.4,5, <u>book</u> lns.3,7, <u>obtrusive</u> lns.21,22, and with a superficial morphological distinction, <u>symbolism</u> and <u>symbols</u> lns.3,10.

However, the linguistically and logically more interesting cases are undoubtedly those founded on only partial synonymy or on some other relationship, involving at least the use of different forms. Probably the straightest type of example of non-repetitious synonymy would be the use of **virtual synonyms** (i.e. different lexical items within the same close range of meaning, as recorded for instance by a dictionary of synonyms). Thus, <u>emblem</u> in ln.4 is a virtual synonym of <u>symbol(ism)</u> in ln.3: certainly, they appear interchangeable in the context of phallic __, (cf. also ln.18), and they would have a large part, if not quite all, of their semantic structure in common. The textual function of such items is fundamentally similar to that of straight repetition, but with the addition of variation at the surface level for stylistic purposes.

A more partial variety of synonymy often takes place when the antecedent term is a proper noun, or refers to an individual. Subsequent reduced items may then be seen to perform two functions: first, the deictic function as before, which is the prime purpose of the whole process, and second, the selection of a different lot of semantic material from the entire possible semantic structure underlying the item in question (cf. our discussion of Mr. Reagan in Ch. 2). This partial information will still be used deictically, but also to present a different facet of the referent:

13. <u>Mr. John Stonehouse, MP</u>, sat in an

[112]

Emphasis

> Australian prison cell tonight ... It was
> a day-long drama for <u>the runaway MP</u> ...
> <u>the MP</u> argued heatedly ... Then <u>the man
> who had been Britain's Postmaster-General
> in the 1960s</u> struggled to a departure
> gate ...
>
> (*The Times*, 10.6.75)

Underlining here indicates referential synonymy of the type being discussed. In terms of emphasis, however, <u>the runaway MP</u> and <u>the MP</u> would certainly be Reduced (since if they were at all stressed, they would be Contrastive). Similarly, the longer definite description in the last sentence, though containing some stresses in the relative clause, will have a Reduced head: the [man]. In fact, when different possibilities of this type have been exhaustively investigated, we believe it will be found that such complexes should count as Reduced, despite containing some subsidiary stresses. A phenomenon closely related, certainly, to this referential synonymy, and possibly simply another case of it, is the pseudo-pronominalisation of so-called epithet nouns discussed by G. Lakoff in (1968b), e.g.

> 14. I was speaking to Max_1 on the phone, but
> [the $bastard_1$] hung up on me.

This sort of example indicates that the attributes subsumed under a proper noun referring to an individual need in no way be inherent or permanent. They may actually be quite casual and occasional (cf. the similar point made in respect of President Reagan in Ch. 2). By virtue of this, the intensional meaning of proper nouns is open-ended and fuzzy.

An even more elusive source of reduction is implication, both logical and pragmatic. An example of the former of these from passage (12) is presumably <u>father</u> in ln.6, since:

> 15. *All* x: *If* $\langle x, y \rangle$ SON *Then Exists* y, $\langle y$
> *Included-in* $z \rangle$ & $\langle y, x \rangle$ FATHER
>
> "If x is somebody's son, then there is a y
> who is x's father"

We ignore problems with tense, orphans, and so on. The material implication in (15) is a necessary

Emphasis

result of human biology: we therefore take it to be logically necessary, though a parthenogenetic Betelgeusan might conceivably (?) disagree. An example in (12) of contingent implication (deriving from encyclopaedic, rather than logical, knowledge) is <u>published</u> in ln.1. The implication operating here can be set out in our logical notation:

16. *All* x: *If* <x> BOOK *Then Exists* y, <y, x> PUBLISH

"If x is a book, then some y has published x".

In this case, however, the operator must be taken to mean not 'all', but something like 'typically'. Not everything we call a book has been published (some may be individual scribal copies, some circulated etc.). However, it may safely be assumed that the vast majority of books are published. Therefore, the item <u>published</u> may be Reduced without having been explicitly mentioned before, since it is implicit in <u>book</u>. Another pair of examples of contingent implication leading to Reduction are <u>early</u> and <u>late</u> in ln.20. The implicational steps are somewhat as follows:

17. (a) *All* x: *If* <x> BOOK *Then* <x> DURATION & <x> FINITE

"If x is a book, then x has duration and is finite".

(b) *All* x: *If* <x> DURATION *Then* <x> CHRONOLOGY

"If x has duration, then x has chronology".

(c) *All* x: *If* <x> CHRONOLOGY & <x> FINITE *Then* Exists y,z, <y, x> BEGIN & <z, x> END

"If x has chronology and is finite, then x has a beginning-point and an end-point".

(d) *All* x: *Exists* y,z, *If* <y, x> BEGIN & <z, x> END *Then All* j: *If* <j, y> NEAR *Then* <j, x> EARLY & *All* k: <k, z> NEAR

[114]

Emphasis

"If x has a beginning and an end, then any j near the beginning is early in x, and any k near the end is late in x".

For the coherence constraint of Ch. 5.4 to work with the above examples, the sledgehammer requirement would be that ALL implications of predications, including the contingent ones, be stated as part of their semantic structure, (cf. a comparable requirement for entailments in Wilson and Sperber 1979). This would indeed be a tall order, and perhaps impossible even in principle. However, Clark and Marshall 1981, writing about mutual knowledge, suggest that a similar condition for the interpretation of definite reference is in actual practice considerably simplified. They propose that references are sorted out by consulting several kinds of mental "file": some containing knowledge particular to each of the several "communities" to which the speaker belongs; some recording those experiences which are relevant to the establishment of mutual knowledge with a given listener. Then implications such as those of (17) would be contained in particular community files. In actual psychological fact, we may suppose that such implications would be stored among the speaker's general linguistic/ontological knowledge, and actuated when required. Actuation in this instance would involve the subsequent use of a PF from the implicational structure as though it were from the main semantic structure. Cf. our remarks on common ground in Ch. 3.

6.5 Nature and behaviour of Accent

One problem (at least) remains, and that is: how should the grammar distinguish between the semantic links which exist between items and their Reduced counterparts, as described above, and those undoubted links which exist between Accented items in a connected text? Take passage (12) again: there are presumably clear links of a pragmatic-encyclopaedic type between <u>Freud</u> (3), <u>sexual symbolism</u> (3), <u>phallic</u> (4), <u>Oedipus</u> (9) and also within the same "pragmatic field" of psychoanalytical language, <u>frustrated</u> (5), <u>hates</u> (6), <u>death</u> (6), <u>adolescence</u> (12) etc. Why should these remain unReduced, when other equally pragmatically-linked terms such as <u>published</u>, <u>early</u>

[115]

Emphasis

and <u>late</u>, all with <u>book</u> as their antecedent, get Reduced?

Ultimately, the answer is probably outside the scope of a grammar of linguistic competence: it is is probably intimately involved with the intention of an individual act of speech. However, there are some comments of a general nature which can be made about these examples. If we consider the initial item in each **"coherence-chain"**, we note that in the case of <u>published</u>, <u>early</u> and <u>late</u>, the initial item is **book**, since this is the central thematic concept of this part of the text. The text is "about" the book at this point, and details of its content, its socio-cultural role, and its proper divisions, whether explicit or implicit, are all dependent upon the prior evocation of the book. But this same item is also central so far as its semantic structure goes: PUBLISH is implicationally derivable from BOOK, as are EARLY and LATE. So the thematic and semantic dependencies coincide here.

In the case of the psychoanalytic vocabulary listed above, however, we can see that the initial item, central to A's argument, is **sexual**, and <u>Freud</u> and all the other items are thematically subsidiary to that. Yet it is the semantic and contingent structure of FREUD which draws all of the others together. So in this case the thematic and semantic dependencies do not coincide: therefore, no Reduced sequences. If <u>Freud</u> had been thematically as well as semantically central, however, we might have expected the other terms to be Reduced or at least Reducable:

> 18. I wonder whether when it was FIRST [published] in *1927*, the [average reader] *recognised* the strong *Freudian overtones* in the *book* — because of course the *lighthouse* is a [phallic emblem], and *James* [hates his father], and is a *classic case* of [Oedipus complex].

This seems to read perfectly naturally, as predicted. Notice the content of our claim: that Reduction based on contingent implication only takes place when the semantic and the thematic antecedents coincide. This does not imply that it MUST take place in these circumstances: indeed a "listing-intonation" would require As instead of Rs in most instances[14]. But it does imply that R cannot take place when these circumstances do NOT obtain:

[116]

Emphasis

> 19. *I wonder whether when it was FIRST
>   [published] in *1927*, the [average reader]
>   *recognised* the *very strong sexual
>   symbolism* throughout the *laundry-list*.

We would maintain that (19) with [published] Reduced, is highly improbable, on the grounds (a) that laundry-lists are not normally published (though, of course, like any written material they MAY be), so there is no contingent implication to this effect; so that (b) if this one WERE published, contrary to usual expectation, <u>published</u> would be Accented. So in this case <u>laundry-list</u> is thematically, but not semantically, central whereas in the case of <u>Freud</u>, it was semantically — at least, implicationally — central but not thematically so. Since theme and semantics do not coincide, the prediction is that there will be no reduction, explaining the awkwardness of (19). These four cases may be shown in table form:

Example	Semantic centrality	Thematic centrality	Emphasis
(11) book... published	book	book	A...R
(11) Freud... sexual symbolism	Freud	sexual symbolism	A...A
(18) Freudian... phallic emblem	Freudian	Freudian	A...R/A
(19) laundry-list ... published	?something published	laundry-list	A...A

TABLE 6.3

We have tried to show, therefore, that the application of the coherence constraint in positive cases — i.e. cases of synonymy, complete or partial — is realised by Reduction. In the less accessible instances involving not primary semantic structure but its implications, logical or contingent, the machinery is essentially the same, but there are constraints which enable the distinction to be drawn

Emphasis

between partially-synonymous items (which Reduce) and semantically-related items (which may be Accented). The distinction is between, in fact, partial synonyms and partial non-synonyms — for the division is not an absolute one.

The notion that the carrier of Accent is "completely new", i.e. "unexpected", information, tends to collapse upon examination. "Newness", like "repetition", cannot be an absolute category. Rather, it occurs along a scale from full synonymy to complete heteronymy, someway towards the latter end. Necessarily, though, it cannot be at the extremity of completely different meaning, since the notion of thematic, or coherency, linkage requires some semantic structure to be carried over from the preceding discourse, i.e. from the common ground.

6.6 Nature and behaviour of Contrast

Superficially, as we saw in section 6.22, Contrastive items may be either lexical or grammatical. If we assume this conventional distinction, lexical categories consist of nouns, full verbs, adjectives and adverbs, while the remaining categories — determiners, auxiliaries and modals, conjunctions (co-ordinating and subordinating), prepositions, pronouns and other pro-forms, quantifiers, and various particles and 'expletive' elements (e.g.infinitive <u>to</u>, 'impersonal' <u>it</u>, <u>there</u>) — are grammatical. In Ch. 7.1-2, we shall take a closer look at Contrast on items in each of these traditional categories.

There can be little doubt that of the three emphatic categories, it is C which is the most complex. As compared to A and R, its effects are more "staged" and lead us to suspect that ultimately C has to be explained in terms of **intentionality**. For an illuminating discussion of this concept, see Searle 1983. In addition, the very interesting notion of "Dominance" developed by Erteschik-Shir and Lappin in, for example, their 1983 paper, is also ultimately based on speaker intentionality. Nevertheless, we believe that it is possible to go quite far in the investigation by examining the semantic-pragmatic context of C, including the common ground of the discourse. In the final analysis, we presume, the common ground will include an important component modelling speakers' intentions, as well as the hearer's inferences and

[118]

Emphasis

hypotheses about them. However, we devote Ch. 7 to the more immediately attainable goal of investigating the "public" features of Contrast.

An important concept in all of the ensuing chapters will be that of the **SET**. We shall be using this term not in the strict mathematical sense of any nominated group of entities, but in the more restrictive (and more useful) sense of a group of entities sharing some empirical properties, and defined by these.

6.7 Review section

The earliest technical use of the term **focus** that we have been able to locate is in Halliday 1967a[15], where it is a semantic notion. However, notionally, it probably owes much to discussion surrounding the main sentence-stress, particularly the position and function of the **nucleus** or **tonic**[16]. The history of these notions is undoubtedly of some venerability but an important figure in making some of the crucial distinctions was H.O. Coleman. In a paper dated 1914, he distinguishes between "emphasis of prominence" and "emphasis of intensity". It is the term prominence which is relevant to our study of emphasis (since in emphasis of prominence he includes both Accent[17] and Contrast, in our terms):

> Prominence is by no means confined to the purpose of contrast. In nearly every sentence some word is regarded as the chief word (or, as we shall now term it, the prominent word) namely that word which constitutes the logical predicate - the informing word, denoting the fact to which one's attention is called, the word that answers the actual or imagined question, the last word that one would sacrifice to save a halfpenny on a telegram.
> (1914:9)

Thus for Coleman, prominence is roughly equivalent to what we have called 'focus'.

Schubiger 1935 takes a similar position, but adds the principle of **relative prominence**:

> In unemotional speech intonation serves to mark the relative importance of the different parts of the utterance. The psychological predicate[18], which is the weightiest element, gets the intonation turn, and round this nucleus are

[119]

Emphasis

grouped the other parts of the sentence, and
intoned according to their relative prominence.
(1935:9)

Essentially similar are Stannard Allen 1954,
Kingdon 1958, O'Connor and Arnold (1961 and 1973
editions, though the former uses "prominence" and
the latter substitutes "accent"), D.Jones (1967, and
the earlier editions we have checked), and in
general, the European tradition of intonation-study
up to the 1960's.
The American Structuralist tradition on the
other hand, did not operate with the concept of
'prominence'or 'nuclear tone', but was instead
concerned with the enumeration of pitch and stress
phonemes (cf. Pike 1945, Trager and Smith 1957).
Generative linguistics has, by and large, concerned
itself with the rules and constraints governing
stress placement in syntactic constructions, and the
extent to which this placement is governed by
syntactic considerations.
It has uniformly been assumed that stress
assignment is phonological, but that since the
syntactic bracketing of the surface-structure is
available to the phonological component, the rules
of stress-assignment may be governed by it (and not
by deep-structure or, certainly, semantics). It is
quite clear that any notion of 'prominence' or
"semantic importance" has no part in this tradition,
so that when the phenomenon of focus comes to be
tackled (as in Akmajian 1970, Jackendoff 1972,
Chomsky 1972), it is taken to be completely separate
from the question of stress-assignment. However,
since it apparently involves stress, it is assumed
by these linguists to be post-phonological.
A further problem for this recent use of the
term has been that it confuses what we have here
distinguished as Accent and Contrast. This, we
assume, is because in superficial terms (notably in
phonetic terms) they are often indistinguishable. We
argue, however, that it impoverishes linguistic
theory here as elsewhere if one ignores semantic
considerations.
Focus as a notion, then, seems to derive from
Halliday's (1967a) use of it, as is assumed for
example by G.Lakoff (1971a: 260 sqq.), who refers to
"the Halliday-Chomsky account" of the phenomenon.
But in fact, Halliday's version is quite different
from Chomsky's[19]. As we noted above, focus for

[120]

Emphasis

Halliday is a semantically-determined entity:

> ...points of information focus which indicate
> what new information is being contributed. ⟨...⟩
> This system of information focus is thus
> dependent on the information structure; it
> involves the selection, within each information
> unit, of a certain element or elements as points
> of prominence within the message. ⟨...⟩
> Information focus reflects the speaker's
> decision as to where the main burden of the
> message lies... Information focus is one kind of
> emphasis, that whereby the speaker marks out a
> part (which may be the whole) of a message block
> as that which he wishes to be interpreted as
> informative.
> (1967a: 202sqq.)

Halliday makes it quite clear that this has no
necessary connection with constituent structure:

> ...the tone group is a phonological unit that
> functions as realisation of information
> structure. It is not co-extensive with the
> sentence or the clause or any other unit of
> sentence structure; but it is co-extensive,
> within limits determined by the rhythm, with the
> information unit.
> (*ibid.*)

"Speaker's decision" is not, of course, an
objectively capturable diagnostic, (but cf. our
remarks on intentionality in section 6.6). Halliday
defers this problem by relating the placement of
focus to the occurrence of new information:

> What is focal is "new" information; not in the
> sense that it cannot have been previously
> mentioned, although it is often the case that it
> has not been, but in the sense that the speaker
> presents it as not being recoverable from
> preceding discourse.
> (*ibid.*)

This does not, of course, entirely dispel a
certain circularity of definition in the
relationship between focus and new information:
focus marks new information; information that is
marked by focus is deemed to be new. But this,
perhaps, reflects an indeterminacy in the linguistic

Emphasis

data themselves, rather than in the system of focus (and cf. our distinction above between information- and attention-Accent). However, as we have attempted to show in section 6.3, this problem can be avoided by assigning focus, (i.e. Accent and Contrast), and Reduction through an ordered set of rules. In this way, ALL semantic elements start out as potentially Accented (or Accentable), and then, according to contextual information, i.e. common-ground propositions, some elements remain Accented, others become Reduced or, eventually, Contrastive.

Next, we turn to Chomsky's account (1972), owing much to work by Jackendoff, published as (1972). For Chomsky, the focus is "the phrase containing the intonation centre" (1972: 91 sqq.). Thus consider the sentence:

> 20.(a) Was it an ex-convict with a red SHIRT that he was warned to look out for?

In (20a), the full phrase containing the intonation-centre <u>shirt</u> is (20b):

> (b) an ex-convict with a red shirt.

However, it is also properly contained in (20c-e):

> (c) with a red shirt
> (d) a red shirt
> (e) shirt.

This means that appropriate denials can concern any of these phrases:

> 20.(b') No, he was warned to look out for an AUTOMOBILE salesman.
> (c') ...an ex-convict wearing DUNGAREES.
> (d') ...with a CARNATION.
> (e') ...red TIE.

In all of these, notice, the stress is CONTRASTIVE; however, as we have seen, the "intonation centre" can equally well be simple Accent. But Chomsky assumes that:

> Rules of phonological interpretation assign an intonational contour to surface structures. Certain phrases of the surface structure may be marked, by grammatical processes of a poorly understood sort, as receiving expressive or

[122]

Emphasis

contrastive stress, and these markings also
affect the operation of the rules of
phonological interpretation. If no such
processes have applied, the rules assign the
normal intonation. In any event, phrases that
contain the intonation center may be interpreted
as focus of utterance, the conditions perhaps
being somewhat different and more restrictive
when the intonation center involves expressive
or contrastive stress, as noted... Choice of
focus determines the relation of the utterance
to responses, to utterances to which it is a
possible response, and to other sentences in the
discourse.
(1972: 99sq.)

The complementary of focus for Chomsky is
presupposition (and it is in this dichotomy that the
term 'focus' has received its most widespread recent
attention). Chomsky warns that presupposition in
this relationship cannot easily be equated with the
familiar, much-debated, though nevertheless elusive,
philosophical use of the term:

Note that we are using the term "presupposition"
to cover a number of notions that should be
distinguisted. Thus *it was JOHN who was here*
expresses the presupposition that someone was
here in the sense that truth of the
presupposition is a prerequisite for the
utterance to have a truth value. On the other
hand, when we replace one of the foci of *John
gave Bill the BOOK* by a variable it is not at
all clear that the resulting expression
determines a presupposition in the same sense,
though it does characterise "what the utterance
asserts" and to which utterances it is a proper
response, when so understood.
(1972: 100, fn. 27)

But it will readily be seen that this is only a
problem for S-grammar. The "two kinds of
presupposition" resolve into a single phenomenon:
contextual givenness, the duplication of previous
information, which has entered the common ground and
has subsequently been Reduced. Therefore the second
of Chomsky's types of presupposition in the above
quotation simply assumes the "given" information
that John gave Bill something, or that John did

[123]

Emphasis

something. However, the requirement that the truth of the whole proposition be conditional upon the truth of these "presupposed" expressions is not a requirement of textual coherence, and so its non-observance or rather non-applicability, makes no difference to the meaning of the sentence. Cf. Ch. 3 for further remarks on presupposition as a contextual notion.

Chomsky uses the term 'focus', therefore, only to make a sentential bipartition (very reminiscent of Prague School practice, cf. Ch. 9) into an assumed portion and a portion under consideration. To do this, he mistakenly assumes that the focus is the constituent containing the "intonation centre". For remarks having a critical bearing on this, see Bolinger 1958, 1961. He further assumes that the focus is a constituent , and that it is determined by surface-structure. For criticisms of these positions, see McCawley 1975, Hope 1973: 84, Contreras 1976: 19 sqq., Esau 1975. Chomsky briefly considers an alternative position (1972:90 sqq., 101 sq.), that focus is determined at deep structure, but dismisses it as a notational variant of his proposals. Nevertheless, it is this alleged "notational variant" that we are pursuing in the present study, and we claim that it provides a more adequate account of the process than Chomsky's does.

Chomsky assumes that focus is derivable without difficulty from the phonological phenomenon of "intonation-centre", which in its turn he assumes is determined by the stress and intonation rules of the phonological component. These rules provide for "normal intonation", but as is widely argued in the literature, the concept of normal intonation has no basis in linguistic reality (see Schmerling 1974a, and Bolinger 1958, 1961 and 1972). In fact, sentences like (21) are well known in the literature, appearing in most of the European works on intonation cited in this section, as well as in Bolinger and Schmerling:

21.(a) The *kettle's* boiling.
   (b) Suddenly, a *policeman* appeared in the doorway.
   (c) The *baby's* crying.   (said by e.g. a neighbour)
   (d) The baby's *crying.*   (said by e.g. the babysitter)

[124]

Emphasis

In such examples, (with the exception of (21d)), the usual intonation – as opposed to the "normal intonation" – has its centre on a lexical item other than the final one. Chomsky's rule for distinguishing the focus and presupposition from each other fails here. It may be said to work in (21d), since a baby-sitter may be considered to utter sentences presupposing (at least pragmatically) that the baby is doing something. But it is clear that far from being the "normal" situation, this is the sociolinguistically most marked case. (21c) represents the unmarked case, where the focus is on the event of baby-crying, leaving nothing for Chomsky's presupposition. We certainly cannot draw from it the presupposition that somebody is crying, except in a specific – and therefore marked – context. Much the same is true of (21a,b). See also Allerton and Cruttenden 1979.

Furthermore, Chomsky overlooks the distinction between Accent and Contrast, except for the observation that:

> When expressive or contrastive stress shifts intonation center, the same principle applies as in normal cases for determining focus and presupposition, but with the additional proviso that naturalness declines far more sharply as larger and larger phrases containing the intonation center are considered as a possible focus.
> (98sq.)

Contrastive stress is therefore for Chomsky a phenomenon which operates at some point (presumably in the phonological component – but under what conditions?) to shift the intonation centre, thus changing the determination of focus post-phonologically. Focus and contrast can therefore be co-extensive in Chomsky's system, but they occur at different levels of analysis.

Finally, he makes no connection between presupposition and Reduction – in fact, he does not mention the latter phenomenon at all. However, intuitively, it seems quite clear that presupposition in Chomsky's use is contained in the D-grammar notion of "given linguistically or situationally in the discourse", a notion which we have attempted to provide more substance for in Chs. 2-3.

[125]

Emphasis

In general, the weakness of Chomsky's system can be traced to the relationship he claims between intonation-centre and focus. As we have seen in the present chapter, neither this relationship nor either of the concepts involved can be determined by surface-structure alone. Moreover, the notion of intonation-centre depends on the separate assumptions of "normal intonation" and "contrastive stress", neither of which does Chomsky define even to his own satisfaction (cf.1972: 89, fn. 21; 100).

There appears, therefore, to be ample room for the alternative suggestion we have advanced in the foregoing sections. Instead of assuming - invalidly, as we claim - that intonation-centre underlies focus, let us assume the reverse. We are then free to postulate that the placement of focus takes place at the semantic level[20]. Intonation would then be one of the surface-structure manifestations of focus and Reduction. However, we shall have little more to say on the question of intonation in the present work.

To sum up, then, the present work regards the processes of emphasis not as superficial manifestations of stress and intonation (as in Chomsky 1972) but as constitutive operations deriving from the semantic connectivity of the discourse. The role of discourse is therefore seen as crucial and the interplay of Accent, Reduction and Contrast both help to explain and to some extent are constrained by the deployment of propositional information within sentences.

NOTES TO CHAPTER SIX

1. Cf. Dahl 1976 on the term <u>information</u>, which is used here in his sense of 'propositional information'.
2. Hesitations etc. have been omitted, and the emphasis-marking remains as described in Ch. 1, fn. 1. Any notation, of course, presupposes some sort of analysis of the primary data. Though we make no claims about our representation of the relationship between stress and intonation, nevertheless our notation reflects certain observations and decisions bearing upon this. A series of Accents tends, in terms of pitch, to drift

[126]

Emphasis

down (a well known phenomenon in African tone-languages). This seems to apply even to two Accents juxtaposed, with the effect that the second may seem less prominent than the first. Contrasts often seem to have the effect of "depleting" the remaining emphatic elements in the constituent, with the result that they apparently reduce their stress. Again, we have taken this to be a mere proximity phenomenon, and we normally mark such items as Accented. For interesting work on intonation, see Brazil 1975, 1978, and Ladd 1980.

3. Note that this is problematical for accounts of focus or stress which relate it to 'new' ([-given]) information. Cf. Lehman 1977: 318 sqq., who distinguishes further between "controlling the mechanisms of the discourse" (e.g.turn-taking, holding the floor etc.), and "directing the flow of information" (e.g. sustaining the topic, returning to a previous topic).

4. Note that the "perceptual strategy" accounts of surface-structure parsing (e.g. Bever 1970, Kimball 1973) also make the same minimal assumption.

5. See Ch. 7 for some discussion of such items.

6. Including verbs that are not, strictly, performatives in Austin's (1962) sense, since they do not express locutionary acts . In particular, we would include verbs of "propositional attitude", cf. fn. 8 below.

7. The proviso is that the forms we are talking about can sometimes be used quasi-anaphorically:

> (i) There's a certain someone₁ I'm longing to see, someone₁ like me...

In such cases, the form is not in fact being used as a weak impersonal, but as a straightforward indefinite NP.

8. Kempson (1977: 64-67) takes the opposite view, arguing that (i) verbs of judgment and belief (such as <u>consider</u>, <u>wonder</u>, <u>believe</u>) are not performatives since they may not co-occur with <u>hereby</u>; (ii) that they nevertheless show the same semantic distiction between simple and progressive present tense as do true performatives; (iii) since they are not actual

[127]

Emphasis

performatives, this distinction may be handled with truth-conditions (iv) therefore performatives may be handled in the same way. But we would argue that Kempson's position is clearly invalid: it is quite trivial to affirm that

(ii) I consider that you are wrong

is True if the speaker goes through some process of "considering" X, (such that X = 'you are wrong' - and its truth-value is irrelevant). The sentence is not, or is only trivially, a report upon the speaker's mental activities. The meaning seems to be much more satisfactorily expressed in truth-conditional terms as something like: "'you are wrong' is true to p probability of reliability". In other words, I consider that ... is a hedge, in the sense of G.Lakoff (1972): it does not itself possess a truth-value, but relativizes the truth-value of any proposition embedded below it. In fact, we would argue that such verbs have a function fundamentally similar to that of true performatives. As we have already remarked in fn. 6, we propose to treat them all as set (b) items. Apart from the fact that both groups of verbs behave similarly with regard to emphasis, we find that both function to contextualize propositions: performatives contextualize them socially (*I declare this bridge open* "places" 'this bridge is open' relative to a clear social situation); judgementals etc. contextualise propositions attitudinally (*I believe this bridge is open* places the same proposition relative to the attitude of the speaker).

9. Miller 1972, and Miller and Johnson-Laird 1976 use TRAVEL rather than MOVE, and assume that:

(iii) Travel$_t$ $\langle x \rangle$ *Equivalent-to* Change$_t$ $\langle$Place $\langle x, y \rangle \rangle$

(Miller and Johnson-Laird 1976: 90). This latter expression is equivalent to:

(iv) Place$_{t-1}$ $\langle x, y \rangle$ & Place$_t$ $\langle x, y' \rangle$ & Change$_{t-1,t}$ $\langle y, y' \rangle$

[128]

Emphasis

(ibid. 87). Compare our formula (11a).

10. Miller and Johnson-Laird 1976 define *to* locationally:

(v) not AT $\langle x,y \rangle_{t-1}$ & AT $\langle x,y \rangle_t$

i.e. x is first not at y, then x is at y. Clearly, this is included in our notation (11a), in that the predicate START combines the notions of location and previous time, while FINISH combines the notions of different location and subsequent time. It also seems reasonable to regard the change-of-state predicate CHANGE in Miller and Johnson-Laird's system as decomposable into an initial state START and a final state FINISH.

11. There is some historical evidence, furthermore, for the identity of TO with verbs of motion. Cf. Shakespeare *King Lear* Iii: "Edmund the base shall to th' legitimate" (i.e. 'attain') - though many editors cannot believe this, and amend it to top. Cf. also Pepys *Diary* (2 Sept. 1666): "So I down to the waterside... I to White Hall... we to a little ale-house on the Bankside".

12. Cf. Kuno (1978: 282sq.) for the distinction between "given, old" and "anaphoric". In his terms, our R-marked items are "old", i.e. predictable and anaphoric, while our C-marked items are anaphoric, but not predictable. This accords with the analysis presented here.

13. The internal numbering of example (12) is based on a combination of tone-group divisions and syntactic constituency. It is not, however, intended to reflect any serious analysis, but is merely for ease of exposition.

14. The phenomenon of 'exhaustive listing focus' (which Alain Bossuyt brought to our attention) is presumably a kind of attention-accent in the case of ordered lists, such as numbers, and information-accent otherwise.

15. Nigel Vincent has discovered an earlier use, in Pike 1963 (see Householder 1972: 197 sqq.), with a somewhat different function: the semantic role (viz., actor, goal, referent) towards which the activity of a predicate may be directed is the "focus complement", and this apparently serves to invest that element

[129]

Emphasis

with contrastive emphasis (Pike's preferred
translations use cleft structures). Pike
traces his use of the term to A.Healey 1958.

16. Strictly speaking, in most cases these terms
refer to the syllable upon which the main
stress (or intonation-turn) falls.

17. Strictly speaking, only those Accents that
remain on the surface after the rule of
Reduction has applied.

18. The term 'psychological predicate', according
to Vachek (1966: 111), is due to G. von
Gabelentz, though Hermann Paul was certainly
using it at about the same time.

19. However, Lakoff quotes from an unpublished
paper of Halliday's which is closer to
Chomsky's version in that it treats the
non-focal part of a sentence having marked
focus as presuppositional; in unmarked focus
sentences, 'the nonfocal components are
unspecified with regard to presupposition'
(quoted by Lakoff 1971a: 261). Since Chomsky
does not make the distinction between marked
and unmarked focus, he does not recognise this
division.

20. Note that it was the facts of focus as he
presented them which originally led Chomsky to
postulate a two-level semantic model (Extended
Standard Theory), though this bears little
resemblance to today's GB model. Nevertheless,
he still maintains his 1972 treatment of focus
in essentially the same form (cf. 1981: 238).

[130]

Contrast

Chapter Seven

CONTRAST

7.1 Contrast on grammatical items

We have seen that Contrast may occur on items in what are traditionally called "grammatical" categories, such as WE and THROUGH in passage (1) of Ch. 6. But can Contrast occur on ALL grammatical items? And how well-defined is the notion of grammatical category, anyway? In fact, if we examine the potential for Contrastiveness across the various categories of grammatical item listed in section 6.6, some interesting variations emerge. We may examine each of these classes in turn: first, the **DETERMINERS:**

1. (a) Are you THE Captain Pugwash ?
   (b) *Mary had an audience with THE Archbishop of Canterbury.
   (c) *Who's just trodden on THE cat?
   (d) * {THE} horse is a large quadrupedal
        { A }
        mammal
   (e) (A man and a woman mounted the podium). *THE woman was carrying a trumpet.
   (f) (I didn't meet just ANY old film producer). I met THE film producer.
   (g) (I wasn't welcomed by HORDES of beautiful blondes). I was welcomed by A beautiful blonde (only).
   (h) *There's A Captain Pugwash to see you, ma'am.
   (i) *Many A brave man has fallen foul of her charms.
   (j) *It's A madrigal which is polyphonic.

Some clear distinctions may be observed here. First, the clearest Contrastible cases appear to have the meaning of 'unique' (in the case of <u>the</u>) or 'single' (in the case of <u>a</u>) — cf. (1a,f,g). Yet other apparently unique cases, e.g. (1b,c,e), are not obviously Contrastible. Generics (1d,j) are in no circumstances Contrastible, and neither evidently

[131]

Contrast

are the other uses, such as anaphorics like (1e). We have to discover the reasons for this extraordinary distribution.

The case for **generics** seems fairly straightforward. Generics, as argued in Hawkins 1978 and Werth 1980c, are content-free in that they merely signal the totality of some set, itself perhaps defined relative to some situational context. So-called **"uniques"**, such as (1b,c), are really generics relativised down to a specific context. That is, they define the totality of the NP-set relative to its context. In (1c) for example, the cat in question is (within certain lax limits) the total feline population of the relevant space occupied by the speaker and the listener and just one cat. **Anaphorics** such as (1e) are precisely similar, except that the context is necessarily textual — but within it, they equally indicate the total membership of the stipulated NP-set. This explains the impossibility of:

> 1. (k) Some men$_1$ came into the shop. *The man$_1$ was wearing a pink carnation in his buttonhole.

How then are we to explain the grammaticality of cases (1a,f) as opposed to (1b,c)? The comparison of (1b) with (1f) perhaps suggests an answer: Archbishops of Canterbury are truly unique at any given time; they occur, that is, one at a time. Therefore a context like that of (1b) is contingently implausible, though not necessarily implausible (there have been two Popes at the same time, for example). This gives us a clue about the significance of a Contrast like (1f): the uniqueness here is of a subjective kind. (1f) could even be said at the Cannes Film Festival, where film producers are ten a penny, and yet still be felicitous. This kind of subjectivity requires that the NP in question be sufficiently salient somehow. For example, in a cats' home, one would rarely have occasion to felicitously say (1l) any more than (1c):

> 1. (l) Who's just trodden on the cat?

perhaps not even in the case where the animal was the Supreme Champion of Champions.

The usual 'totality' meaning of <u>the</u> (cf. Hawkins 1978) is semantically equivalent to *'All'*,

[132]

Contrast

which it should be noted is not a predicate but an operator. But the Contrastive use (as in (1a,f)) implicitly or explicitly denies that the criterion for its satisfaction is either set-totality or simple set-membership. It will be satisfied only by some particular member specified according to subjective criteria of the speaker. Notice that there is no logical difference between (1c) and (11): both claim that the stipulated set is totally satisfied by the referent. But the Contrastive stress appears to signal that the subset criteria are subjective, or at least inexplicit. In fact, the use of the definite article allows the speaker to imply that there exists only one referent which will satisfy ALL criteria for set-membership, crucially including, of course, the subjective criterion. The feasibility of this belief is then to be found in the pragmatic circumstances: Archbishops of Canterbury do not usually have their uniqueness questioned, while for cats, there is normally little reason to assert it.

Where Contrast is possible on determiners, therefore, there is the potential for further content, even if its precise nature is left inexplicit. On the other hand, in the absence of explicit distinguishing criteria, we might relegate these particular forms of Contrast to the category of "intensity emphasis" (for an emotional or subjective purpose), rather than counting it as true Contrastive emphasis.[1]

Next come **AUXILIARIES** and **MODALS**:

2. (a) You MUST do as you're told
   (b) Jean MUST be there by now
   (c) He CAN'T believe that his mother's a freemason
   (d) I MAY decide to decorate the bathroom
   (e) This IS Henry Hall speaking
   (f) Murgatroyd WAS supposed to appear
   (g) DO you believe in miracles?
   (h) Dmitri HAS read *Das Kapital*

All of these are quite clearly Contrastible, as has been recognised from the earliest versions of TG (cf. the EMPH formative). In all cases, it is obvious that the Contrast is attached to some content, whether this is simple polarity (in (2e,g)) or tense ((2f)), or whether it is a more complex

[133]

Contrast

meaning, such as possibility ((2d)) or obligation ((2a)). With <u>may</u>, however, C seems for some reason to select the epistemic (possibility) sense, rather than the root (permission) sense:

    2.(i) Cinderella MAY go to the ball (but I
          don't know for sure)

We may now consider co-ordinating and subordinating **CONJUNCTIONS:**

    3.(a) This happened both at the beginning AND
          at the end
      (b) Bill fell out of bed AND broke a leg
      (c) Do you want coffee OR tea?
      (d) She was poor YET she was honest
      (e) She was poor BECAUSE she was honest
      (f) ALTHOUGH she was poor, she was honest
      (g) IF she was honest, why didn't she report
          the robbery?
      (h) AS SOON AS he opened the door, I burst in
      (i) AFTER June the 12th, this scheme ceases
          to operate

Again, apparently all these conjunctions are Contrastible. The subordinating ones clearly have content: <u>because</u>, for example, does not merely mark subordination. It also contains the predicate REASON (cf. the paraphrase <u>for the reason that</u>). Its complementiser function presumably dates from the loss of complementiser <u>that</u> from <u>because that</u>.

The co-ordinating conjunctions, however, are rather more difficult. The examples in (3a–d) are probably Contrastible because, apart from the logical connectives & and *Or*, they also contain predicates: SUBSEQUENT in (3a,b), EXCLUSIVE in (3c), and CONCESSION in (3d). "Pure" logical connectives are probably not Contrastible, however, though it is difficult to construct good examples:

    3.(j) *Oil floats on water AND my Auntie Jane
          is sick
      (k) *Kelly saw the Supreme Pontiff, OR in
          other words, the Pope

(3j) as a "pure" conjunction presents the conjuncts as simply contiguous; Contrastive <u>and</u> seems to force some further significance, presumably derived from the common ground. (3k) virtually resists the

Contrast

contentful 'exclusive' sense altogether. We can therefore conclude that with conjunctions too, Contrastibility correlates with semantic content.

Let us now look at **PREPOSITIONS:**

4.(a) It's a long way TO St.Louis.
   (b) Luke swam ACROSS the river.
   (c) On this occasion, Cinderella went to the ball WITH her sisters.
   (d) John looked UP the road.
   (e) *John looked the number UP.
   (f) Kate was standing BY the statue.
   (g) * She opened the letter BY mistake.
   (h) ?Ziggy was knocked down BY his fans.
   (i) (Did Ziggy knock any of his fans down?) No, HE was knocked down BY his fans.
   (j) *The tenant asked FOR a rent rebate.

With prepositions too, the distinction is fairly clear: those which are Contrastive are those with semantic content. This may be directional (e.g. (4a,b)), or associated with case-roles (e.g. instrumental or comitative with, as in (4c)), and these have quite often been equated with deep predicates. The non-Contrastible ones, on the other hand, are those without content, such as the by of (4g) or the for of (4j). Again, it seems reasonable to suppose that these lack an underlying predicate, constituting instead semantically unaligned parts of complex lexical items. (However, for a somewhat contrary view, cf. recent work by Lindner 1981, and Brugman 1981, reported upon by Lakoff 1982).
A reasonably clear demonstration of our thesis, however, is the comparison of (4d) with (4e): up in (4d) is directional (contrasting with, for example, down or across), whereas up in (4e) is part of the complex verb look up, and lacks any separate semantic specification of its own. The case of passive by is quite interesting. As (4h) shows, it does not always take Contrast readily. However, it appears that when passive by is Contrastively stressed, it emphasises the notion of agency: and as we have already said, case-roles seem to constitute semantic content.

QUANTIFIERS seem to be uniformly contrastible:

5.(a) ANY friend of Batman's is a friend of mine

[135]

Contrast

(b) You can fool SOME people ALL of the time
(c) I recognised MOST of the people there
(d) SOME cats like fish
(e) EVERY home should have one

Again, there can be little doubt that quantifiers as a grammatical class are meaning-bearing. However, we should not confuse grammatical quantifiers with logical quantifiers. Logical operators as such are not stressable, for two reasons, perhaps: (a) they are abstract, and (b) they do not contain predicates. As is well-known, the natural-language quantifiers are considerably looser in meaning than the equivalent logical operators: in fact, we may postulate that this is not so much "loose" as "extra" meaning. Nevertheless, despite its uniform Contrastibility, this class presents some conceptual problems for our general thesis[2].

We may next examine the **PRO-FORMS:**

5. (a) Liked HIM, hated HER
   (b) That idea was MINE
   (c) *That car WHICH overtook us was a Lotus
   (d) WHAT overtook us?
   (e) A Lotus certainly {DID so }
                         {*did SO}
   (f) *SO I was led to believe
   (g) *I told you SO myself
   (h) *They say Mary's pregnant, but I don't believe IT

Since the class of pro-forms has received such concentrated attention from all theories of grammar, it provides the opportunity of comparing different theories with respect to their treatment of pro-forms, and the predictions they ought to make for our data. If, as used to be the standard treatment, pro-forms are substituted for their equivalent full forms (e.g. pronouns for NPs) by transformation, and under certain conditions, then at some semantically-explicit level, they will consist of PFs containing predicates, and will therefore be eligible to go through the stages of emphasis given in (8), Ch. 6. This is compatible with the Contrastibility of the personal, possessive, and interrogative pronouns, but not with the non-Contrastibility of relative pronouns. Other pro-forms, such as propredicate so and prosentential

[136]

Contrast

it, ought also to behave like personal pronouns, since in such an account, they are substitutes for full predicate-containing PFs. However, as (5f-h) show, they too do not behave as predicted by a transformational account.

Equally, there are problems for an account which base-generates pro-forms: again, such an account attempts to treat all pro-forms uniformly, and therefore draws no relevant distinction between personals, possessives, and interrogatives, on the one hand, and relatives, propredicates, and prosententials, on the other.

To save one or other of these positions, we might claim that the first group are "contentives" while the second group are "empty" (arguing perhaps that so and pro-S it are purely anaphoric). However, this certainly will not account for the relative pronouns, which contain the clear semantic distinction <±HUMAN>.

The explanation we would like to propose for these facts considers the two-fold nature of Contrast. On the one hand, Contrastive items cohere with an antecedent (the anaphoric property); on the other hand, they deny identity with that antecedent (the negative property). Consider next what the domain of Contrastive and antecedent items is: for grammatical items, it is the closed set (or paradigm). As we shall see, this is to some extent true for lexical contrasts too. Thus, the contrastive preposition in *John went OVER the wall* implicitly denies that he went under, round, through, or past it, and simply does not entertain the possibility that he went for, with, or despite the wall, since these are not in the same set as over. But not all grammatical items occur in multiple-member sets. Some are the sole member of their set, either because they are the only item in the language bearing some particular function, or else because their occurrence is externally constrained by some rule (e.g. of concord). Such items might therefore be capable of cohering, since coherence is not class-bound. If it were, the coherence between go and to that we noted in passage (1) would be impossible). If they are in one-member sets, however, they are necessarily incapable of denying, since this is a relationship between set-members. In the pro-form data given in (5), propredicate so and pro-S it are one-member sets of the first type: there appears to be no other item existing within the same functional paradigm.

[137]

Contrast

Relative pronouns, however, are of the second type: although they appear to occur within a small, though several-member paradigm, in reality, each one is uniquely specified by the semantic features of its antecedent. Thus relatives, for all that they occur in a several-member set from a text-book perspective, viewed functionally have no individual possibility of Contrast.

Next we may examine various **PARTICLES**. On the whole, this dustbin-category contains non-Contrastible items: sundry dummy elements, markers and flags having no discernible content:

    7. (a) *Percival tried TO find the grail
       (b) *I want TO be free
       (c) *TO err is human
       (d) *I found IT very difficult to answer the question
       (e) *IT was widely rumored that the Princess was a man
       (f) *IT's very foggy today
       (g) *IT was John who rang
       (h) *THERE was a jolly swagman who camped by a billabong
       (i) *Is THERE going to be a strike?

However, the situation is not as clearly non-Contrastible as (7a-i) would suggest. Infinitival <u>to</u> in particular presents some problems. Of the three forms exemplified in (7), it is perhaps the least likely to have content; yet there are cases where it is clearly Contrastible:

       (j) What shall we eat? – There's nothing TO eat
       (k) I just stood and gawped. What else was I TO do?
       (l) You have a nice touch. – YOU're nice TO touch

There are significant similarities among these cases. First, note that the infinitival verbs marked with <u>to</u> are all anaphoric, in the extended sense of the term used in Ch. 4.2: i.e. they are semantically similar to an antecedent item. Thus, <u>eat</u> and <u>touch</u> are both repetitions, while <u>do</u> is the pro-verb form for <u>stood and gawped</u>. Furthermore, the non-infinitival part of each of these sentences contains a denial of something in the previous context: (7j)

[138]

Contrast

denies the presupposed 'There's something to eat'; (7k) uses the adversative form <u>else</u>; while (7l) Contrasts <u>you</u>₁ with <u>you</u>₂, as well as the different case-roles and the different senses of <u>touch</u>. Finally, we may consider what would happen if Contrastive stress were on any other item than the particle <u>to</u>. Take (7j): <u>there</u>, as we have seen, rejects Contrast; Contrast on <u>nothing</u> would seem to answer the wrong question (e.g. *What is there to eat?*); Contrast on <u>eat</u> would suggest that, however, there is plenty to DRINK, for example. So, putting the Contrast on <u>to</u>, we would suggest, provides the only possibility of Contrasting the whole sentence. Even putting Contrast on every item would only give an oddly insistent pronunciation. Thus, the infinitival particle is not in itself the focus of the contrast, but as in the famous Chomsky example of the ex-convict's shirt (cf. Ch. 6.7 above), is instead merely the formal locus for a Contrast extending over a larger domain. We should also mention that infinitival <u>to</u> is frequently classified as a complementiser, a category to which we now turn.

The **COMPLEMENTISERS** have become an important category in modern generative grammar. Their behaviour under Contrast is mixed:

8.(a) ?I assumed THAT Bert was dead (*but I didn't assume WHY)

  (b) I know THAT Gert won the Cup, but I don't know HOW

  (c) ?James wondered WHETHER it was raining in Acapulco

  (d) James asked WHETHER it was raining, but he didn't ask WHY

  (e) ?The claim THAT Ronald has disappeared with the money surprises me

  (f) THAT Ronald has disappeared is obvious. WHY he has is a mystery

Apparently, the complementisers can sometimes tolerate Contrast, but sometimes not. The solution to this puzzle, we would like to suggest, is related to that proposed for (7j-l), and perhaps sheds further light on the notion of sentential Contrast.

First, it is generally assumed that complementisers constitute a COMP node which occurs in the S^1 construction (= in X-bar notation, S with a single bar). Thus, $S^1 \rightarrow$ COMP S, and S $\rightarrow N^2$ INFL V^2, as exemplified in Fig. 7.1.

[139]

Contrast

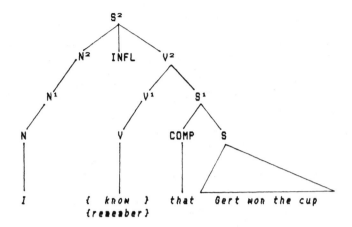

FIG. 7.1

Secondly, the occurrence of COMP structures is governed by the subcategorisation of the lexical items involved[3]. In this case, verbs like know or remember are subcategorised for S^1, but they also allow other varieties of complementation, viz:

> **know:** $[+\_\_\_S^1]$
> $[+\_\_\_N^2 \text{ to } V^2]$
>
> **remember:** $[+\_\_\_S^1]$
> $[+\_\_\_\text{to } V^2]$
> $[+\_\_\_S[N^2 \text{ Poss } -\text{ing } V^2]]$

COMP, too, may take several possible forms, depending upon the controlling verb, and also upon the controlled S: that, whether, if, why, (for)-to, how, what, when, etc. This introduces some complications into the picture:

(i) items subcategorised for S^1 do not necessarily take the same range of complementisers:

>   {that   }
> 9.(a) Linus knows {whether}   there's a Great
>   {if   }   Pumpkin
>   {why   }

Contrast

```
                          {that     }
    (b) Snoopy assumes {*whether}  he's a
                          {*if      }     basic beagle
                          {*why     }


                          {*that   }
    (c) Schroeder wonders {whether}   Lucy will
                          {if      }      go away
                          {?why    }


                          {that    }
    (d) Charlie Brown doubts  {whether} he'll
                          {if      }
                          {*why    }
       ever have any friends
```

This means that subcategorisation for S^1 alone is not enough: at least some items require further specification of permissible COMPs.

(ii) more problematical still, the presence of some COMPs depends not on their governing verb, but upon the further specification of the sister S. So, in a theory such as GB, Move-alpha to COMP, when alpha is a *wh*-element, can only take place if there is a constituent of the right type in S. In other words, the rule must somehow scan S for the presence of a temporal, a locative, a reason adverbial etc., in order to return <u>when</u>, <u>where</u>, <u>why</u> etc. to COMP.

(iii) Yet this situation is not wholly controlled by the constituency of S. Even if there is a constituent of the right type in S, Move-*wh* cannot take place if the governing verb is not subcategorised for the requisite complementiser:

9.(e) I know that Felix went to London: I know where Felix went

(f) I know that he went for a good reason: I know why he went

(g) I assume that Felix went to London: *I assume where Felix went

(h) I doubt that he went for a good reason: *I doubt why he went

No doubt such complications are resolvable in a complex theory such as GB. Our point in bringing them up is not to cast doubt on GB, but rather to demonstrate that it is not because a given item is subcategorised for S^1 that it therefore necessarily takes the full range of complementisers in all contexts — or even, indeed, in any context. There

[141]

Contrast

seem to be, in fact, many contexts for many verbs in which only one specific complementiser is possible. What seems to be happening in the Contrastive cases of (8), then, is that the Contrast is on the entire S^1, with the actual point of focus being on the complementiser. The explanation for this, therefore, is similar to the case of infinitival to: since the complementiser is, in this case, the unique member of a single-member paradigm, it has no Contrastibility in and of itself. Hence it may function as the locus for Contrast on the larger constituent.

The foregoing explanation applies mostly to complementiser that, since, like infinitival to (also known as complementiser (for)-to), that has no content. The other complementisers, for the most part, do have content, though like the relative pronouns, they may be the unique bearers of that content in certain positions. There is a semantic consequence to this: Contrast on COMP that focusses on 'the fact S'; Contrast on COMP wh-, though, focusses on some lesser constituent of S, the remainder of S being presupposed. This presumably explains the impossibility of the following sequence:

(i) *I know WHY Gert won the Cup, but I didn't know THAT she had

There is a formal consequence, too: Contrasts on COMP that have to take place in an antithetical — or at least parallel — construction (cf. (8f) as opposed to (8e)). Furthermore, they cannot occur in second conjunct position, and they cannot occur alone, since the normal way to Contrast the fact of an assertion — its polarity — is to stress the auxiliary. Thus, the only remaining possibility for Contrast on COMP that is the type exemplified in (8b), in which that S precedes, and the other COMP S follows. Given such facts, it seems reasonable to conclude that though Contrast on all other COMPs than that is genuine to the extent that they have content, nevertheless, they tend to function uniquely in most uses. This means that, along with that, Contrast on these items normally constitutes a mere point of focus for larger constituent Contrast.

It seems, therefore, that the claim we have made is fairly clearly vindicated, at least on the positive side: all cases of Contrast on so-called

[142]

Contrast

grammatical items are arguably on underlying predicates. The reverse is almost, but not quite, justifiable, too: grammatical items that cannot be contrasted do not contain underlying predicates.

There is one more type of case which we mention here in the interests of comprehensive coverage, though we believe it to be in fact quite distinct from the examples we have studied so far. We refer to the type of Contrast known as "citation contrast". This takes the form of stress upon sublexical morphological items, as in:

10. (a) I said INcisive not DEcisive
    (b) They were complImentary, though hardly complEmentary
    (c) You mean stationAry, not stationEry
    (d) He was more EXtinguished than DIStinguished

These are founded upon an explicit contrast of forms actually used, and always arise out of a metalinguistic impulse. It is very clear that they are in some sense post-lexical, and indeed post-phonological*. Their mysteriousness derives largely from the artificiality of their usual format, viz. as isolated sentences in linguistic discussions. In context, however, their behaviour is very standardised: the negated member of the pair is always a repetition of an Accented PF in previous discourse, usually having the same surface form. Thus, what we might call the "contrast-trigger" in these cases, usually occurs in some previous part of the discourse (often a dialogue), where it presumably has reached its surface-structure form. The speaker of (10), who may be responding to an interlocutor or monitoring his own utterance, has a surface-structure form against which to assess his intended item. His response is to "repair" the offending item by substituting a corrected form, with the locus of the correction stressed.

What seems perfectly clear, though, is that such constructions are so different from normal Contrasts in the rigidity of their format, and the lack of any connection other than a purely fortuitous physical one between their contrasted parts, that there are no solid grounds for believing them to originate from the same process. Similar conclusions have been put forward by Kiefer 1967: 6 sqq., Jackendoff 1972: 242, and Schmerling 1974a: 70 sqq. For the contrary view, see Dogil 1979: 14 and

[143]

Contrast

passim. However, Mangold 1975: 43 presents what appears to be an unassailable argument for the view expressed above: he points out that Contrastively-stressed inflexional formatives can only be used to contrast MORPHOLOGY and not meaning. Compare:

11.(a) It wasn't oxES, but oxEN.
  (b) *He saw not ONE ox, but oxEN.

7.2 Contrast on lexical items

Because Contrast is constrained textually, by the negative imputation of some preceding element, it is essentially a syntagmatic process. We have shown in the foregoing section that despite the appearance they give of functioning paradigmatically in sets, grammatical items under contrast nevertheless conform to this same general pattern. But there is a sense in which lexical category items also give the appearance of occurring in paradigmatic sets, in that the contrastive items (i.e. the antecedent and the subsequent items) seem to be constrained by the condition that they should be members of the same semantic set. 'Semantic set' presumably is to be defined as any set of all and only those semantic configurations sharing structure, down to a certain level of differentiation. This level has to be determined empirically, and may be variable: most such sets, we would suggest, are fuzzy. But in any case, this paradigmaticity is more apparent than real, as we shall now show. (12) shows the progressively distinct apparent semantic set of <u>strawberry</u>:

12.(a) I like STRAWBERRIES, but not
        {GOOSEBERRIES }
        { APPLES   }
        {BLACKCURRANTS}

   (b) I like STRAWBERRIES, but not {GARDENING}
                                    { CREAM   }
                                    {SHORTCAKE}

   (c) ?I like STRAWBERRIES, but not
        {   LAWN TENNIS   }
        {ROYAL GARDEN PARTIES}
        {   PRIZE DAYS   }

[144]

Contrast

(d) ??I like STRAWBERRIES, but not
    (rubber BOOTS)
    (Elton JOHN   )
    (KIRKEGAARD   )
    (INTOLERANCE)
    (LEXICOSTATISTICS)

(e) ?*I like STRAWBERRIES, but not
    (being WASHED   )
    (having my NOSE pierced)
    (whistling *GRANADA*)
    (arguing with FASCISTS)

    The hierarchy which seems to emerge from (12) is a scale of contingency: (12a) is perhaps necessarily Contrastive, but the subsequent (groups of) sentences rely more and more upon contingent circumstances for their acceptability and interpretability. At some stage, we reach such a point that, in order to accommodate a sentence from (12e) one has to cook up so outlandish a situation that we have to judge it as highly unlikely (rather than highly unacceptable or even ungrammatical). It may, of course, be argued that this is because strawberries do not belong to the same "natural set" as nose-piercing or whistling *Granada*, but while there is undoubtedly some truth in this assertion, it does not throw much light on what is actually going on here[5].
    In our view, the solution is clearly bound up with the notion of COHERENCE as developed in Ch. 5. Firstly, the definition of 'semantic set' given above included the notion of "shared structure". This in fact is precisely what constitutes coherence, particularly in the form underlying both Reduction and Contrast. Thus we can explain the facts of (12) in this way: the sentences of (12) make sense to the extent that the Contrasting items cohere. This is perhaps why (12a) may be regarded as necessarily contrastive, given the high coherence of strawberries with gooseberries and other garden fruit (in terms of shared semantic structure), and the explicit negation of one of them. The subsequent sentences of (12) come to depend progressively more upon their surrounding contexts (which are not, of course, supplied here), for semantic information to "fill in the gaps" between the contrasting items. Thus, the sentences of (12b) require close association of meaning, whereas those of (12c) call for a rather more remote and culturally-restricted

[145]

Contrast

association.

This, then, brings us to our second point arising out of the notion of coherence, and that is, that as we have seen at length, a crucial component of textual coherence is the common ground of the discourse. The common ground functions both on the intensional propositional information provided by the text, and on the extensional information provided by scenes and knowledge frames of various levels of complexity ranging from community knowledge to limited shared experiences of many kinds. Within this welter of potentially and actually relevant information, a text-world gradually gets built up, and **it is through this text-world that all textual operations are filtered.** This is an extremely important point: not only do reference-acts take place within the domain of the text-world (or worlds), as we will show in Ch. 8, but all of our emphatic relationships operate in respect of it too (via their adherence to the coherence constraint). Consider (12c): for many readers, perhaps, this is no better than the examples of (12d). But there are some people for whom there exists a "ready-made" world in which strawberries are naturally associated with lawn tennis, i.e. the world of the Wimbledon Championship. For these people, the simple mention of one or the other NP from (12c) will be enough to evoke the Wimbledon scene as a potential text-world. Other people, though, will require such a world to be more painstakingly built up in the text. This is the case, probably, for the sentences of (12d-e): in order for the Contrast to be really salient, a text-world has to be constructed in which the NPs are in some relationship. The degree to which this operation presents problems is, of course, in inverse proportion to the probability that some such knowledge-frame already exists for the speakers. Our epithet "outlandish", therefore, represents our prediction that such a prefabricated framework of knowledge for a given situation has a very low probability of prior existence.

When such a text-world is successfully contrived, however, the procedure is exactly the same as before, i.e. syntagmatic rather than paradigmatic. In the ensuing sections, though, we will continue to refer to these relationships as 'sets', but the reader should bear in mind that these are defined in terms of coherency, and not as opaque and *sui generis* paradigms.

[146]

7.3 Summary: Contrast on grammatical and lexical categories

We can summarise the foregoing data on Contrast in a diagram:

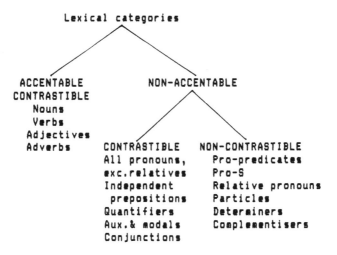

FIG. 7.2

Fig. 7.2 marshalls the facts of sections 7.1-2 in terms of the lexical/grammatical distinction and Contrastibility. Notice that no category is <+A -C>, and that our hypothesis predicts this: <-C> marks the set of contentless forms; A, by the rules of (8) in Ch. 6, marks only content-elements, i.e. predicates. By extension, the same is true of R and C also, again by the stipulations of rule (8), together with the positive and negative coherence constraints. It is the latter of these which operates with respect to C, and it is to this that we now turn.

7.4 Semantic properties of sets

We have seen then that contrast consists of the non-identity of similars, and that this definition involves two factors: (i) negativity, and (ii) set-membership. We will look at the characteristics of negativity in section 7.5, but at this point, let

Contrast

us examine the semantic notion of **set-membership** .

By definition, the members of a set are **mutually exclusive**. Furthermore, if the set is semantic, rather than (merely) mathematical, then the members are **non-unique**, i.e. there must be at least two. Finally, a semantic set is **specified**, i.e. there exist criteria for set-membership other than mere nomination. We shall examine these properties in turn.

Exclusiveness. Unlike Accent, as we have seen, Contrast operates between similar, i.e. partially identical items, or in other words is **anaphoric**. On a Contrastive item, C not only emphasises that item, it also excludes the other items in that particular semantic set. For example:

> 13.(a) It's STRAWBERRIES I like (and not gooseberries, raspberries...)
> (b) It was the DOCTOR who examined the Pope (and not the dentist, obstetrician, chiropodist, TV repairman...)

This property seems to characterise all kinds of potential opposites (cf. Ch. 5.3), as long as the contrast is expressed positively. With overtly negative contrasts, however, (which we call 'contradictions' in section 7.5), the situation is quite different:

> 14.(a) It's not STRAWBERRIES I like
> (b) It wasn't the DOCTOR who examined the Pope

In the case of isolated sentences such as these, all we know is that the negated item itself is excluded. But we have no idea about what it is that the speaker DOES in fact like. However, by now it should be abundantly clear that observations based on isolated sentences are to be treated with a great deal of suspicion. The Chomskyan presuppositional account (see Ch. 6.7) will have us believe that a cleft sentence like (14a) presupposes that 'I like some x', and asserts that 'x is not strawberries'. The essence of a sentence like (14a), however, is that it CONTRADICTS a previous assertion that the speaker likes STRAWBERRIES. There is also, it is true, some presuppositional content. But this is NOT the completely unspecified 'I like some x', but rather 'I like some member of the *specified set*'.

[148]

Contrast

The set-specification, as we have seen, is a function of the common ground. Contradictions, then, assert that some previous claim is untrue, while preserving a textually-specified presupposition.

In the positive cases, we can test for exclusiveness by conjoining such sentences as (13) with conjuncts expressing non-exclusiveness: the result ought to be unacceptable.

15. (a) *It's STRAWBERRIES I like, and all other fruit too
    (b) *It was the DOCTOR who examined the Pope, and so did everybody else

In the negative cases, non-exclusive negation gives equally weird results:

16. (a) *It's not STRAWBERRIES I like, and no other fruit either
    (b) *It wasn't the DOCTOR who examined the Pope, and nor was it anybody else

The cleft structure has been used in all of these examples since, as will be suggested in Ch. 9, its stressed element is normally C. Non-clefts, whose focal element may be either A or C, distinguish between the absence and presence, respectively, of exclusiveness:

17. (a) The *doctor* examined the Pope, and so did everybody else
    (b) *The DOCTOR examined the Pope, and so did everybody else

Non-uniqueness. Since contrast involves denial within sets, it follows that the C-marked element cannot be the unique member of a single-member set. If such must logically be the case, then contrast will be impossible. Possible instances of this include sets whose membership has already been exhausted in a given context, and genuine single-member sets. Here are some examples:

18. (a) *I find the former difficult to accept, and it's the LATTER I find difficult to accept also
    (b) *Out of everybody here, it's ALL of them I've met
    (c) The President I've met is Gerald FORD

[149]

Contrast

(d) *The Supreme Pontiff I've met is the POPE

Thus, (18a) has already exhausted the two-member set of its sole alternative. (18b) divides the set of {everybody here} into the two implicit subsets {those I've met} and {those I haven't met} and declares the second to be empty, thus effectively leaving a single-member set. (18c) is acceptable, since the set of Presidents contains several members, each of which is potentially Contrastive with Gerald Ford. (18d), on the other hand, nominates a set with just one member: the Pope (though if the example had named names, e.g. '... John the Twenty-THIRD', this would have constituted a different set, whose members are those individuals who have been Supreme Pontiff).

Specificity. The contrastive element must also belong to a semantic set, that is to say, one whose members share at least one semantic property other than belonging to that set. This has the effect of ensuring that contrast is semantically specified from among the properties which the set-members have in common. It also means that the C-marked element refers to some entity which is distinct, non-analytic, and semantically informative:

19. (a) *It was SOMEONE who stole my cheque-book
    (b) *It's PEOPLE who say that George is a genius
    (c) *What Sid discovered was SOMETHING
    (d) *It was a MURDERER who killed John
    (e) *It's a MOTHER that Maud is to her daughter

Notice that where a reading for any of these sentences is possible, the Contrastive element must be understood as specific. Thus to be interpretable, (19d) must use murderer in the sense of 'a professional assassin', and not simply 'one who has become a murderer by virtue of having murdered'. In other words, the analytic use is non-Contrastible (cf. Donnellan 1978 on 'referential' vs. 'attributive'). This is not a surprising finding, in view of our conclusion in sections 7.1-3 that Contrastibility requires content: analytic items, of course, lack content to the extent that they are alternative locutions, i.e. completely specified by

[150]

Contrast

the remainder of the expression in which they occur. Similarly, <u>mother</u> in (19e) is tautologous when analytic, but may be specific in the sense of 'one who displays the motherly virtues', and <u>someone</u> in (19a) could be specific in the sense 'a person of consequence'. The requirement that the C-marked element must be specific predicts that analytic uses such as definitions will reject contrastive marking, and such appears to be the case:

> 20.(a) *It's the CAT that is a domestic feline
>   (b) *It's a TRIANGLE that is a three-sided figure

If these are acceptable at all, it is as citation-forms, somewhat in the sense of, for example: 'The term for a three-sided figure is "a triangle"'.

In terms of our discussion in sections 7.1-3 above, the specific sense can be regarded as contentful, i.e. bearing at least one underlying predicate. The analytic use, on the other hand, is empty of content, thus bearing no predicates. The claim is, therefore, that examples like (20) are non-Contrastible because in each case the item in capitals provides no information beyond that already provided elsewhere in the construction.

The notion of specificity referred to here is presumably related to the syntactic notion 'specificational', introduced by Akmajian, and developed extensively by Higgins 1976. We shall return in Ch. 9 to this and other properties of certain syntactic constructions whose form is determined by the textual impulse of emphasis, and particularly of Contrast.

7.5 C and negative coherence

All of the types of 'contrast' distinguished by Lyons (cf. Ch. 5) are capable of entering into, or of forming the environment for, C. But what of our tentative suggestion that such an environment consists of a matching semantic structure in the scope of some form of self-negation? Van Dijk's coherence constraint (Fig. 5.3 above) ensures that the matching PFs are terminal ones, which fits the arrangement we require for C so far. We want now to investigate the hypothesis concerning negation.

[151]

Contrast

The first point to be made is that the proposed negation may occur on either the antecedent or the subsequent item, without in any way affecting the claim. But are the pairs (or multiples) of items affected by C susceptible to such an analysis?

The role of markedness. One phenomenon which perhaps suggests the requisite positive-negative relationship between contrastive pairs is that of markedness[7]. Markedness, like many other linguistic phenomena, is seemingly a matter of degree, according to the items involved, and their contexts, (cf. Lyons 1977: 311). However, taking clear-cut cases among gradable adjectives (Lyons' 'antonyms'), we have such examples as <u>tall</u> (unmarked) — <u>short</u> (marked), <u>high</u> (u) — <u>low</u> (m), <u>deep</u> (u) — <u>shallow</u> (m), <u>long</u> (u) — <u>short</u> (m), <u>far</u> (u) — <u>near</u> (m), <u>wide</u> (u) — <u>narrow</u> (m), among dimension terms; and <u>good</u> (u) — <u>bad</u> (m), <u>fresh</u> (u) — <u>stale</u> (m), <u>clever</u> (u) — <u>stupid</u> (m) among evaluative terms. If the negation hypothesis is correct, such pairs should share semantic structure up to a point where it is negated in the marked term. In simple terms, this would mean that short ought to be equivalent to 'not tall', low to 'not high', bad to 'not good', and stupid to 'not clever'. (Lyons 1977:277sq) notes that there is a sense in which these equivalences seem to hold true, and this stems from "a general human tendency to categorise experience in terms of dichotomous contrasts", even when the particular realm of experience is gradable. Thus a negative reply to *"Is Trevor clever?"* suggests that he is stupid, rather than merely average. However, it is clear that there is really an excluded middle operating in such cases, since (21a) makes sense, whereas (21b) (a true dichotomy — medical science notwithstanding) does not:

  21.(a) Trevor is neither clever nor stupid
    (b) Trevor is neither dead nor alive

(given, of course, that Trevor refers to a human being).

  With complementaries, marking seems to be culturally determined: Lyons examines the example of gender-markedness (307 sqq). In domesticated animals, it seems that the unmarked term reflects the use or value of the animal in a given culture. Gender-differentiating terms do exist in most cases, but the generic also has a gender-sense,

[152]

Contrast

corresponding to the unmarked case (e.g. dog, which is masculine, and duck, which is feminine). A similar point may be made with human occupation-terms, e.g. nurse, typist, dancer *vs.* doctor, executive, conductor: the genders expected here reflect cultural roles, rather than logical implications. Converses seem not to display markedness generally, while directionals appear to behave similarly to gradables in this respect. Multiple taxonomies show no clearly defined marking tendencies, though as Lyons points out (p. 288) the assertion of one item in a many-member set tends to imply the denial of all the others. This is particularly the case when it is asserted as the complement of be:

22. (a)   This is a rose *Implies* 'This is not a tulip/daffodil/geranium...'
    (b) Today is Monday *Implies* 'Today is not Sunday/Tuesday...

He also points out that the implication of denial is clinched, as it were, when the item in question is contrastive (i.e. marked 'C'); but since this would render our attempt to characterise C circular, we obviously cannot use this as a test, (cf. Ch. 7.4).

It seems clear, therefore, that the negation hypothesis, as tentatively suggested above, is too strong. Markedness perhaps reflects cultural and cognitive behaviour rather than linguistic competence (insofar as these can be distinguished, of course, which is not very far), and in any case it only applies to some kinds of Contrast. But there is no reason to suppose that, given two Contrasting items, one contains the semantic structure of the other, but within the scope of a negative. We do not need to postulate, that is, actual negation in one of the semantic structures involved, even when one is unmarked relative to the other.

However, that is not to say that examples involving actual negation cannot be Contrastive. We shall call such Contrasts simple contradictions, and they are of two types:
(A) where an item is used twice, and on one of these occasions is explicitly negated, e.g:

23. Where's your friend Charles, the deep-sea diver? Charles isn't a DIVER

(B)   where the two items belong to a single lexical

[153]

Contrast

set (perhaps exclusively); then, the second is used to contradict the first, e.g:

24. Tom is tall, isn't he? No, he's not, he's SHORT

(24) is equivalent to: *No, he's NOT [tall]*, i.e. type (A), with the repeated gradable Reduced in the scope of an explicit negative, itself the focus of the Contrast.

These constitute the most clear-cut cases of negativity in contrast. By the same token, perhaps, they are less interesting than the cases involving negative implications, which we will examine shortly.

(C) a further set of cases show the contrastive item attracting the negation semantically, though not syntactically (cf. (25b,d)):

25.(a) *All* the *boys didn't go*
   (b) ALL the [boys] [didn't] [go]
   (c) I *didn't* marry you because I *love* you
   (d) I didn't [marry] you because I LOVE you

The notion we want to follow up now is that which we have variously expressed as the "imputation of denial, or falsity, or negativity" upon the Contrastive item. Notice the word "imputation": the idea is that Contrast can involve implied, as well as actual, negation, a state of affairs whose counterpart we have already seen with Reduction.

Let us, then, examine this variety of Contrast by looking at some examples a second time. From (1) in chapter 6:

26.(a) You *pass* THROUGH the [country]

In chapter 6, we characterised this contrast as follows:

(b) <ADDRESSEE+OTHER>$_i$ <i MOVE>$_j$ & <j CONTINUOUS> <j THROUGH k> <COUNTRY>$_k$

where THROUGH contrasts with <u>to</u> in:

(c) ...(when) we *go* to the [country]

(26c) is represented as:

[154]

Contrast

(d) <SPEAKER+OTHER>ₐ <A MOVE>ₑ <B TO C>
<COUNTRY>𝒸

We commented at that point that the semantic relationship between <u>through</u> and <u>to</u> was presumably one of implication: 'If x goes through y, then x goes to y (and further)'. We can perhaps express this a little more carefully: 'If x goes through y, then x starts at some point w and finishes at some point z, and at some intermediate timepoint is located in y'ᵉ. An implication we can draw from this is 'x does not stop in y'. Compare this with <u>to</u>: 'If x goes to y, then x starts at some point w, and finishes at y'⁷. Clearly, if this is the case, then 'x stops at y'. Since these implications of <u>through</u> and <u>to</u> are mutually denying, we seem to have identified a case of contrast between a positive and a negative implication. In terms of Lyons' categories of contrast, however, we can perhaps classify <u>through</u> and <u>to</u> as orthogonal directionals.

Another example from (1) in chapter 6 is:

27.(a)...we have a *place* to *go* and we don't sort of STOP...

The first conjunct in (27a) may be represented along the lines of:

(b) <SPEAKER+OTHER>ₐ <A HAVE B> <PLACE>ₑ &
<A MOVE>𝒸 <C TO B>

i.e. something like (26d) embedded as a relative clause in 'we have place'. As we have already seen, (26d) — or rather, one of its predicates, (<TO>) — bears the implication 'x stops at y'. In this case the variable x is satisfied by we, and the variable y by the unspecified goal. The second conjunct in (27a) may be represented as follows (ignoring <u>sort of</u>):

(c) <SPEAKER+OTHER>ₐ NOT <<A STOP>ₑ <B IN C>
<COUNTRY>𝒸>

In this case,of course,the sentence asserts (rather than implies) 'x does not stop before y' (where y in this case is not "in the country"), giving a contrast between a positive implication and a negative assertion.

[155]

Contrast

A third example from the same passage is:

28.(a) This might NOT be so in AUSTRALIA...?

The reference of <u>this</u> is to the preceding sentence:

(b) ...we think of it as *important* and an *event* when we *go* to the [country]

Let us call this antecedent sentence $\langle X \rangle$. We may then represent (28a) as:

(c) $\langle\langle NOT \ X \rangle_A \ \ \langle A \ POSSIBLE \rangle\rangle_B \ \ \langle B \ IN \ C \rangle$ $\langle AUSTRALIA \rangle_C$

"It is possible that not-X is the case in Australia".

Presumably, the focus of the Contrast on <u>Australia</u> here is opposed to:

(d) This...is *perhaps* a very ENGLISH [thing] to *talk* about...

Since we are here dealing with proper nouns, it is evident that the Contrasting terms (ENGLAND, included in <u>English</u>, and AUSTRALIA) firstly are not analysable in the same way as our previous examples, and secondly, do not bear implications in the same way as our previous examples — but cf. our remarks on the semantics of proper nouns in Chs. 2 and 6.

ENGLAND and AUSTRALIA, then, are both members of a multiple taxonomy, and are incompatible (semantically speaking). We have already seen that the assertion of one member of a multiple taxonomy tends to deny each of the others: whether this is a material or a contingent implication, however, or something perhaps even weaker, is very difficult to decide. Clearly these possibilities are vitiated if the set is a very large one, (such as "all the nations of the world", in this case). However, a factor which will delimit a much smaller sub-set of this large set — and we take it as given that Contrast is more salient within a smaller set — is the common ground. It happens in this case that the participants are English, Australian, American and Norwegian, though only the first two of these are represented in our actual extract. It seems

[156]

Contrast

reasonable to hold that this is the relevant set in the present case. Furthermore, it seems reasonable with such a small set to postulate that the assertion of one member in a proposition will implicitly deny the others in that proposition. This not only explains the contrast on <u>Australia</u>, with its explicit antecedent <u>English</u>, but also the contrast on <u>English</u>, with no explicit antecedent, though with the same small set in the common ground.

Let us now consider an example from passage (12) in Ch. 6. Segment (8) reads as follows:

29.(a)   But just at the *end* there's a RECONCILIATION (viz: 'between James and his father')

Here the contrast is with the preceding assertion in segment (6):

(b) *James...explicitly hates* his [father]

Leaving out any representation of <u>explicitly</u>, (29b) may be represented as:

(c)   <JAMES>$_A$ <A —EMOTION B> <FATHER-of-A>$_B$

The semantic form of (29a), including the implication, will be something like:

(d)   <<<JAMES>$_A$ <A   +EMOTION   B> <FATHER-of-A>$_B$>$_C$ <C AGAIN>>$_D$ <D AT E> <END>$_E$

"James likes his father again at the end (of the book)".

It is possible that the notion of reconciliation, in other contexts, incorporates reciprocity. The important thing here is that, however one represents it, <u>reconciliation</u> will contain in a PF the predicate underlying <u>like</u>, which, borrowing somewhat from Leech, we have called <+EMOTION>. A clear implication relating these two propositions can then be formally expressed as:

(e) *All* x,y: *If* <+EMOTION <x, y>> *Then* <NOT <-EMOTION <x, y>>>

[157]

Contrast

"If x likes y, then it is not the case
that x dislikes y".

Note that <u>like</u>, <u>hate</u>, etc. are antonyms (gradables)
in that they are scalar. They are somewhat special
in that the scale is differentiated elsewhere than
simply at its extremities (cf.among adjectives,
<u>hot-warm</u> / <u>cool</u>-cold). The Contrast in (29a)
nevertheless relies upon a negative implication, but
we shall return presently to the effect of the
middle ground in antonymous contrasts.
      Of all the types of opposition set out in Ch.
5.3, we still have not looked at any examples of
complementaries or converses under Contrast.
Complementaries.
Complementaries, like incompatibles, tend to be
mutually exclusive. More precisely, we may say that
linguistically they are mutually exclusive, but
ontologically there may be a fuzzy middle ground[10].
The assertion of one thus tends to deny the other,
since its assessment as a genuine implication
depends upon the validity of the negative of its
reverse. For example:

30. *All* x: *If* <ALIVE <x>> *Then* <NOT <DEAD
    <x>>>

Consider, for example:

31.(...*Stephen Biko died* on the *night* of...)

   (a) One of the *terrible ironies* of *South
       African politics today* is that [Biko]'s
       DEATH has *probably accomplished* more
       for his *cause* than anything he did when
       he was ALIVE

   (b) Biko did things (for his cause) when he
       was alive

   (c) Biko's death has accomplished more (than
       (b))

Part of the contrast here is obtained by way of the
implicational pragmatic relationship between
<u>accomplish</u> and <u>alive</u>: (i) 'if x accomplishes y, then
x is (normally) alive'. In other words, the normal
agency of an accomplishment is human and living at
the time. But, as (30) states, (ii) 'if x is alive,
then x is not dead'. So, (31c) asserts a

[158]

Contrast

contradiction to the first of these implications: 'Biko accomplished some things; therefore, he was alive at the time' (by (i)); 'Biko accomplished more by his death; therefore, he was dead at the time' (a necessary entailment); 'if he was dead, he was not alive' (the reverse of (ii)); 'but if he accomplished something at this time, he should have been alive' (by (i)). The Contrast is therefore between 'not alive' and 'alive', and is carried by way of both logical and pragmatic implications.

Converses. Converses, too, tend to be mutually exclusive in most cases. So that 'if x is the wife of y, then it is not the case that y is the wife of x'. Some, however, are not quite so clear:

32. *All* x,y: *If* <BEFORE <x, y>> *Then* <NOT <AFTER <x, y>>>

Where x and y are complex and perhaps discontinuous chains of events, it is not obvious that the lefthand side of the implication could ever be asserted. Nevertheless, in context — as we have by now seen — Contrasts may have to be inferred from a complex series of implications. Take, for example, segment (2) in example (12) of Ch. 6:

33. *...1927* was, after all, AFTER *Freud...*

The converse of <u>after</u> occurs nowhere in the vicinity, so clearly this is not a simple contradiction-type contrast. In this case, it seems, we have to look ahead in the discourse for the contrast to become clear, and we have to look at, among other things, the semantics of <u>recognise</u>, and the pragmatic implications on <u>Freud</u> and <u>sexual symbolism</u>. The semantic structure which is lexicalised as <u>recognise</u> contains the predicate KNOW, which is generally accepted to be a factive. This means that its y-variable is a true fact, that is, a state of affairs existing in w_j. Now we come to the pragmatic implication, based on the assumption that Freud revealed the existence of sexual symbolism (whether this is true or not is immaterial): 'if Freud revealed the existence of sexual symbolism at time x, then other people did not recognise its existence before time x'. But 1927 is after time x; therefore people ('the average reader') should have recognised its existence at that time. Nevertheless, the speaker 'wonders

[159]

Contrast

whether' (i.e. to some extent, doubts) this was the case: that is, to some extent, he believes it might not have been the case that the average reader recognised the sexual symbolism at that time. (We briefly discussed the modulatory function of performative-type verbs like <u>wonder</u> in Ch. 6.23). So, despite the fact that 1927 was after time x, he implies that readers' ignorance ('not knowing') of these facts might suggest they lived before time x. But since before, by (32), implies 'not after', we again have a Contrast.

Gradables. Finally, how do antonyms (gradables) behave under Contrast? Recall that such pairs are not mutually exclusive, except superficially in certain contexts which might well be regulable by Gricean conventions of co-operation. However, given that they are normally scalar, one might expect Contrast to reveal rather more subtle distinctions than with mutually exclusive pairs. In the case of <u>hate</u> vs. <u>reconcile</u> ((29) above), we saw that the assertion of <+EMOTION> did not allow the implication of <-EMOTION>. But the converse is not the case:

> 34. *All* x,y: *If* <NOT <-EMOTION <x, y>>> *Then* ?<+EMOTION <x, y>>
>
> "If x does not dislike y, it is not necessarily the case that x likes y".

If the Contrast in (29) had been the other way round, how would (34) have affected it?

> 35. A: At the *end* of the [book], *James expresses* his *lack* of *dislike* for his *father* in these *words...*
> B: But *right through* the [book], he *explicitly* doesn't LIKE his [father].

An initial observation would be that there is something a little strange about B's intervention here. We are prompted to wonder why he would even utter his Contrastive statement. In fact, as we shall see, such examples throw some rather interesting shafts of light on the whole question of negativity in Contrast. Presumably, in this case, (35A) would include part of the structure of (29c), but negated:

[160]

Contrast

36.(a) NOT <<JAMES>ᴀ <A −EMOTION B>
        FATHER-of-A>ᴮ>

(35B), on the other hand, would be identical to part
of (29d) but negated:

    (b) NOT <<JAMES>ᴀ <A +EMOTION B>
         <FATHER-of-A>ᴮ>

The sole difference between (36a) and (36b), then,
is   the   predicate-polarity (as opposed to the
propositional polarity) on <EMOTION>. There are two
points to   make   here,   one semantic and   one
observational. The semantic point is that   the
Contrast in (35B) depends on the assumption that it
is stating something antonymous to (35A). But as
(30) makes clear, this is not the case: there is no
necessary opposition between 'lack of dislike' and
'not liking'. There may be, of course: not liking
someone includes the possibility of hatred   or
dislike, but not exclusively; and it is this middle
ground which robs the Contrast of its salience. This
brings us to the observational point: the above
comments lead to the prediction that (35B) should be
at the most only weakly contrastive, and such does
indeed seem to be the case, as we have already
remarked. We might check this out, though, against
more straightforward gradable adjectives:

    37.(a) The *full story* of the *events* of that
           [night] is too *long* and *complicated* to
           recount within *present limitations.*
        (b) However, BRIEFLY, what *appears* to have
            [happened] is *this...*

Whatever its full representation, we take it that
(37a) will contain a semantic structure much like:

    (c) <STORY>ᴀ <A LONG>

while (37b) will contain:

    (d) <<to-EXTENT>ᴮ <B SHORT>>

That is, "to a short extent". In other words, the
surface sentence-adverb <u>briefly</u> is here represented
by part of a proposition containing the predicate
<SHORT>. LONG in (37c) and SHORT in (37d) are an
antonymous pair, related implicationally by:

Contrast

      (e) *All* x: *If*   <SHORT <x>>   *Then*   <NOT
      <LONG <x>>>

This   explains the contrast in (37b). However,
suppose the implicit polarity of such an opposition
is made explicit, bearing in mind that:

      (f) *All*   x: *If*   <NOT   <LONG   <x>>> *Then*
      ?<SHORT <x>>

and also:

      (g) *All* x: *If* <NOT <SHORT <x>> *Then* ?<LONG
      <x>>

The strength or weakness of a contrast is directly
bound up with this question of negative-scope in
implications. Such an example as (38) is relevant:

    38.(a) The *full* *story...* is *not* too *long* or
        complicated to *recount.*
      (b) However, without being BRIEF, what
      [happened] is *this...*

(38a) contains the partial representation:

      (c) NOT <<STORY>ₐ <A LONG>>

and (38b) contains:

      (d) NOT <<to-EXTENT>ᵦ <B SHORT>>

  (37g) tells us that if something is not short, this
does not necessarily imply that it is long. If this
were not the case, then (38) would provide strong
Contrast, since (38c) negates LONG and (38d) negates
its antonym SHORT. Thus the situation ought to be
identical to a straight Contrast between LONG and
SHORT. But as (37f,g) show, there is middle ground
between an antonymic pair, ground which is revealed
by negating both terms. Therefore the Contrast is
predicted to be at the most a weak one, and this
does seem to be borne out by the data.
      Contrast on gradables is therefore executed
under somewhat different conditions from Contrast on
the other categories of opposition. Complementaries,
converses, orthogonals etc., display no distinction
between Contrast when they are explicitly negated
and Contrast when they are implicitly denied, or
when they implicitly deny their antecedent. For

[162]

Contrast

maximum contrast, however, gradables (antonyms), and to some extent, motionals have to be stated positively. If either item is stated or implied negatively, then the unexcluded middle of gradables causes problems for interpretation.

NOTES TO CHAPTER SEVEN

1. We are indebted to both Steve Harlow and to Anne Mills for many of the points in the discussion of Contrastive the.
2. In the cases where logical quantifiers have explicit expression in surface structure, Contrast appears to have the opposite effect from that which our hypothesis predicts:

> (i)   Cows have four legs
> (ii) All cows have four legs
> (iii) ALL cows have four legs

We can interpret (i) and (ii), that is to say, as being inherently hedged with typically. Example (iii), though, seems to allow less latitude of interpretation: Contrastive stress appears to restrict the meaning of all to logical universal quantification, which in other circumstances (e.g. the determiners) is seemingly not enough to support Contrast.

3. Subcategorisation apparently remains the mainstay of Chomskyan generative grammar, albeit in a somewhat different form than in Chomsky 1965. In his 1981 book, he incorporates the machinery of subcategorisation into his Projection Principle (p. 29), which states that the subcategorisation properties of lexical items must be satisfied at each syntactic level (i.e. LF, D-structure, and S-structure).
One such possible property is the selection of the Poss -ing complementiser. This, however, is now handled via case-assignment (p. 64).
For another view of complement selection, arguing that it is semantic rather than syntactic, see Grimshaw 1979. This accords with our brief discussion in section 8.65 below. The papers in Hoekstra *et al.* 1980 offer a variety of approaches to these questions.

[163]

Contrast

4. In fact, they are for Chomsky (1972: 99) important evidence that interpretation of focussed elements must occur at surface-structure. But it is surely unlikely that forms like those of (10c) would ever be phonologically distinct. Further cases presenting even more profound problems include the reinterpretation of graphology into phonology found in:

(iv) I meant [aʊ]ral, not [ɔ]ral.

5. Chomsky 1972: 94, fn. 25, mentions equivalent cases:

(v) Is John certain to WIN? - No, he's certain to drink BEER

Here, the unnaturalness of the Contrast is "a matter of pairing of foci", just as it is in cases of unnatural co-ordination. Such a pairing, to be natural, "must use as focus items that are somehow related - exactly how is not clear, but the relation surely involves considerations that extend beyond grammar". That depends on one's theory of grammar, of course, and within that, on one's definition of semantics. Since such an association as that between Wimbledon fortnight and strawberry teas is obviously pragmatic rather than strictly logical, however, sentences such as these pose problems for semantic theories which seek to be well-defined objects. Seemingly, we must now accept that a theory of meaning (as opposed to one of truth-function) cannot be a well-defined object, and that semantics is therefore necessarily fuzzy and open-ended.

6. Hetzron 1977 distinguishes between "opposition to something" (= Contrast), and "opposition to anything" (= Accent, his 'emphasis'). Neither of these characterisations appears to capture the full range of properties of Contrast and Accent, however. The former makes no mention of the necessary coherency link between the "something" and the item under Contrast. The latter, by embracing everything, actually defines nothing. As we have seen, Accented items too have to maintain coherency.

[164]

Contrast

Schmerling 1974b argues against the existence of contrastive stress, except as a pragmatic entity. This is similar to our position here, but we attempt to define the relevant pragmatic conditions.

7. Cruse 1976 makes a distinction between 'marked' terms and 'committed' terms, the latter being one type of the former. Committed terms are those which, when used comparatively, imply or presuppose their positive: e.g. *X is worse than Y* presupposes *Y is bad*, according to Cruse (p. 283).

8. For more formal representations of these prepositional meanings, see Leech 1969: 180 sqq. and Bennett 1975: 85 etc. Note that y is taken to be three-dimensional, hence <u>in</u> is used. The equivalent two-dimensional preposition would be <u>across</u> (cf. Leech, loc. cit.); w and z need not be specified.

9. Cf. Leech 1969: 191 sqq. and Bennett 1975: 90.

10. In the case of <u>dead</u> vs. <u>alive</u>, the progress of medical science, changes in the legal requirements for certification of death, etc. are often cited as obscuring the distinction. But this is not actually true: neither in medicine nor in the law is there yet a category of 'neither dead nor alive'. The recent discussion about brain-death as opposed to the cessation of autonomous functions has helped to redefine the point at which death can be pronounced. Until that point is reached, however, the individual is still, medically and legally, though presumably not functionally, alive.

[165]

Anaphora

Chapter Eight

ANAPHORIC CONNECTIVITY

8.1 Resumé of anaphora

In Ch. 4.21, we briefly reviewed the range of senses in which the term "anaphora" has been used in recent studies. The definition of anaphora which we are going to assume from now on stipulates that, in the A (antecedent) – B (anaphor) relationship:

(i) **A may be linguistic or extralinguistic.** In practice, most of our examples will be linguistic, for ease of exposition. However, we assume that extralinguistic instances will fall in with linguistic ones (and cf. our remarks in Ch. 3). Accordingly, we shall assume until evidence to the contrary that situational anaphora ("pragmatically-controlled anaphora", "exophora") is semiotically equivalent to the linguistic kind – though, admittedly, we need a much deeper understanding of the significant elements of situations, and their interrelationships, before this can be corroborated.

(ii) **The AB link may be one of reference** (cf.(1)), **sense** (cf.(2)), **or implication** (cf.(3)):

$$
1.\ \text{Basil called the waiter}_i\ \text{but}\ \begin{Bmatrix} \text{he} \\ \text{the man} \\ \text{the waiter} \\ \text{the idiot} \end{Bmatrix}_i
$$

had gone home

$$
2.\ \text{The modern waiter}_{(x)}\ \text{is likely to be Spanish}
$$

$$
\text{or Italian, and}\ \begin{Bmatrix} \text{he} \\ \text{?the man} \\ \text{?the waiter} \\ \text{*the idiot} \end{Bmatrix}_{(x)}\ \text{may speak}
$$

almost no English

Anaphora

3. Basil was in a cupboard$_{(i)}$,

examining { the hinges }$_{(i)}$
{*some hinges}

KEY: subscripts i = identity of reference, x = identity of sense, and (i), (x) = coinciding implication from referential and non-referential antecedents respectively.

Example (2) shows that repetition-anaphora and epithet-anaphora occur clearly only with identity of reference. In (3), <u>the hinges</u> is anaphoric to <u>cupboard</u>, allowing of the implication that "if x is a cupboard, then x has hinges". <u>The hinges</u> is thus "bound" (though not in the narrow sense of the term) to "hinges" in the implication. The indefinite <u>some hinges</u>, on the other hand, is likely to be a first-mention, and therefore non-anaphoric. However, it would be possible to force an anaphoric interpretation even here (= 'some of the hinges'): this might depend on pragmatic factors such as the number of items expected in the set.

(iii) **the degree of relatedness between A and B may vary from complete identity to some empirically-determinable degree of partial linkage.** Most current approaches assume simple identity of sense or reference; we, on the other hand, have shown that it is not necessary for A and B to be any more than "sufficiently-connected". Thus, as well as being an example of connection by implication, (3) is also an example of partial identity of reference, the referent of the anaphor corresponding to a part of the referent of the antecedent known by implication. Partial identity of sense anaphora is also possible, as in (4):

4.(a) To ensure high standards of hygiene in all hotels$_{(x)}$, the kitchens$_{(x)}$ will be regularly inspected.
 (b) The fact that the horse$_{(x)}$ is a herbivore can be established by examining the teeth$_{(x)}$.

We can perhaps express the implications of this view of anaphor more clearly in communicative terms. Considered thus, anaphora is a phenomenon of the common ground, which, as we saw in Ch. 3.5, is that

[167]

Anaphora

information, both permanent and cumulative, which is mutually recognised by both speaker and hearer in a discourse (cf.Werth 1981a, Smith 1982). In these terms, A, the antecedent, has a ground (or world) establishing function, while B, the anaphor, has a ground referring function (using refer here in a non-technical sense, as is allowed by the assumption of possible worlds, cf. Ch. 3.4 above). Complete identity between A and B means that the latter refers to the whole of A; partial identity is then reference by B to the common ground using only some of the information embodied in A.

We must, however, emphasise again here the point we made in Ch. 2.1. Identity of semantic structure does not in itself tell us anything about coherence, and still less does it guarantee anaphora. The condition on the sharing of common-ground is crucial: to cohere, items must be in the same text-world, defined in the common ground, or in accessible worlds, again as defined in the common ground. For anaphora, the condition is even more demanding: an anaphor refers to an entity previously singled out in the text-world (though contrary to the general view, the relationship is not necessarily one of identity, but may be part-whole, member-set, or subset-set, for example).

8.2 Reference

So far, we have been treating the "dangerous term" **reference** in a somewhat cavalier fashion. In the last section, we spoke of "identity of reference", and elsewhere in the book, we have talked about anaphors "referring" to such different things as Noun Phrases, semantic structures, and situational entities. A basic distinction which is normally drawn is that between 'reference' and **'sense'**. Reference is a deictic process linking a linguistic item with some element of the "real world". This element may be a concrete and palpable entity, like a shoe or a carburettor, or it may be a conceptual entity of some type, such as an attack or a rest. In any event, given an "act of reference", that is, a particular instance of use in a situation, then that which is properly and successfully "referred to", can also be said to exist.

Reference is an aspect of the **extension** of a semantic structure. Sense, on the other hand, is

[168]

Anaphora

intensional, that is to say, it is the "internal" or "dictionary" meaning which is associated with a given linguistic expression. This is habitually extended to include all non-existent cases, such as mythical objects, stipulations, generics, and indeed, non-referential uses of all kinds. The property of reference,then, is bound up with the property of existence. But existence, as any philosopher will testify, is a can of worms. Nevertheless, speakers have the embarrassing ability to slip at will and with no apparent effort or conceptual contortion from referential to non-referential meanings. What is more, hearers can usually follow them with no trouble:

> 5.   A: Do you think Reagan's going to win next time?
> B: Well, I know this: whoever DOES win, he's going to have to put up with a more hawkish attitude from the Russians.
> A: What, even if it's another Republican?
> B: Yeah, well, ANYBODY, whether he's Republican or Democrat, has got to face up to the disarmament question without all the hogwash and doubletalk we've had up to now. And don't forget, the Chinese are as anxious as anybody to see some sort of agreement. Deng's successor could be someone who's less prepared to stay in the background.

This is a completely unexceptionable conversation, such as any competent speaker of English could handle any day of the week. <u>Reagan</u> and <u>Deng</u> refer to known, existing individuals, and other referring expressions in (5) include <u>the disarmament question</u>, <u>the Russians</u>, and <u>the Chinese</u>. The exact extension of these last two sets, though, is somewhat fuzzy, and presumably not co-extensive with those sets taken in isolation. Practically all other NPs and pronouns in (5), however, are non-referring in the philosophical sense, since they are generic or stipulative or universally quantifying. Yet there is nothing particularly odd about a conversation like (5).

Similarly, writers of science fiction and other forms of speculation (and indeed of all fiction to some extent), manage to write about non-existing states of affairs quite convincingly, and without apparently mystifying their readership.

[169]

Anaphora

6. (a) Vegetation that looked something like trees — but no trees of Earth — blocked part of his view. Through the branches and fronds he could see a bright green sky. He lowered his eyes to take in the scene on the ground beneath the trees. Six or seven nightmare creatures were gathered at the base of a giant boulder. It was of red, quartz-impreganated rock and shaped roughly like a toadstool. Most of the things had their black furry, misshapen bodies turned away from him, but one presented its profile against the green sky. Its head was brutal, subhuman, and its expression was malevolent. There were knobs on its body and on its face and head, clots of flesh which gave it a half-formed appearance, as if its Maker had forgotten to smooth it out. The two short legs were like a dog's hind legs.
(Philip José Farmer)

(b) ...these horses are born and bred to the service if the Dark Lord in Mordor. Not all his servants and chattels are wraiths! There are orcs and trolls, there are wargs and werewolves; and there have been and still are many Men, warriors and kings, that walk alive under the Sun, and yet are under his sway. And their number is growing daily... here in Rivendell there live still some of his chief foes: the Elven-wise, lords of the Eldar from beyond the furthest seas. They do not fear the Ringwraiths, for those who have dwelt in the Blessed Realm live at once in both worlds, and against both the Seen and the Unseen they have great power.
(J. R. R. Tolkien)

We take it to be obvious that it is this sort of fact about linguistic behaviour, and not centuries of philosophical problems with the notion of 'existence', that should guide us in our treatment of reference.

Speaking particularly of anaphora, one of the problems much discussed in this area is the

[170]

Anaphora

distinction between "de re" and "de dicto" reference (McCawley 1981a: 285sqq), or "referential" and "attributive" descriptions (Donnellan 1966, 1978, Cole 1978). Another problem concerns the fact that pronouns appear to be somewhat promiscuous in their links with referential and non-referential expressions alike (cf. "sloppy identity", "pronouns of laziness" etc.). We shall in fact seek our solution to such problems in the concept of 'possible worlds', discussed in Ch. 3.4.

Consider the following cases, all falling within our broad definition of anaphora:

7.   Who on earth's he? (Pointing at someone)
8.   What is this I see before me? (Macbeth: an imagined dagger)
9.   I saw John, and Fran saw him too. ("Ordinary" identity of reference)
10. I last saw her only three weeks ago. (A remembered entity)
11. I saw John last week – Really? Well, I saw him yesterday. (Cf.(10), but antecedent in preceding S)
12. The man who owns a donkey beats it.(Non-referential: stipulative)
13. The horse is a herbivore, and it lives for about 40 years. (Non-referential: generic)
14. Unicorns are bald, and they live on potato-crisps. (Non-referential: mythical)

We can make some general observations about the states of affairs that these examples allude to: (a) the antecedent (A in our definition) may be linguistic, as we have already stated, but of course need not be; (b) in either case, the referent of both A and B may be "real" or not; (c) if not, it may be imaginary, classificatory, or stipulated; (d) if real, it may occur in the immediate situation, or be "displaced" (cf.Hockett 1958: 579) in time and/or place. We may diagram these distinctions with respect to examples (7)–(14), (see Table 8.1).

[171]

Anaphora

	COMMON-GROUND CONTEXT (world)	COMMUNICATIVE FACTORS	REFERENT (exophoric antecedent)	LINGUISTIC ANTECEDENT	ANAPHOR	REMARKS
(7)	Wo immediate context	Visual cue + pointing	'some ind-icated man'	None	<u>he</u>	Exophoric, "real"
(8)	World of the play; within this, world of Macbeth's imagination: $W_0(W_j(W_m))$	Inference by audience: "suspension of disbelief"	'vision of dagger'	None	<u>this</u>	Exophoric, "unreal"
(9)	Wo displaced	Explicit naming	'John'	<u>John</u>	<u>his</u>	Normal, unmarked case
(10)	Wo displaced	Implicit: memory of speakers	'some mut-ually known woman'	None	<u>her</u>	Like (9), but inexplicit
(11)	Wo displaced	Explicit naming	'John'	<u>John</u>	<u>his</u>	Like (9), but textual
(12)	All worlds in which there is at least one event of a man owning a donkey	Understanding situation to be stipulative	'any donkey in a world'	<u>a donkey</u>	<u>it</u>	Stipu-lative, "real"
(13)	All worlds in which the spec-ies <horse> exists	Understanding intension of <u>horse</u>	'any mem-ber of the class <horse>'	<u>the horse</u>	<u>it</u>	Generic, "real"
(14)	All worlds in which the spec-ies <unicorn> exists	Understanding intension of <u>unicorn</u>	'all mem-bers of the class <unicorn>'	<u>unicorns</u>	<u>they</u>	Generic, "unreal"

TABLE 8.1

We may now see that in all cases, "real" or "imaginary", the unitary definition of anaphora given above applies. Thus, B corresponds to A, or alternatively, the referent of B may be identified with A or its referent. To do this, though, it is necessary to make an adjustment of viewpoint from

[172]

Anaphora

"real" states-of-affairs to "unreal" ones, where "unreal", as we have seen, includes all kinds of non-referential and imaginary uses.

We saw in Ch. 3 that displacement brings about a world-shift. It follows then that anaphoric connections can be made not only within worlds, but also between worlds:

15. I know the defendant very well (t_o). He and I grew up together (t_n, where n is before now).

16. Stoner imagined that far-off in the distance he could see Afghanistan, where the hill tribesmen still fought for independence, as *they* had fought against the armies of Alexander the Great. (Ben Bova)

For they in (16), (our italics in the quotation), read "their counterparts at time a (a before now, or specifically, the time of Alexander the Great)". The pronoun they, in other words is used as a bridge between two worlds separated by time, though perhaps not in many other ways. The reference of they is a set of counterparts of today's hill tribesmen, occupying the same sort of cultural niche two thousand three hundred years ago. In non-possible-world terms, it would be difficult to reconcile this sort of use with either identity of reference, (which it clearly is not), or with identity of sense, (which would be extremely problematic).

Despite this rather extreme (though by no means improbable) example, however, we can assume that time-displacements are in most cases rather conservative. In any event, the theory of possible-world logic allows us to posit a subset of w_n (perhaps corresponding in psychological terms to speakers' memory and belief systems), which is highly accessible from w_o; (for the notion of **accessibility**, see the references below, and also Rescher 1964, Hughes and Cresswell 1968, Lewis 1973, Van Dijk 1977, and McCawley 1981a).

It seems reasonably clear, therefore, that the notion of possible worlds by extending the relationship of reference from the actual world to any conceivable or displaced state of affairs, and removing from reference the prerequisite of existence in our world, allows us to treat identity of sense and situational identity in the same terms

[173]

Anaphora

as identity of reference. (For further treatments of the notion of possible worlds in general, see Rescher 1975, Bradley and Swartz 1979, and Kripke 1972. For applications to tense and modality, see Werth 1981b. On counterparts, see Lewis 1968, Lakoff 1968a, McCawley 1981a: 290sqq.).

8.3 Types of anaphor

8.31 *Pronouns*

Anaphoric pronouns are bound variables which are minimally-specified along other semantic dimensions, such as gender and number. Communicatively, these have the function of providing extra "clues" to facilitate the correct antecedent-anaphor connection. On the narrowest definition of binding, A and B are restricted to a single sentence (necessarily complex, except in the case of reflexives), and to a single world, w_o, the "actual" world. This latter restriction excludes anaphoric relationships from holding across conditional contexts, for example. A wider interpretation will include non-referential cases, but exclude non-textual cases ('exophora' or 'pragmatically-controlled anaphora'), which are deictic though not anaphoric. We might also mention at this point other "pro" processes in which A is other than a nominal, notably a sentence or a predicate. In such cases, the B element may take several forms, including <u>do so</u>, <u>do it</u>, and <u>do Ø</u>. Hankamer and Sag 1976 contains some particularly interesting observations about the behaviour of these forms. (cf. too Dorrity 1981).

8.32 *Definitisation*

As Hawkins 1978 points out, the basic sense of the definite determiner is relativized universal quantification. This is not the contradiction in terms it appears; in a structure $_{NP}$[Det $_{NOM}$[...]], the Nominal defines a set, or a set-intersection, and the Determiner indicates how much of that set is to be considered. Thus, <u>a</u> selects one and only one member; <u>sm</u>, more than one member, or part of a mass; and finally, <u>the</u>, all of the designated set. (See further Werth 1980c). There are two special cases of the last of these: first, the so-called 'unique' (or

[174]

Anaphora

'homophoric') use (e.g. the Queen, the Pope, the milkman, the sun) in which **the set is designated by the situation down to one member**. The situation may in each case be characterised deictically, as **the minimal circumstances containing both the specified object, the speaker, and the hearer**. The second special case is more directly relevant to the question of cohesion: anaphoric the picks up a set (which may be a one-member set or an intersection) designated previously in the text. A point not often noted is that a can be anaphoric too, in the rather special sense that it can indicate one member of a designated set, as in:

> 17. A herd of elephants were browsing in the long grass. As our Land Rover approached, *a young elephant* turned to face us

The italicized phrase is anaphoric in that it picks out one unidentified member of the previously-designated herd (and is therefore equivalent to 'a young one of the elephants').

8.33 *Epithets*

These are what we have been calling 'virtual synonyms', and they include super-ordinate terms and co-referential NPs. As anaphoric elements, they share with their antecedents some crucial portion of semantic structure or specification in a world. In communicative terms, epithets may be alternative locutions bearing the same reference, in which case, they may have the same or similar meaning, or may denote some other aspect of the referent:

> 18. (a) *The Prime Minister of Canada* started an official visit to Britain today ... At a press conference, *the Canadian Premier* said ...
>
> (b) ... At a press conference,
> { (i) *Mr Trudeau* }
> { (ii) *the leader of the* } said...
> { *Canadian Liberal Party* }

In non-referential cases, clearly epithets cannot be related only by reference, as they are in (18b). The anaphoric relationship will then of necessity be based on at least partial semantic similarity (including less specified but not more

[175]

Anaphora

specified forms):

19. (a) *The dog* has been the companion of humans
for many thousands of years. Remains of
the animal have been found in human
habitations dating back to .

$$
\text{(b) @Remains of}
\left\{
\begin{array}{l}
\text{(i) } Rover \\
\text{(ii) } the\ pooch \\
\text{(iii) } next\ door\text{'}s\ boxer
\end{array}
\right\}
$$

have been found in human habitations
dating back to ...

8.34 *Zero anaphora*

In certain circumstances involving identity of
meaning (though not necessarily reference, cf.
Grinder and Postal 1971) between A and B, B may be
zero. In ST, this was handled by deletion-rules of
various kinds (Conjunction-Reduction, Gapping etc.)
whereby B was represented in deep structure as a
copy of A. In particular, B was said to have the
same semantic representation as A, though
incidentally the same form as well (this was seen as
arising naturally out of the general constraint of
Recoverability). In various current models, B is
regarded as a **gap** which has to be bound by some
formal device in the grammar. This gap is in some
models base-generated (e.g. Gazdar 1979, Brame
1979). In other models it is the result of a
transformational rule whereby some element — either
a copy of the antecedent or a pronoun, but in both
cases anaphorically bound to the antecedent — has
been deleted or moved from the site, leaving a
(filled) gap, (e.g. Chomsky 1977a, 1977b, 1981,
Chomsky and Lasnik 1977, Fiengo 1977, Lightfoot
1976, 1977, 1979, Reinhart 1983). These latter
scholars posit that such rules leave behind them a
"trace", an abstract element that may be used as a
variable for binding at subsequent stages in the
derivation. (For arguments against trace theory, see
in particular Postal and Pullum 1978, Pullum and
Postal 1978).

Trace, as Wasow (1979: 9) indirectly points
out, is a global device allowing surface-structure
interpretation by means of a deep-structure item no
longer present at surface structure. Hankamer too,
in a paper dated 1976, shows that it becomes
possible to talk about "surface structure
interpretation" of anaphora only if such a device as

[176]

Anaphora

trace allows one to keep track of NP-movement. However, as he points out, trace admits a measure of global information into the surface structure. In other words, surface-structure "enriched" with trace contains more than information available at surface-structure, since the only function of trace is to maintain pre-surface-structure information at the surface-structure level. Thus, there is some doubt as to the legitimacy of trace as a device.

Furthermore, since there is evidence (cf. Hankamer and Sag 1976, Williams 1977) that some zero-anaphora is extrasententially, and even pragmatically, controlled, it would appear unlikely that the theory of trace can be generalised to account for all cases of zero-anaphora. This would require not only that trace be a transderivational device, but also that discourse-processes of deletion (if not movement) be incorporated into REST. Thus the very device which triggered off the latest generation of transformational grammars may well provide a strong argument against their restriction to the sentence level.

8.35 *Repetitions*

In circumstances which are vaguely understood, and not at all quantified, lexical elements may recur in a text, with identical reference if they are referring elements, or having the same range of meaning if they are non-referring. The problem, which makes repetitions difficult to pin down, is that their appearance often runs counter to the other anaphoric processes described here. Thus, pronouns, epithets and zero anaphora in particular operate to minimise repetition, and even the process of definitisation has the effect of marking an NP in a formally distinct way. However, it may be argued that the impulse behind the non-repetitious varieties of anaphora is not primarily grammatical, but STYLISTIC. This would suggest that their implementation needs to recognise two elements: the element of **anaphoricity**, common to all; and the element of **form** (or formation), which, in marking the distinction between A and B, distinguishes one type of anaphora from another. Repetitions then may be seen as bearing the element of anaphoricity but lacking any further mark to distinguish A from B. However, we shall be modifying this in the next subsection.

If the occurrence of anaphoric elements, as

[177]

Anaphora

distinct from their interpretation, is a stylistic matter, then the question still remains: under what conditions does this stylistic impulse fail? Possibly the answer might involve the concept of "defeated expectation", or "foregrounding", a notion of Prague School stylistics. According to this theory, an expected pattern is violated, yielding some stylistic effect (e.g. of prominence). Indeed, we may say that foregrounding is to stylistics what conversational implicature is to pragmatics. To investigate such issues, let us consider typical cases of repetition, as commonly found in non-literary discourse. We may look again at passage (12) from Ch. 6, repeated here as (20). Note the repetition of <u>the lighthouse</u> in (20), as compared to the pronouns in the "rewritten" version (20'):

20. T.D.   ...*the lighthouse* is a phallic emblem, and James, the son, the little boy James, who wants so badly to go to *the lighthouse* and is frustrated all the time, explicitly hates his father and wants to stab him to death, which occurs both early and late in the book.
   D.P.   But just at the end there's a reconciliation.
   T.D.   It's this Oedipus thing really.
   J.M.   *The lighthouse* does raise all sorts of questions about what exactly the symbols are, whether in fact you invent your own rather, and put them in. Certainly one of them is the little boy who, now in adolescence, steps on to *the lighthouse* and that is his coming to manhood, presumably.
    (From a radio discussion)

20'.   *The lighthouse* is a phallic emblem, and James ...., who wants so badly to go *there* ...
   It does raise all sorts of questions ... Certainly one of them is the little boy who ... steps on to *it*

In (20), repetition seems to have at least two functions, neither of them exactly foregrounding. First, a text-structure function: the third occurrence of <u>the lighthouse</u> in (20) is uttered by a

[178]

Anaphora

new speaker after a brief altercation on a somewhat different topic by two other speakers. We may therefore regard it as signalling the initiation of a new sub-text, (or rather, the restatement of a previous topic, which has been digressed from).

Secondly, material intervening between potential A-element and B-element may contain other possible antecedents for a pronoun form. This factor is probably active in all of the cases in (20), but particularly in the third and the fourth. We can, indeed, see from (20') that it is particularly prone to multiple interpretability since it can refer to anything singular which is not specifically gender-marked. In such a case, the repetition of a full NP solves the problem completely. However, in speech, we find that the repetition is not exact in all respects, which brings us to a particular feature of anaphora which is common to all types: namely, its relationship to the phenomena of EMPHASIS. (See Bolinger 1979 for further discussion).

8.4 The role of emphasis

To simplify the situation, we may say that emphasis is a VEHICLE for anaphora. All of the five types of anaphor discussed in the previous section crucially use emphasis as part of their mechanism for signalling anaphora.

We have already discussed the different categories of emphasis, and in some detail, their relationship to each other and to texts (see Ch. 6). In particular, as has already been mentioned, Reduction and Contrast are both anaphoric, whereas Accent is necessarily non-anaphoric. As we have been using them, these are abstract notions whose concrete realisations may take one of several forms. Among these, for English and languages which use sentence-stress, is the presence or absence of **phonetic stress**, usually manifested as pitch-variation. That is, we can signal anaphora in English by departing from normal degrees of stress (-cum-pitch-variation) in either direction: by increasing it, for some manifestations of Contrast, and by reducing it for some manifestations of Reduction. Thus, in the cases of repetition discussed in section 8.35, we should expect the B-element to show reduced stress. In fact, it is a commonplace of descriptive linguistics (cf. Postal

[179]

Anaphora

1971: 230 sqq., G.Lakoff 1971b: 333) to point out that stress can disambiguate questions of co-reference:

    21.(a) (The American administration has been concerned about its relations with Israel, recently)... However, the *President*₁ was able to assure newspaper correspondents at a Press conference at the White House that the relationship between the *Prime Minister* and the [President]₁ was as cordial as ever.

    (b) (The American administration has been concerned about the relations between Thatcher and Mitterand recently).... However, the *President*₁ was able to assure newspaper correspondents at a Press conference at the White House that the relationship between the *Prime Minister* and the *President*ⱼ was as cordial as ever

Thus surface-stress MAY sometimes disambiguate such occurrences, though the possibility of reAccenting <u>President</u> in (21a) (giving an utterance superficially identical to (21b)) cannot be discounted. Furthermore, the presence of stress on an item tells us only that it is focussed; it does not necessarily distinguish between Accent and Contrast, as we have already seen in Ch. 6.1. We shall in fact go on to argue now that the proper distinction between these terms is basically semantic.

    We have established that two of the three kinds of emphasis, C and R, are anaphoric – in the sense that they mark semantic material as having been taken up previously in the discourse. This is compatible with the standard theory of anaphora (cf. Lyons 1977), in maintaining a distinction between anaphora and reference. Non-referring items can be anaphoric, though as we have seen, it is convenient and desirable to regard them as manifesting reference between one possible world and another.

    We have also seen that, from the formal point of view, anaphoric relationships are not necessarily restricted to a single syntactic category, nor do A and B have to be in the same syntactic category. Yet current accounts of anaphora seem to assume that it uniquely concerns co-reference in NPs:

[180]

Anaphora

> I assume there is a procedure for introducing
> variables for NPs in LF, including pronouns,
> and that the notions 'anaphoric',
> 'non-anaphoric' will be understood as
> determining the choice of variables as the
> same or different
>   (Chomsky 1977: 73)

> It is only the cases where the assignment of
> referential values to NPs is restricted by the
> form of the sentence, regardless of the
> discourse or the situation in the world, which
> concern us here
>   (Reinhart 1979: 111)

Furthermore, as these quotations show, there are further restrictions. The limitation to the single sentence is one which we have already commented on at length (particularly in Chs. 2 and 4). Moreover, the recognition of only two values of indexation, viz. "same" or "different", or "coreferential" vs. "disjoint", shows that these scholars are confining themselves to form at the expense of function (cf. Wasow 1979: 144sqq.). Then, there is their unexamined assumption that anaphora is a property of whole NPs. We, on the other hand, have already suggested that any account of coherence is forced to recognise partial similarity and other types of association as well as full identity. This is only possible in a semantic, as opposed to a syntactic, account of anaphora. (But see Thrane 1980: 45 who rejects, in our view on insufficient grounds, the possibility of partial reference). Thus, if it is possible for anaphora to be based on the partial similarity between A and B, then it must be some subpart of one of them which is identical to the whole or part of the other. If A and B are NPs, then obviously we cannot reasonably insist on anaphora being a relationship between whole NPs (although naturally, only whole NPs actually occur). Consider the following examples:

22. (a) **Max* is an *orphan*$_{(i)}$ and he *really
         misses* them$_{(i)}$ (i = 'parents')
    (b) *Max* is an *orphan*, but BILL's [parents]
         are ALIVE
    (c) **Max* is an *orphan*, but BILL's *parents
         are alive*

[181]

Anaphora

Assuming that the semantic structure of orphan contains the PF <x's parents are dead>, then (22a) shows that lexical items are "anaphoric islands" as far as pronoun-anaphora is concerned (cf. Postal 1969). However, (22b) shows that another manifestation of anaphora, emphasis-marking, is not only possible, but obligatory. (Compare the unacceptable (22c), with non-anaphoric Accent on parents and alive). Note in particular, the second conjunct of (22b), which is identical to the second conjunct of (22d):

    22.(d) *Max's parents* are *dead*, but BILL's [parents] are ALIVE

By the rules of (8) in Ch. 6, the R on parents and the C on Bill and alive are all quite normal: parents is repeated, and therefore Reduced; Bill, being a co-member of the same set as Max (defined in the text-world), is Reduced, and then, since he is different from Max, is Contrasted; similarly, alive is Reduced because it shares semantic specification with dead (= <NOT <ALIVE>>, say), and is then Contrasted because the shared part is denied. Since (22b) shows an identical pattern of emphasis, we can only conclude that emphasis-anaphora is sensitive to sublexical semantic structure[1]. (Cf. also Werth 1979: 243 sq.).

The recent accounts that we have cited, therefore, restrict the scope of their attention, illegitimately in our view, in at least six directions. They take into account only:

    (i)   identity of reference anaphora
    (ii) NP-anaphora
    (iii) certain anaphors (namely, pronouns and zero-anaphors)
    (iv) whole NPs
    (v)   sentential anaphora,

and they assume anaphora to have only:

    (vi) syntactic constraints.

Note that these are not restrictions on the power of the grammar or on the form of the grammatical theory, but merely limitations on admissible data. We shall comment on this in a little more detail in

[182]

Anaphora

the next section.

At this point, however, it will be useful to compare the anaphoric function of emphasis with that of pronouns, in the light of the above restrictions on REST/GB. Emphasis-anaphora, comprising Reduction and Contrast, does not comply at all naturally with this set of restrictions. Let us take R and C separately, and also, for the time being, identity of sense and identity of reference. Example (1) above, repeated here as (23), shows R with identity of reference, and (24) shows identity of sense[2]:

23. Basil called for the waiter$_1$, but the
    {[man$_1$]}
    {[waiter$_1$]}
    {[idiot$_1$]} had gone
24. Manuel dropped a bottle$_x$ of wine and a [bottle]$_x$ of KETCHUP

Moreover, as we have already seen, R can involve partial and implicit relatedness:

25. Basil took a stiff drink$_1$, but after the first [sip]$_{(1)}$ passed out
26. Sybil called$_x$ her friend up, and was [on the phone]$_{(x)}$ for two hours

C, on the other hand, can only occur with partial relatedness:

27. *Basil called for the waiter$_1$, but the
    {MAN$_1$ }
    {WAITER$_1$}
    {IDIOT$_1$ } had gone
28. *Manuel looked for a bottle$_x$ of wine but didn't want a BOTTLE$_x$ of WHISKEY
29. Basil called for the waiter$_1$, but only the smell of GARLIC$_{(1)}$ remained
30. Manuel looked for a bottle$_x$ of wine but didn't want a CARAFE$_x$ of [wine]
31. Sybil called$_x$ her friend up, but had to LISTEN$_{(x)}$ for two hours

(27) shows full identity of reference, and (28) full identity of sense; both are impossible with C as indicated, and for reasons which should be obvious. Given that Contrast, as we have shown in Chs. 5-7, is a denial of identity, clearly we cannot expect C

[183]

Anaphora

on items which show full identity. (28), to go through, would require some previous assumption that Manuel fancied a bottle of whiskey, and even then this particular form would constitute a rather strange denial (cf. Ch. 9.6). (29)-(31), though, are all acceptable: (29) shows partial identity of reference, in that the smell of garlic is presented as part of the referent waiter. (30) shows partial identity of sense, in that bottles and carafes are both containers, but a carafe is nevertheless different from a bottle. (31) is the implicational type: call up normally suggests talking; listening is in the same semantic field as talking, but obviously is different, hence the Contrast. These examples show that emphasis anaphora is neither confined to referential identity, nor to whole NPs.

In fact, neither R nor C is, self-evidently, confined to NPs at all. For C, as we saw in Ch. 7, almost any word-class is available. For R, the situation is rather more unclear: however, we can say that all items in lexical classes are reducible. For further discussion, see Ch. 6.4. The third restriction is not applicable to this account, of course, though it should be said that since pronouns and gaps are at least bound to their antecedents, and in the case of pronouns, also contain some attenuated semantic structure, while at the same time being non-Accentable, they represent the point at which Reduced emphasis and absence of emphasis come together.

Also, neither R nor C imposes any requirement confining antecedent and anaphor to a single sentence. In fact, though sentential examples are readily available, intersentential examples are much more obviously the norm, statistically speaking. Finally, as for syntactic constraints, it seems clear that there are none on emphasis-anaphora. Instead, there is a very far-reaching semantic constraint, that upon coherence, which applies to all forms of anaphora, as we shall go on to see. In fact, we will go further than that: in section 8.7, we will attempt to show that the types of anaphora which are most constrained syntactically, and therefore offer the best case for a syntactic account, namely, reciprocals (and reflexives, too) actually respond rather naturally to the same coherence constraint governing emphasis and textual connectivity in general.

Let us now briefly compare pronominal anaphora in the same terms. Firstly, as is well known,

[184]

Anaphora

pronouns are not confined to referential cases (indeed, it was just this point which led to the abandonment of the co-reference theory of pronominals):

> 32. (a) Basil called for the waiter$_1$, but he$_1$ had gone
> (b) The elephant$_x$ is the largest living species of land-mammal, and it$_x$ is much used as a beast of burden.

Secondly, although pronouns often have NPs as their antecedents, they do not necessarily do so. Nor, incidentally, do the other pro-forms, as the present sentence and the previous one clearly illustrate.

> 33. (a) Jeremy says <that England will win the World Cup>$_x$, but he doesn't really believe <it>$_x$
> (b) Bill often <chases other women>$_x$ but he doesn't <do it>$_x$ when his wife's around

Again, the third restriction does not apply. Fourthly, although personal pronouns are normally anaphoric to whole NPs, implicational antecedents are possible:

> 34. (a) Whenever I redecorate, I always get it all over myself
> (b) Mrs Jones went to get her prescription filled, and they advised her to take it three times a day

Furthermore, <u>one</u>-anaphora can never be whole-NP anaphora, and is necessarily identity of sense:

> 35. (a) John has a slim wife$_{x/*1}$, and Bill has a PLUMP one$_{x/*1}$
> (b) George sold <a copy of Government and Binding>$_{x/*1}$, and he BURNT one$_{x/*1}$

Fifthly, pro-formation is not only possible between Ss, but we would maintain that this is its characteristic mode (with the exception of reflexives and reciprocals). Furthermore, as is well known, pro-forms can have non-verbal ("pragmatic") antecedents, though there are differences in behaviour between these and the verbal antecedent type. Thus, they are no more bound to a syntactic characterisation than are the emphasis-forms.

[185]

Anaphora

8.5 Anaphora as coherence

The definition of anaphora we are employing, then, is solidly semantic, and the constraints on anaphora are, we shall argue, the ordinary semantic constraints on any elements in discourse, namely, the **coherence constraint** (cf. Ch. 5.4). To recapitulate, this semantic requirement on a discourse, distinguishing it from a random collection of sentences, is approximately that all the elements in it should cohere, (slightly more precisely, that each of the constituent propositions should cohere with another, each pair thus formed cohering with another proposition, until all the propositions and proposition-pairs are accounted for). We shall assume that coherence, then, is a matter of semantic relationship, and we proposed in Ch. 5 that there is a requirement on all propositions forming the semantic structure of a text that they must be semantically related to another proposition in the same text, (or,more accurately, in the common ground of the text).

As for anaphora, we claim that it is simply a special case of coherence. The process of discourse consists of the establishment of a common ground, against which each new utterance is assessed for **relevance** (by means of the coherence constraint), and if adjudged sufficiently relevant, is added to the common ground. (See Werth 1981a, and Ch. 3.5-6 above). An utterance is relevant to its common ground either if it brings new information which is related to information already present, or else if it brings further information about items already present. "Bringing" information may be by direct or indirect means, e.g. a question may pave the way to new or further information; "information" may include other types of speech act than statements of fact. Relevance of the second type crucially involves anaphora, i.e. the marking of an utterance as concerning either an entity or a concept already referred to in the common ground.

The crucial difference between anaphora and non-anaphoric coherence, we may suppose, is that the latter merely requires that two items belong to the same conceptual domain, whereas anaphora requires that two items are, at least for the present purposes of the discourse, related to the same conceptual entity. To put this another way, we can

[186]

Anaphora

say that for two items to cohere, they must allude to the same text-world, in terms of a set or field or frame or scene – but in any case more or less defined in the common ground. For two items to be anaphorically related, however, the anaphor must cohere down to a single choice of antecedent, whether this is an individual, a set or subset, or a part or implication of one of these.

Given these theoretical assumptions, it follows that sentential anaphora is merely the thin end of discourse anaphora, and any apparent syntactic restrictions are to be explained either as obeying the coherence constraints themselves, or as in fact emanating from a different and coincident cause, or in some cases from a full or partial syntacticisation of the coherence requirements, (cf. Givòn 1979: Ch. 5).

8.6 Reciprocal anaphora: two views
8.61 *The view from G-B*

To test the various claims made in the foregoing sections, we will now look at a type of anaphora which is usually assumed to be among the most sententially-restricted of all, namely **Reciprocal** or <u>each other</u> anaphora. Furthermore, we shall contrast the discourse-based account with the most narrowly-restrained of current sentence-based accounts, namely, that of REST/GB. We have already commented on the narrowness of the REST definition of anaphora; in fact, even this undergoes further straitening in Chomsky 1981: firstly, by distinguishing between "full anaphors" (reciprocals, reflexives and certain idiomatic occurrences), which are overtly marked, and other forms (such as pronouns, zero-anaphors), which are not necessarily bound in the same sentence. Thus in Chomskyan terms, the latter are not bound at all (but either **"free"** or **"disjointly-referring"**). Secondly, as we have already observed, there is a, perhaps unconscious, restriction on admissible data: only identity of reference anaphora (marked by the rule *"Co-index"*); only intrasentential anaphora; only Noun Phrase Anaphora; only pronoun and zero-anaphora; only full identity of reference anaphora. Conversely, what is not admitted is: identity of sense and situational anaphora; discourse anaphora; Verb Phrase Anaphora (e.g. <u>do</u> <u>so</u> forms); definite NP anaphora, epithets, repetitions, and Contrastive forms (see Ch. 7 and section 8.3); partial identity anaphora. Given such

[187]

Anaphora

severe restrictions, REST accounts of the phenomenon can appear to be highly constrained, when in fact they are, rather, extremely limited.

Let us now consider the context of Chomsky's account of Reciprocal anaphora. Briefly, (and for a fully-detailed version, the reader is, of course, referred to Chomsky 1981), the grammar he espouses consists of a Base, having Phrase-structure rules and a lexicon, a Transformational component, containing just the rule *"Move-alpha"* (the nature of *alpha* and its destination being defined by the Base plus general constraints on the grammar), and two interpretive components, Phonetic Form (PF) and Logical Form (LF). The various components are subject to a number of separate "subsystems of principles", or sets of rule-constraints. The most important of these for our present purposes is **Binding Theory**, which "is concerned with relations of anaphors, pronouns, names and variables to possible antecedents" (1981: 6). In other words, despite the narrowing of the term "anaphor" itself, which we have pointed out earlier, Binding Theory purports to be a theory of anaphora.

The "relations...to possible antecedents" which Binding Theory is concerned with are in fact two in number: a positive relation ("binding"), and a negative one (absence of binding). The latter then has two subtypes, "free" and "disjointly referring". "Free" in a governing category (roughly, in the domain of c-command), means that the antecedent may, but need not, be in the governing category. "Disjointly referring", on the other hand, means that an item MUST not be bound in its governing category.

Binding itself is defined configurationally:

> It is a configurational property - presumably, c-command- that determines the operation of the binding theory, not a requirement that anaphors (or pronominals...) search for subjects or objects as antecedents, in some sense of this notion that has any independent sense apart from the configurational properties (1981: 154)

Freedom, on the other hand, is defined simply as the complementary of binding: "a is X-free if and only if it is not X-bound" (1981: 185). Disjoint reference, though, is rather problematic and variable: in 'On Binding' (Chomsky 1980), it is

[188]

Anaphora

equated with "freedom" under the concept 'free(i)'. However, in Chomsky 1981 (e.g. 211), it appears to be regarded rather as the equivalent in pronouns to binding in anaphors (in the narrow sense): "linking involves coreference for an anaphor and disjoint reference for a pronoun".

To sum up, there is a subset of all anaphors (i.e. items having a deictic relationship with an antecedent) which in addition appear to be syntactically restricted: these are the so-called bound anaphors. A subset of these are overt anaphors (reciprocals, reflexives, certain idiomatic constructions), the remainder having zero phonological representation. Everything else is either free, and therefore not configurationally-defined, or else configurationally-definable, but obligatorily unbound. We may indeed observe that these cases are not really catered for at all in Binding Theory. A cynical view of this situation would surely comment on the wholesale spawning of all these zero-forms: to trace, PRO and AGR, we can now add lack of binding and non-binding, and as our discussion of Contrast has shown, we might have to add negative binding to the list as well...

Central to this syntactically-defined notion of anaphora is the property of **c-command**, originally due to Tanya Reinhart (e.g. 1979, 1983), but much-employed in the subsequent development of REST. Chomsky gives a version of the configuration (1981: 166)[3]:

> a c-commands b if and only if
> (i) a does not contain b
> (ii) Suppose that $c_1,....,c_n$ is the maximal sequence such that
> (a) $c_n = a$
> (b) $c_1 = a$[3]
> (c) c_i immediately dominates c_{i+1}
> Then if d dominates a, then either (I) d dominates b, or (II) $d = c_1$ and c_1 dominates b

As far as Reciprocal Anaphora is concerned, c-command predicts the following constraints:

> 36.(a) They introduced each other to Bill
> (b) *Each other introduced them to Bill
> (c) *They expected me to introduce each other to Bill
> (d) They pointed the guns at each other

Anaphora

(e) They expected me to point the guns at each other
(f) They'd prefer (for) each other to win
(g) *They expected Bill to prefer (for) each other to win
(h) We believed each other to be incompetent
(i) *We expected him to believe each other to be incompetent
(j) ...their stories about each other
(k) *...his stories about each other
(l) ...some stories about each other
(m) We read each other's books
(n) *They expected me to read each other's books
(o) *They read my reviews of each other's books
(p) They read the reviews of each other's books

(These are almost identical with the set of examples discussed in Chomsky 1981:154). A further type of example discussed by Chomsky (ibid.) is not excluded by c-command though ungrammatical:

37. *We thought (that) each other gave the books to Bill

(37) is excluded by the former Nominative Island Condition (NIC) — see Chomsky 1980: 36 — which in Chomsky 1981 is eventually amalgamated into the revised Binding Theory. This is contrived by the expedient of incorporating into the binding conditions the notion of nominative case (in the guise of "SUBJECT", a somewhat elusive concept (p.209)), such that the anaphor has to be in the c-command domain of SUBJECT (p.220).

Nevertheless, it seems fair to say that this additional condition to the Binding protocol changes its nature from an objective configurational constraint to one considerably more dependent upon special pleading (notably in the case of the possible SUBJECT-manifestation AGR, or agreement). It will be useful to look at this device of the GB model a little more closely.

Chomsky argues (p.52) that AGR (i.e. the person-gender-number complex) is "basically nominal in character" and "identical with PRO". The nature of this "identity", however, is never more than asserted. The situation is complex and constantly

[190]

Anaphora

under modification, but it would appear that the position AGR = PRO is open to a number of inconsistencies, not the least of which is that in a sentence like:

> 38. John [INFL past AGR] win (= *John won*; Chomsky 1981: 209)

AGR governs (and c-commands) the subject, John, and is co-indexed with it, but at the same time, as a pronominal (p.102) anaphor (p.64), it should be bound in its binding category. Chomsky shows (p.221) that this is a self-contradictory requirement, and that PRO (and hence AGR too) cannot have a binding category. Thus, PRO (and AGR) is free in reference, either arbitrary or with remote antecedent (p.78). Nevertheless, there is a distinct difference between these possible referential states. When PRO is arbitrary, as in:

> 39.(a) It is unclear [what PRO to do t] (p.56)
> (b) John was asked t [what PRO to do] (p.75)

it shows no agreement features, i.e. its potential for person-gender-number marking is unfulfilled (with partial conventional exceptions, cf.Chomsky 1981: 61). But when the person-gender number marking of PRO can be determined (as in all cases of AGR, it seems), then it is necessarily the case that it is not arbitrary, but has an antecedent, albeit remote. It is this antecedent which controls the person-gender-number marking in a very direct way: thus Chomsky finds himself at one and the same time claiming that AGR governs its subject, and that the subject controls AGR.

Whether or not this position is really as illogical as it sounds, it seems clear that the argument for introducing AGR into the conditions for Binding Theory (namely, its alleged nominal character) is based not on configurational considerations, but on the semantic features of person, gender and number. This means that the apparent contradiction between Chomsky's claim (quoted above) that binding theory is "not a requirement that anaphors (or pronominals...) search for subjects or objects as antecedents)" (p.154), and his claim that "an anaphor or pronominal searches for the closest SUBJECT to which it can be linked" (p.211), is in fact a genuine contradiction, since the restriction to configurational statements

[191]

Anaphora

cannot be maintained. Thus in order to appreciate – and assess – the full-blown configurational nature of Binding Theory, we shall ignore the last revision (incorporating NIC), and return to the version (p.188) employing only configurational notions:

40.(A) An anaphor is bound in its governing category
   (B) A pronominal is free in its governing category
   (C) An R-expression (i.e. a referring expression) is free

It is within this context, therefore, that we may look at the examples of Reciprocal Anaphora in (19) above. In an earlier version of the Pisa lectures, Chomsky presents a Reciprocal Rule (1979:15 sqq.), which stipulates that each other is:

-an overt anaphor
-case-marked
-argument-bound

Though this characterisation as such does not appear in Chomsky 1981, it is in fact implicit in (40A). An "overt anaphor", according to Chomsky, is an antecedent-bearing element having no intrinsic reference; he often uses the term "anaphor" simply to refer to overt anaphors. Case-marking (the later *theta*-marking) is subsumed under the notion of "governing category" since the "governor" controls whether an anaphor (for example) is Nominative, Objective etc. "Argument-binding" (the later "antecedent-" or "A-binding") is what is meant by "bound" in (40A), and signifies that the element is co-indexed with a c-commanding argument (cf. Chomsky 1981: 184).

The expectation for each other, therefore, is that it will always occur within the c-command domain of its antecedent. It is further assumed that its antecedent will be properly plural, and that each other constitutes a single item (like its counterparts in Dutch and German, historically phrases, but now single words)[4]. Thus in:

41. They expected each other to leave

each other is indeed c-commanded by they, which is plural, so the sentence is grammatical. On the question of the single-item status of each other, however, no arguments in support of this claim are ever adduced, apart from the assertion that each

[192]

Anaphora

other is in a rule of sentence-grammar, while the separate form each ...the other(s) is not (Chomsky 1976: 322sqq.). This is obviously the very claim that we wish to challenge here with regard to anaphora in general. It is, of course, true that no simple substitution argument is possible with respect to each other (hereafter the "phrasal form") and each ...the other(s) (the "periphrastic form"):

    42.(a) The men like each other
       (b) Each of the men likes the other(s)
       (c) *The men want John to like each other
       (d) Each of the men want John to like the other(s)

(examples from Chomsky 1976). Thus, as is clearly shown by (42), the phrasal form is more restricted than the periphrastic form, though there appears to be no obvious reason why (42c) should not be grammatical. For Chomsky, of course, the reason lies in the Theory of Binding: in (42c) each other is c-commanded by John, which is not plural; the sentence therefore fails on that interpretation. The preferable interpretation with the men as antecedent is impossible since it is outside the c-command domain which includes each other.

    Nevertheless, we will put forward an alternative explanation which makes the stronger assumption that the phrasal and periphrastic forms are subject to the same rules, not because they are both single items, the one proximate, the other discontinuous, but because they are both made up of more than one item, namely the quantifier each and the disjunctive or negative anaphor (the) other(s). As such, they play different roles in the communicative process, as sketched out previously. We shall, accordingly, now examine these elements separately.

8.62 *Each*

As a quantifier, each should display certain characteristics. It should bind some NP, which semantically must be a variable rather than a name (in the logical sense); its fundamental meaning is universal quantification, which is, however, distributive ("one at a time") rather than comprehensive ("all at once"), cf. McCawley 1981a: 98sq.; because of this, it is basically singular, though its universalist meaning sometimes attracts

[193]

Anaphora

plural concord. Like the other quantifying elements, each may also function as an anaphor (in Chomskyan terms, a pronominal anaphor). In that case, it is a bound element, in the sense that it has an antecedent, (i.e. not in the strict Chomskyan use of the term), rather than a binding element:

43. The members of the committee remained silent
44. (a) Each knew what he was doing
    (b) Each was thinking his own thoughts

In (44), each is anaphoric to the members in (43). However, it is anaphoric in a way not accounted for by any current theory of anaphora that we know of. That is, in any extension of (44) which is true (i.e. for each case contributing to the eventual truth of (44)), the meaning of each requires a sum of partial anaphoric links until the antecedent-set is exhausted. Thus, in any verification of (44), each necessarily takes us through a series of steps, none of which is actually anaphoric in the standard sense with the set {the members}. Hence the fact that, in both (44a) (in the sense in which he is bound by each) and (44b), the anaphoric link between each and the pronoun has singular concord.
    Furthermore, let us consider (44c):

44. (c) Each of them was aware of the risks involved

Here, we find that them is anaphoric in the standard sense with the members, but that each is now anaphoric, in the way distinguished above, with them. Let us call all of these cases examples of **d-anaphora** (for "distributive anaphora"). Now consider the standard definition of quantifier-binding above and for example, Chomsky's distinction between argument/antecedent binding, or A-binding, and operator binding, or $\bar{a}$-binding (1981: 184). A puzzle to bear in mind at this stage is that with the following PP, a quantifier $\bar{a}$-binds the NP of the PP and is A-bound by it. Yet as we can see from (43)-(44c), the NP them is not a variable, since it is co-indexed with the members. How, then, can the relationship with each be one of operator-binding? Furthermore, a moment's thought will reveal that each is not at all unusual in this respect. In fact, this is the normal situation for ALL quantifiers: the set over which quantification

[194]

Anaphora

takes place is normally defined contextually, under conditions which guarantee that it is already a name (in the logical sense) and not a variable. Standard "out-of-the-blue" examples of the *all men are mortal* type do not serve to disprove this assertion, since we can argue that generic sets like {men} are inherently universal (as in *Men are mortal*), which is what makes them generic (cf. Werth 1980c for a detailed analysis along these lines).

Example (44c) introduces the possibility, apparently not previously considered, of a sort of "mutual binding" relationship between a quantifier and the subsequent NP in an NP construction with a quantifier (i.e. in X-bar terms , an N^1 in an N^{1+1} construction with Q^1). What is very interesting for our present purposes is that the post-quantifier PP of (44c) and (45a) below may be matched by a post-quantifier N, as in (45b):

> 45.(a) Each of the members was aware of the risks
> (b) Each member was aware of the risks

These quantified NPs may also occur in oblique positions:

> 46.(a) The Chairman asked each of the members for his opinion
> (b) The Chairman asked each member for his opinion

It should particularly be noticed that none of the sentences in (44)-(46) is fully interpretable (in the sense of establishing reference) without such a context as (43), providing a set-antecedent of the type required for d-anaphora. Under these normal conditions, it is the N^1 of the quantified NP which bears the standard anaphoric relationship with the antecedent set, while the quantifier quantifies into that N^1.

Furthermore, "quantifying" seems to be a fundamentally anaphoric process, although not necessarily standardly anaphoric (i.e. involving co-indexation). Each, as we have seen, is distributive ; one in *one of the members* is partitive; none is negative; and few is quasi-negative. We may speculate therefore, that quantification is fundamentally a process of stipulating HOW the antecedent should be referred to: holistically, partitively, distributively, etc.

[195]

Anaphora

8.63 *Other*

We may now consider how <u>other</u> fits this pattern. The term "mutual binding" used above is, of course, rather significant: we have seen that in such examples as (45b), the N member is anaphorically linked to the antecedent-set {the members of the committee}, while being quantified by <u>each</u>. <u>Each</u>, however, is then d-anaphoric to <u>member</u>. But <u>each other</u> seems, structurally at least, identical to <u>each member</u>. We are going to assume, therefore, that <u>other</u> is anaphoric to an antecedent (which for reasons which we will explore must be in the same sentence), and that <u>each</u> both quantifies and is d-anaphoric to <u>other</u>.

Semantically, this seems about right. In (48) as compared with (47), <u>the others</u>, whatever its precise reference, is in any case disjoint from <u>the members</u>:

47. The members of the committee support each other
48. The members of the committee support the others

From these examples, we may confirm that <u>other</u> is a negative anaphor (henceforth, an **n-anaphor**). That is to say, it takes its value to be the converse of the value of its antecedent. The resulting value may be contextually defined, or simply equivalent to "not-antecedent". Thus, in (48), <u>the others</u> may be contextually-defined (e.g. the ordinary members of the golf-club as opposed to the committee members – information which would have to be in the common ground), or else it may simply be equivalent to 'those who are not members of the committee'. The second sense may be clearer with a different verb:

49. The bees in the hive repelled the others

Given this essential negativity, then, it seems obvious that <u>other</u> is n-anaphoric. N-anaphora is better-known as Disjoint Reference in REST, and according to Chomsky, it is what characterises pronouns as opposed to (overt) anaphors when in their governing category (cf. above and Chomsky 1981: 188). Yet it makes a considerable amount of sense to view Reciprocals not as bound (what we have been calling "standard") anaphora, but rather as

[196]

Anaphora

mutual disjoint reference. The use of each other, that is to say , guarantees that for each individual in the antecedent-set considered in turn, there is precisely no co-referent in the anaphor-set. Only when the process of disjunctive matching is complete is there a full correspondence between the two sets. But this correspondence is not standardly anaphoric, since it is achieved by a process which is fundamentally disjoint. Thus, the combination of distributive each and n-anaphoric other results in the Reciprocal meaning, or "distributed disjoint reference".

We are claiming, therefore, that each other, just like any other Q-N combination, takes the ordinary meaning of other and quantifies it with the ordinary meaning of each. Crucial to both of these ordinary meanings, however,is the notion of the set and its subsets: thus each seeks to match the members of the antecedent-set pairwise in turns, while other defines the complementary of an antecedent subset.

8.64 *Quantifier-floating*

Next in our review of the quantifier-behaviour of each, we may look at the question of **Quantifier-floating**. This phenomenon was originally characterised in transformational terms (hence the dynamic terminology), and under various names (see e.g. Dougherty 1970: 877 sqq., Postal 1974: 109 sqq.). It involves the universal quantifiers all, both and each, though not every. These share a peculiarity of distribution, namely, that they can occur in several alternative positions, while maintaining the same binding relationship. Schematically:

> 50. (Q of) The boys (Q) have (Q) bought me (Q) a pen (Q)

> 51. (a) Each of the boys bought me a pen
> (b) The boys each have bought me a pen
> (c) The boys have each bought me a pen
> (d) The boys have bought me each a pen
> (e) The boys have bought me a pen each

To these we may add:

> (f) Each boy has bought me a pen

[197]

Anaphora

The acceptability of each of these variants is, to be sure, not always equal, but what is of great interest here is the similarity between these positions, and the possible positions for <u>each</u> in the periphrastic reciprocal:

52. (a) Each of the boys has bought the other a pen/a pen for the other
    (b) Each boy has bought the other a pen
    (c) The boys each have bought the other a pen
    (d) The boys have each bought the other a pen
    (e) The boys have bought a pen each for the other
    (f) The boys have bought a pen each for the other
    (g) *The boys have bought for the other each a pen
    (h) *The boys have bought for the other a pen each
    (i) *The boys have bought the other each a pen
    (j) *The boys have bought the other a pen each

To these we may, of course, add:

    (k) The boys have bought each other a pen/a pen for each other

It is interesting to compare the asterisked forms here. In every case, even with <u>other</u> in a PP, the meaning of distributed disjoint reference is impossible when <u>each</u> follows <u>other</u>. As (51d,e) show, however, this is not due to the position of the quantifier towards the end of the sentence, or in an equivalent syntactic environment. It is, however, due to the interaction between the quantifier and the neighbouring NP:

53. (a) *The boys have bought the girl each a pen
    (b) *The boys have bought the girl a pen each

In all of these cases, the second NP (the indirect object) forms part of a predicate-unit, and the subject <u>the boys</u> is quantified with respect to this unit. Thus, when <u>each</u> is d-anaphoric to the set {the

[198]

Anaphora

boys}, it treats the predicate as an anaphoric island (of sorts). The whole predicate, that is to say, is applied to the members of the set in turn. Boy_1 has-bought-the-girl-a-pen, boy_2 has-bought-the-girl-a-pen,... boy_n has-bought-the-girl-a-pen. We may note, incidentally, that in all these cases, the form with _each_ following the whole predicate-unit is better than the form where _each_ "penetrates" the predicate-unit. With simple transitives, this tendency is confirmed when the predicate is non-anaphoric, but with anaphoric predicate NPs, we get an awkwardness parallel to examples (52g-j, 53). However, due to the semantic properties of _each_, as we have described them here, the predicates must allow multiple occurrence:

    54.(a) The boys bought a hot-dog each
       (b) The boys kissed a girl each
       (c) ?The boys studied the Renaissance each

    55.(a) *The boys bought the hot-dogs each
       (b) *The boys kissed the girl each

The assumption with the "unitary" predicates of (54) is that there were as many acts of doing that predicate as there are members in the subject-set. This then pragmatically implies as many hot-dogs as boys, (assuming no hot-dog is bought more than once), though not necessarily as many girls as boys. It also explains the awkwardness of (54c), which is non-anaphoric, but unique (cf. our discussion in Chs. 2.1 and section 8.3 above). The implication that there are as many Renaissances as boys is difficult to satisfy, given the presumption of uniqueness. In (55), however, there is nothing to prevent the predicate from denoting a multiple event. We must assume, therefore, that it is the anaphoricity of the predicate NP which stops these sentences from going through.

    This conclusion is very relevant in the explanation of our asterisked Reciprocal examples (52g-j). We have seen that _other_ is n-anaphoric, applying always to the complementary of an earmarked subset. Thus, if set A contains members {a,b}, and member a is nominated, then _other_ will refer to member b, and correspondingly, _others_ for set-residues of two or more. If this process of nomination is controlled (i.e. quantified: see section 8.62) by _each_, then the members of A are nominated in turn, and _other_ refers to their

[199]

Anaphora

complementaries in turn. If it is <u>other</u> which is quantified by <u>each</u>, then the process of n-anaphora operates on the relevant set, taking each possible subset in turn, the exact combinations being regulated by the precise form of the <u>other</u>-phrase (sg. or pl., definite or indefinite). We will discuss this latter aspect presently. In a precisely parallel way, when <u>each</u> quantifies a predicate N, it is the resulting NP which determines the number of times the event takes place:

56. John kissed each girl

In such a case, the number of girls (an item of information which might be in the common ground) determines how many events of John kissing a girl there are.

So far, then, all the peculiarities of Reciprocal anaphora fall out from the intensional meanings of <u>each</u> and <u>other</u>, together with the operation of anaphora, which we will sum up presently. First, however, we will clear up some undiscussed problems.

8.65 *Reciprocals in complex sentences*

The examples of Reciprocal anaphora that we have chiefly been considering, while complex semantically, have not had the added complication of syntactic complexity. Let us now expand our data, therefore, to include this:

57. (a) They expected to buy a gift
    (b) They expected to each buy a gift
    (c) They expected to buy each other a gift
    (d) They expected me to buy a gift
    (e) *They expected me to each buy a gift
    (f) *They expected me to buy each other a gift

58. (a) They promised me to each buy a gift
    (b) They promised me to buy each other a gift

59. (a) They seemed to John to each dislike their mother
    (b) They seemed to John to each dislike the other
    (c) They seemed to John to dislike each other

Anaphora

The examples in (57) show rather clearly that although, as is well-known, (57f) is ungrammatical, so is (57e) without Reciprocal anaphora. But like (57f), (57e) contains each; (57d), on the other hand, is identical except for the occurrence of each. We take it, then, that it is the item each which is somehow responsible for the ungrammaticality of both (57e) and (f). As we have seen, each functions by operating upon a set in its environment distributively. The question now is: how is the relevant set selected?

We suggest that the procedure is as follows:

A. First choice: NP of immediately following of-PP;
B. Second choice: immediately following count N;
C. Third choice: (with certain provisos), the nearest preceding NP.

Thus, to illustrate the straightforward cases:

60. (a) The winners hoped to kiss each of the girls
    (b) The winners hoped to kiss each girl
    (c) The winners each hoped to kiss the girls

The provisos spoken of concern cases where an NP other than the nearest preceding one is the antecedent, including some ambiguous examples.

61. (a) The winners hoped to kiss some girls each
    (b) Bactrian camels have two humps each
    (c) The pirates tied the girls to each other

(61a,b) both ignore the immediately preceding NP, despite the fact that it denotes a set, in favour of another NP. (61c) is ambiguous between pirates as the antecedent to each other, and girls as the antecedent. The cases which do not meet the terms of our generalisation are, therefore, (61a,b) and the interpretation of (61c) with pirates as the antecedent. Choice of subject appears to be a possible answer, but is clearly not in fact the governing circumstance, (since (61c) is possible with girls as the antecedent, and it is in fact quite easy to find non-subject-antecedents). Rejection of object will not work either, for similar reasons.

[201]

Anaphora

The proviso to the third choice ((C) above) is undoubtedly to be sought in the machinery of Verb Control, a full treatment of which is beyond the scope of the present book. However, we may indicate the outlines of a theory of verb control sufficient to suggest a solution to the problem. In our view, verb control, i.e. the distributional preferences which verbs impose on their complements, is a direct effect of the intensional meaning of the verb in question. Let us consider the approximate meaning of some of the verbs we have used in our examples (we will examine only verbs with S^1 or V^2 complements):

62. (a) $\langle$A EXPECT $S^1\rangle$ = $\langle$A BELIEVE B $\langle S^1$ HAPPEN$\rangle_B\rangle$

(b) $\langle$A PROMISE $S^1\rangle$ = $\langle$A UTTER B to-C $\langle$A ASSURE $S^1\rangle_B\rangle$

(c) $\langle$A SEEM $V^2\rangle$ = $\langle$B APPEAR-TRUE to-C $\langle$A $V^2\rangle_B\rangle$

These are general semantic formulae with variables at all argument points. Let us, however, particularise them to examples from (57-59):

63. (a) They expected to buy each other a gift

(b) $\langle$THEY$\rangle_A$ $\langle$A BELIEVE B $\langle S^1$ HAPPEN$\rangle_B$ $\langle\langle$X BUY for-C D$\rangle_{B1}$ $\langle$EACH $\langle$OTHER {A}$\rangle\rangle_C$ $\langle$GIFT$\rangle_D\rangle\rangle$

64. (a) *They expected me to buy each other a gift

(b) $\langle$THEY$\rangle_A$ $\langle$A BELIEVE B $\langle S^1$ HAPPEN$\rangle_B$ $\langle\langle$I$\rangle_E$ $\langle$E BUY for-C D$\rangle_{B1}$ $\langle$EACH $\langle$OTHER {E}$\rangle\rangle_C$ $\langle$GIFT$\rangle_D\rangle\rangle$

With <u>expect</u>, any intervening NP will be inside S^1, that is B in the semantic structure. If it shows the necessary set properties (which <u>me</u> in (64a) does not), it may act as antecedent. The variable X in (63b) marks an argument-slot with no name specified to fill it: this device is simply to aid exposition; in fact, X is no different from A or C. The first name (i.e. predicate with no variables) preceding the slot may then be read into it — which is perhaps true for all variables in pre-predicate position.

65. (a) They promised me to buy each other a gift

[202]

Anaphora

    (b) $\langle$THEY$\rangle_A$ $\langle$A UTTER B to-C $\langle$A ASSURE S$^1\rangle_B$
           $\langle\langle$X BUY for-D E$\rangle_B{}^1$ $\langle$EACH $\langle$OTHER {A}$\rangle\rangle_D$
           $\langle$GIFT$\rangle_E$ $\langle$I$\rangle_C\rangle\rangle$

66. (a)   They seemed to John to dislike each other
    (b) $\langle$THEY$\rangle_A$ $\langle$B APPEAR-TRUE to-C $\langle$A -LIKE D$\rangle_B$
           $\langle$EACH $\langle$OTHER {A}$\rangle\rangle_D$ $\langle$JOHN$\rangle_C$

In the cases of <u>promise</u> and <u>seem</u>, the semantic structure shows that the superficially-intervening NP is in fact peripheral. Another way of putting this is to say that the intervening NP of <u>expect</u> is an argument of the embedded predicate (i.e. BUY), while for <u>promise</u> and <u>seem</u>, the intervening NP is an oblique argument of the controlling predicate. The rule that seems to be emerging, then, now looks like this:

    C′.   Third choice: the nearest preceding set-denoting NP which is not an oblique argument.

This leaves the ambiguity of (61c) to be explained: in this case, both NPs are set-denoting and non-oblique. Perhaps, therefore, we should relax the condition "nearest"? But consider (67):

    67. The boys gave the presents to each other

Here, both <u>boys</u> and <u>presents</u> are set-denoting and non-oblique. Yet <u>presents</u>, the nearest, cannot support the Reciprocal anaphora. Or can it? It appears plausible to hold that at this point we encounter a pragmatic filter, which says: "You can't give a present to an inanimate object". But what if the present is itself human?

    68. To show his contempt for the Union, Colonel Beauregarde gave his slaves to each other

This suggests that a remodified strategy (C") would come close to covering all the problem areas we have discussed:

    C".   Third choice: a preceding set-denoting non-oblique NP, subject to pragmatic constraints.

In other words, (C′) applies more or less as stated,

[203]

Anaphora

unless there exist any pragmatic constraints on the particular predicates involved. Such pragmatic conditions would be available in the common ground of the unfolding discourse, and specifically would form part of the scenes (Idealised Cognitive Models) evoked by the propositional content of the text.

8.66 *Ambiguity of the phrasal form*

The phrasal Reciprocal, <u>each</u> <u>other</u>, which is the subject of most of the literature on Reciprocals, is in fact severely ambiguous, corresponding in any given use to several possible periphrastic forms. For example:

68. (a) The players praised each other

    (b) Each of the players praised the other (= 2 players)

    (c) Each of the players praised the others (= >2 players; exhaustive mutual binding)

    (d) Each of the players praised another (= >2 players; non-exhaustive single distribution)

    (e) Each of the players praised some others (= >3 players; non-exhaustive plural distribution)

The non-exhaustive cases (68d,e) are two interpretations of (68a), corresponding to:

68. (f) There was praising going on among the players

We can characterise what is happening here by saying that <u>each</u> divides the set it quantifies (by the selection-procedure outlined in the previous section) into two subsets: a focal subset of just one member, and a residue. Due to the essential shifting nature of <u>each</u>, both of these subsets are constantly varying until every member has occupied the focal subset just once. In the periphrastic Reciprocal, the form of <u>other</u> depends on the cardinality of the residue-subset, and on whether <u>other</u> is exhaustive or not. If the n-anaphoric link with the residue-set is exhaustive, then the definite article will be used (since the meaning of the definite article is 'totality of some defined

[204]

Anaphora

set or subset', cf. Hawkins 1978). Otherwise, <u>other</u> will be indefinite. If the residue-subset contains just one member, then <u>other</u> will be singular; otherwise, it will be plural. Definiteness and plurality, in other words, behave here exactly as they do elsewhere in the language. The phrasal form <u>each other</u>, as we have already pointed out, may be several-ways ambiguous, and is not necessarily exhaustive. That is to say that when <u>each</u> focusses on the set member by member, <u>other</u> does not necessarily refer to every member of the residue-subset.

Thus, while it undoubtedly remains true that, whatever the precise interpretation of <u>each other</u> in any given instance of (68a), the anaphoric link is always with <u>the players</u>, nevertheless complete interpretability is always preferable to partial information. Conversely, it is no counterargument to say (as does, e.g., Dougherty 1974: 15) that sentences with the phrasal form are "more vague" than sentences with the periphrastic form. In fact, as we have seen, the phrasal form suppresses all indications of exhaustiveness or plurality. Thus, it is formally indeterminate, but semantically, it corresponds with some definite state of affairs, which for practical reasons may be difficult to disentangle. Any disentanglement possible, however, will obviously come from the common-ground context in which the sentence in question is embedded. It will not normally be derivable from within the sentence itself.

8.67 *Reciprocals and discourse*

<u>Each</u> and <u>other</u> separately, and the periphrastic Reciprocal too, are all fully capable of referring into a discourse context. The phrasal Reciprocal, however, is among the most strictly sentential elements in English, hence its popularity with S-grammarians. Part of the reason for this we have already touched on: the complex of semantic behaviour which characterises the two forms separately and in association combines to prevent occurrence in the matrix subject position. Hence, since it is also strictly anaphoric (in the Hallidayan sense), it follows that there will always be at least one preceding NP in the same sentence.

Nevertheless, there are some interesting indications that a pragmatically-controlled variety is possible. We leave them to our readers to

[205]

Anaphora

explain:

69. (a) (Prison regulations): Messages to each other must go via the Warden's Office.
    (b) (Youth club leader): And no kissing each other on the back row, please!
    (c) Who dislikes each other more: Mum and Dad or you and me?
    (d) The Christian message is to love each other
    (e) Rover doesn't do that when he's by himself. — Neither does Fido. I think it must be because of each other
    (f) Hitting each other never solves anything
    (g) It was very stimulating to massage each other, wasn't it?

Nevertheless, it must be said that the phrasal Reciprocal, like the Reflexive, represents the thin end of the wedge as far as discourse anaphora is concerned. These forms, that is to say, operate in general in accordance with the ordinary discourse requirements on anaphora, but for a constellation of reasons which we do not yet fully understand, have a strong tendency to confine themselves to the domain of the sentence. However, we claim that this tendency is, saving a fuller understanding of the processes involved, a further idiosyncracy of an already idiosyncratic category. It is a serious tactical error to regard this behaviour as diagnostic for anaphors, and thus to justify Procrustean attempts to force all anaphora into the same inappropriate bed.

8.7 Anaphora and coherence

We have seen that Reciprocal anaphora, whatever its syntactic form or behaviour, brings a particular complex of semantic processes into the discourse. The quantifier <u>each</u> has the function of distribution (itself in certain circumstances anaphoric: what we called 'd-anaphora'); this selects one member of the antecedent set at a time (the 'focal subset') until the set is exhausted. The n-anaphoric element <u>other</u> then operates upon all or some of the membership of the 'residue subset', depending upon its overt marking for definiteness and plurality, or, in the absence of marking, upon pragmatic factors in the common ground. (We should say, rather, that it

[206]

Anaphora

always depends upon common-ground factors, but that these sometimes receive overt marking in the shape of definiteness and plurality). We may express the general outlines of this explanation in the form of a postulate:

> 70. *All* y,z: *Exists* X \>1\ <y *Included-in* X, y \1\> & *If* <z *Complementary-to* y> *Then* R <y, z>

In (70), y corresponds to each, z to other, and X is the antecedent-set, having at least two members. y is a single member of X and z is the complementary of y. Given that these conditions apply in a given case, then y bears the given predicate relationship to z. For example, given a sentence like (71a), then (71b) is the appropriate specific case of (70):

> 71. (a) They expected each other to leave
> (b) <THEY>$_x$ <A <A *Included-in* X> EXPECT B <C <C *Complementary-to* A> LEAVE>$_B$>

What the postulate (70) does not make clear, however, is (i) the "rotation" of y until X is exhausted, and (ii) the role of common ground information in determining the exhaustion of the residue-set z. Deficiency (i) requires a "procedural" notation of some sort; nevertheless, (70) adequately represents each separate stage of the procedure. Deficiency (ii) is repaired in the full coherence constraint (cf. Ch. 5), of which any anaphoric postulate, including (70), is simply a special case. Let us now satisfy ourselves that this is indeed the case.

The argument-binding for each other which Chomsky claims is, as we have tried to show, quantifier-binding with special properties due to the intensional meaning of each (cf. Vendler 1967, McCawley 1981a: 98sq.). When each is separated from its antecedent-set (as in all cases of the phrasal Reciprocal), we may also recognise a relationship of d-anaphora between the quantifier and the set, a relationship which is presumably always present, but is masked when the quantifier and the set-denotatum are in the same phrase. Other has a relationship of n-anaphora with the residue of the set left after each application of quantification. The set-each relationship is that of X-y in (70), the set-other relationship is that of X-z, while the each-other relationship is that of y-z. Since these

[207]

Anaphora

relationships are all essentially anaphoric, they all fall under the coherence constraint, which we repeat here in its essential form:

72. All y: Exists x <R <y, x> & W <x, y>>

that is, "for any y (a PF), there exists an x (a set of common-ground propositions), such that y has some logical or pragmatic relationship with x, and x and y are in worlds accessible to each other". The antecedent-set X of (70) and they of (71) represent a common-ground proposition of the general form '<x> = <OTHER PERSONS>', and in the case of they, specific contextual information will be available from the anaphoric link which it has with its antecedent in normal circumstances (i.e. excluding being cited in isolation in a linguistics book). Other bears a relationship of negative inclusion with its antecedent; its anaphoric link, that is to say, is rather similar to that we examined for Contrast (Ch. 7). The quantifier each, on the other hand, which has propositional content by virtue of the meaning it has over and above its quantificational meaning, is not only included in the antecedent-set, but is also distributively rotated through that set, as we have seen.

Other relevant information, such as the cardinality of the set, (shown by '\\' in (70), or the probability of exhaustiveness, may be read from x, the common ground. An example may help:

73. L.A.G.B. wine parties are always rather lively affairs. At the last one I went to, there was a vocal bunch of Generalised Phrase Structure Grammarians in one corner, and a vociferous group of Government Binders in another. (a) From time to time, they would eye each other suspiciously. A couple of waiters were gliding around serving the wine. (b) As the evening wore on, people began to mingle more with each other. Suddenly, two voices could be heard above the hubbub. (c) They were shouting at each other about wh-movement. (d) And on top of this, the waiters started complaining to each other about people leaving traces in the empty glasses

As this text unfolds, the reader will be involved in

[208]

Anaphora

augmenting his stock of information relevant to understanding the text. The text-opening depicts a world (an 'L.A.G.B. wine-party' world) with which he may or may not be familiar. If he has that particular "community knowledge" (Clark and Marshall 1981) or something similar, he will already be able to create conceptually the broad outlines of that world. If not, he can nevertheless form some sort of picture from the intensional meanings alone (for the benefit of such readers, L.A.G.B. means "Linguistics Association of Great Britain"). In either case, the defining propositions of that outline-world will include the information that linguists are present, and this in its turn may or may not trigger off further information. There will also be expectations and assessments of probability etc. of a more general kind, e.g. on the behaviour of people who drink, what happens at parties, and so on. Then there follow the specific propositions added by the unfolding text itself: for example, that there are representatives of at least two schools of thought present, that they do not easily mix, and that there might be some hostility between them (we are, let it be said, strictly for purposes of dramatic exposition, doing an injustice to both these schools of thought!). We may also add to our common ground knowledge the information that there were two waiters, that wine was being consumed, that it was in glasses, that these were probably served on trays, that there was a lot of noise, and so on.

There are four phrasal Reciprocals in (73); in all four cases, the identification of the antecedent is unproblematical. However, in all four cases, the precise signification of each other cannot be determined from the sentence it appears in. Take (a): the antecedent is they; as far as that sentence is concerned, each other is "vague", indeterminate, or multiply ambiguous. But the text-grammar (and specifically the coherence constraint) searches for an antecedent for they, and finds two possibilities: either the two groups of grammatical theorists, or else the members of the group of Government Binders. But general principles of relevance (cf. Werth 1981a, Wilson and Sperber 1981) suggest that there is some motive for having mentioned BOTH groups: thus a contrast or comparison reading is preferable to the otiose mention of one of the groups. (a) means, therefore, that the two groups would eye each other suspiciously. Further interpretation depends on general knowledge of such a situation: that it

[209]

Anaphora

most probably does not mean, for example, that every now and then, the members of one group would turn round in unison, and with one accord stare at the other group. Nor does it mean that each member of the group would take turns to look at the other group, who would themselves be doing the same thing. Such possibilities are rather ridiculous in our culture, though not necessarily in other cultures. We know that the probable situation is that individual members of each group would randomly look at the other group from time to time, with no particular system or method. (b), too, is rather of the same type. The general conclusion we can draw from such examples is, contrary to Dougherty 1974, and Fiengo and Lasnik 1973, that precision of interpretation may not necessarily be of great importance: it will suffice merely to draw an interpretation which is consistent with the common ground, including all pragmatic systems of expectation contributing thereto. If a more precise interpretation is required or indicated, it will be inferrable either from the form of the Reciprocal (which will then be in the more explicit periphrastic form) or from the verbal or immediate situational context.

This is indeed the case with (c) and (d) in (73). <u>They</u> in (c) has only one possible referent, namely <u>two</u> <u>voices</u> in the preceding sentence. This in turn defines the meaning of <u>each other</u> in (c) precisely. Much the same can be said of (d), except that the relevant information for determining the cardinality of the set {waiters} occurs several sentences earlier.

We have tried to show, therefore, that all instances of anaphoric or deictic connection are simply special cases of the coherence constraint upon the elements of discourse. Sentential forms of anaphora are extreme cases of the normal variety, which is textual. The behaviour of these forms falls out from a combination of their internal meaning, and the syntactic effects which are predictable from it, together with the requirement of textual coherence which governs all propositional material[5]. In Ch. 9, we will see how the same principles apply to phenomena which are conventionally thought to be quite "safe" from the point of view of autonomous syntax, namely the "movement" constructions.

[210]

Anaphora

NOTES TO CHAPTER EIGHT

1. In fact, as our previous and subsequent discussion of Contrast makes clear, the antecedent and anaphor in a C-marked relationship CANNOT be identical, since the essence of Contrast is the non-identity of similars.

2. An account of sense-anaphora using the notion of text-world or scene would be as follows:

      (i)   Manuel dropped a bottle of wine. [He] also [dropped] a [bottle] of KETCHUP

      Scene 1 (focus of attention 1):

W_1

> *Manuel drops a bottle* containing *wine*

      Scene 2 (focus of attention 2):

W_2

> [Manuel]
> [drops] a
> [bottle]
> containing
> KETCHUP

Anaphora here is an aspect of accessibility between the two worlds, and involves several decisions that the entities (objects, events, actions etc.) in W_1 have counterparts in W_2. To count as a counterpart, an entity in W_2 must have the same level of specificity as its correspondent in W_1. Levels of specificity extend from individuals at the most specific end, through set-members, to whole classes at the least specific end. In W_2 above, Manuel is one and the same individual, let us say, as the Manuel in W_1, the action of dropping something is a token of the same action-type as that occurring in W_1, and the bottle referred to in W_2 is a member of the same set

[211]

Anaphora

as the bottle referred to in w_1 (whereas a "bottle" of straw would presumably not be a member of that set). All of these entities are therefore counterparts, and will be Reduced. The contents of the bottle, however, differ from one world to the other, despite the fact that they are sufficiently similar to appear in the same context. For this reason, ketchup receives Contrast.

Note that in this explanation, we have used the notion of world to talk about two subsequent actions, or perhaps even simultaneous actions, occurring in the same setting. We have in fact extended the definition of world so as to include a single focus of attention, enabling us to isolate a single incident, a collection of objects, or indeed any entities capable of being grouped together to the exclusion of others.

3. There are, however, important differences between the Reinhart formulation of the condition and the Chomsky formulation. See Reinhart 1983: 24 sq.

4. A few words of caution at this point: (i) Some languages have lexicalised the phrasal form into a single word (e.g. Dutch, German), while also preserving the periphrastic form. (ii) English has another apparently similar phrasal form, one another, which, however, loses its reciprocality in the periphrastic form.

5. For an approach to the resolution of pronoun reference which in many respects is similar to the one put forward here, see Hobbs 1978. Some interesting and compelling psychological evidence for a broad theory of anaphora, such as is presented above, may be found in Marslen-Wilson and Tyler 1980.

Syntactic variation

Chapter Nine

SYNTACTIC VARIATION: GETTING MOVEMENT INTO FOCUS

9.1 Introduction: "Movement" in recent grammatical models

The so-called movement-rules (most of which were exemplified in Ch. 1.3), are part of the legacy of Standard Theory. However, the notion of movement has undergone some shrinkage since the discussions in Ross 1967 and Postal 1971, for example. An early example of this trend is G.Lakoff 1971a, which advocated the notion of a derivational constraint, as we have seen: since this is viewed as a set of well-formedness conditions between a preceding and a succeeding tree in a derivation, no movement as such ever takes place. Extended Standard Theory did not banish the notion of movement rules completely, but it severely limited the distinctive nature of such rules. Thus, both the REST/GB school of Chomsky and the (related) Lexicalist-Functionalist school of Bresnan (e.g. 1978) reduce the syntactic transformational component to just one highly-constrained rule. All ex-Standard Theorists, at least to some extent (following the lead of Emonds 1976), now generate in the base most of the structures that were formerly the output of movement rules, and attempt to handle their specific conditions by referring surface structures to constraints of an extremely general kind (see Chomsky 1973, 1976, 1977b, 1980, 1981), or deep structures to lexical government of lesser (e.g. Jackendoff 1975, 1976) or greater (e.g. Heny 1978) severity. None of these various schools, however, has ever (to our knowledge) attempted to constrain such structures in terms of their possible environment, i.e. on external rather than internal grounds. (There are, to be sure, occasional exceptions to this generalisation, such as the work of Jorge Hankamer).

The rules of Emphasis-placement and the contextual constraints discussed in Chs. 5 and 6 above are neutral on the question of movement-rules, since they may with equal facility be regarded

[213]

Syntactic variation

either as providing the stipulative conditions for movement rules to take place, or else as constituting either the derivational or output constraints on particular structures. The cost of this will be the inclusion of emphatic marking in syntactic structure, this marking being the manifestation of the effects of context upon the structure of individual sentences in it. Despite the neutrality of the subsequent analyses to the question of movement, however, we shall continue to use the terminology of movement ('shifting', 'fronting', 'dislocation' etc.) for convenience and familiarity. Our remarks may always be formulated in terms of constraints as well as movement, however, and from time to time we will make this explicit.

A constraint that we have barely alluded to so far is one which sorts the information in a particular utterance into that which is already in memory and that which is presented for inclusion. The notion of a basic "psychological" division of sentences into "what the sentence is about", and "what is said about this" is an idea of some venerability in linguistics. In a basic, unmarked sentence-type, the division corresponds to the fundamental division of Subject/Predicate, the Subject corresponding to the **Topic**, and the Predicate to the **Comment**[1] — at least in a simplified world. But as we shall see, a number of phenomena appear to intervene between this picture and reality: notably Contrast and movement. In fact, we will see that these phenomena are intimately bound up with the topic-comment notion, which itself generalises the ideas of emphasis which we have developed in the preceding chapters.

9.2 Topic-comment articulation: review section

Topic andcomment did not really attract mainstream attention in generative linguistics before the early seventies. Like most pragmatic notions, (even more than semantic ones), the division was largely ignored by the American Structuralists (with the exception of Charles Hockett, cf. fn. 1) and their inheritors. However, a great number of insights into this subject have been achieved over forty years or more in European linguistics, and notably in Prague School theories (particularly on this subject, V. Mathesius). The academic inheritors and developers of this tradition today are the investigators of Functional Sentence

[214]

Syntactic variation

Perspective (cf. F. Daneš 1974a) orTopic-Comment Articulation (notably Sgall et al. 1973): the terms are — different approaches aside — practically synonymous. **Functional Sentence Perspective** (FSP) tends to denote the older Prague-influenced approach, in which the sentence is divided into its two functioning parts, **Theme** (Topic) and **Rheme** (Comment)[2]:

> The rheme shows its significance as the conveyor of the "new" actual information, while the theme, being informatively insignificant, will be employed as a relevant means of the construction.
> (Daneš 1974b:113)

Thus the theme links each sentence with what has gone before, while the rheme cumulatively moves on the meaning which the discourse is to communicate.

The more recent Prague-descended approach is characterised by the terms **Communicative Dynamism** (CD) and **Topic-Comment Articulation** (TCA). The first of these belong to J.Firbas (e.g. 1974), and has been developed out a refinement to the basic Theme-Rheme division mentioned above. In this later approach, some scholars (see Firbas, 1974: 25) work with a transitional segment between Theme and Rheme. Firbas refines still further, and assigns a CD value to each element in the S; thus, in an S independent of context:

> the subject carries the highest, the adverbial element the lowest degree of CD, the verb-ranking between them.
> (Firbas, 1974: 19)

However, in context, if the subject is contextually dependent (i.e. thematic) in a subject-verb-object structure, then the object will have the highest degree of CD, the subject will carry the lowest, and the verb will again be intermediate. Contextually independent adverbials will also rank higher than the verb in such sentences, though Firbas does not rate them in respect of the object (e.g. p.20). He sums up this extension of the Theme-Rheme version of FSP:

> As I see it, the distribution of the degrees of CD over the sentence elements, which makes the semantic and grammatical structure func-

[215]

Syntactic variation

tion in a definite kind of perspective, is an outcome of a tension between, or rather interplay of, the tendency towards the basic distribution of CD on the one hand, and the context and the semantic structure on the other.
(Firbas 1974: 22)

The tension, or interplay, he speaks of is set up by the contextual dependencies of the discourse. In our terms, anaphoric links have low degrees of CD, since semantically they mark known information (which may occur in previous discourse or derive from the common ground); and Accented progressions have high degrees of CD, since they move the informative development of the text forward.

The notion of CD is, it its turn, taken up and developed into the TCA theories of Sgall et al. 1973. These scholars regard the dynamics of communication as consisting of the progressive modification by the speaker of the knowledge which he assumes the hearer to share with him:

Thus, the speaker specifies the items of knowledge he shares with the hearer that he wants to be modified - we shall call them the established items - and he specifies, further, what properties should now be assigned to them by the hearer, in what relationship with what other items of knowledge they should be introduced, or which other modifications they should undergo.
(Sgall et al. 1973: 39sq.)

They implement these ideas with a very much more detailed scale of CD (p.67) plus the notion of **contextual boundness**. This is approximately the same as themacity or topicality (and is realised as cohesion), but their innovation is to devise an algorithm (in the form of a flow-chart) deriving the CD of sentences, attaching a boundness marker to some element, and allowing the rules to adapt the CD in the appropriate direction.

The disappointing aspect of their approach is its failure to incorporate the notion of contextual boundness into a principled theory of context, or even into a text, or discourse, grammar, i.e. a theory of linguistic context. On pp. 156 sqq., and again on p. 251, the authors take the line, rather,

[216]

Syntactic variation

that textual study would benefit from TCA, whereas we would argue the reverse. In fact, they appear to be of the opinion that since "there is hardly any hope that a purely linguistic theory of text (not operating with such notions as situations or stock of knowledge) could provide for the phenomena characterised here by means of contextual boundness" (p. 159), there is no justification for arguing that "a theory of text is a necessary precondition for the systematic study of TCA" (p. 158). This pessimistic conclusion seems to imply that a full theory of context is a pipe-dream; however, as we have suggested in Ch. 3, some progress might be made in this direction. This issue aside, it seems clear that Sgall et al. present, albeit in embryonic form, an approach which is in many ways equivalent to our own.

9.21 *TCA and emphasis*

Having briefly reviewed some of the approaches to Topic and Comment in the literature, let us now look at their connection with emphasis in discourse (contrary to the views of Sgall et al.). The unmarked Topic-Comment pattern shows Reduction on what we may call "Grounded" elements, i.e. both conventionally-recessive and subsequently- mentioned semantic configurations (M_1 to M_3 in fig. 9.1), figuring in the common ground. On first-mentioned or revived configurations (M_2 to M_4 in Fig. 9.1), the emphasis is Accent, giving sequences (S_1) to (S_3) in (1) with the Grounded-Accent structure shown:

	M_1	M_2	M_3	M_4
S_1	Grounded	Accented		
S_2		Grounded	Accented	
S_3			Grounded	Accented

FIG. 9.1

1. S_1: Do [you] *want* to *eat?*
   S_2: [We] [want] to [eat] *whelks*
   S_3: [Whelks] are *off*, [dear]

[217]

Syntactic variation

This means that the unmarked emphatic structure of a sentence (assuming that it is not a text-initiator) is:

    2.(a) Topic   Comment
          R.................A
      (b) (John and Bill came to see me yesterday)
          They've just acquired a new car
            R   A   A   A

However, as we have seen, the important thing about topics is not that they display reduced stress, but that they are anaphoric, i.e. they repeat or refer back to some element in the common ground. This property of "groundedness" is shared by R and C, but not by A:

      (c) (John and Bill came to see me yesterday)
          JOHN'S just acquired a new car
            C   A   A   A
      (d) (John and Bill came to see me yesterday)
          Fred's just acquired a new car
            A   A   A   A

Notice that there is nothing actually unacceptable[3] about the discourse (d), but that in order to be understood as a discourse, it must cohere (cf. Grice's Maxim of Relation). One possible way in which this may be effected is to regard the sentence beginning "Fred" as representing the gist of John and Bill's communication, in which case it is the beginning of a new subtext, and therefore not subject to TCA. Alternatively, John, Bill and Fred could form a set in that particular text-world.

We can see, therefore, that the unmarked emphatic structure, which corresponds to Topic-Comment by way of the same processes we have been examining, incorporates anaphoric elements to the left (R and C), and non-anaphoric elements to the right (marked A).

9.22 *The TCA constraint*

Topic and comment are terms used in the description of surface-structure word-order. But we must be careful to distinguish between the **description** of surface-structure, and the **motivation** for surface-structure. Why, in other words, does the division take place, and by what processes? Otto Behagel (1923, quoted by Stockwell 1977:

[218]

Syntactic variation

69) expresses the Topic-comment division as a "law" (Behagel's second law). Stockwell puts it thus:

> the sentence element that is the subject of discussion, the topic of that part of the discourse - either because it has been mentioned previously or because it is conspicuous in the environment - tends to come first and to be destressed ... in subsequent references to it, whereas the new information, the comment, tends to come near the end ...[4]

This is, of course, largely a description of the phenomenon, similar essentially to that given in the previous section. For explanation, it provides some comments on the deployment of given and new information — again somewhat resembling what has been said previously in this chapter (though lacking, of course, the explicit machinery provided here). It therefore alludes to the processes involved, without considering the reasons behind those processes. (This is common enough practice, particularly in introductory textbooks, and our remarks should not be taken as adversely critical of Stockwell's useful book).

We would argue that the reason for Topic-Comment Articulation is to structure one's contribution to the discourse in order to make it maximally effective in transferring meaning. Assuming that human short-term memory is analogous to a push-down store, the principle of recall is "last in, first out". This explains why the important material should be concentrated at the end of the utterance, making it easier to recall, and first to be processed. Therefore, it will be more salient. Pragmatically too, it accords with Grice's Maxim of Manner, particularly with the sub-maxim, "Be orderly".

Thus, the speaker proceeds (ideally) by relating each sentence in his discourse to what has gone before and what may be presumed from the common ground. Each sentence is, therefore, related to the discourse by coherence-links (manifested as R or C), and carries the cumulative meaning forward by means of fresh (including refreshed) semantic material (manifested as A). Thus in a simple discourse such as (1), semantic material is rearranged from the right to the left when it occurs a second time, since by then it will already have been processed, and requires only to be alluded to (i.e. used

Syntactic variation

anaphorically) in order to remain in the discourse.

The "rearrangement" of semantic material we have spoken about may take different directions, and may result in alternative surface-structures. Exactly which will depend upon a number of factors, including emphatic structure and other constraints (such as the well-known ones of Ross 1967). To put this in another way, we are claiming that, in context, syntactic movement, (or, in a non-movement account, the choice between syntactic variants), is a device to deploy elements in the order "anaphoric – non-anaphoric", i.e. unmarked topic-comment order. There are undoubtedly other pressures on surface-structure order, but this one at least is controlled by objectively and empirically verifiable factors. Thus movement rules or choice of variants are here regarded as largely contributing to a "conspiracy" towards Topic-comment articulation:

3. THE TCA CONSTRAINT

> Semantic material is deployed in a discourse so as to respect the order: Anaphoric – Non-anaphoric. This corresponds to the emphatic structure
>
> {R}.......A
> {C}
>
> Corollary: to maintain this order in surface structure, syntactic elements may be moved, or a variant allowing the order may be preferred to one which loses it.

If (3) is correct, then certain predictions about the movement rules may be made. In context, we would expect left-shifted/leftward elements to be anaphoric, and either Reduced or Contrastive. We would expect rightward elements to be non-anaphoric, and Accented. We stress "in context", because anaphora, and therefore emphatic structure, depends as we have seen upon the contextual evaluation of semantic material. The orthodox linguistic practice of giving sentence-examples in isolation and judging them for grammaticality etc. depends we would claim, crucially upon one aspect of linguistic competence that generally goes unrecognised: namely, the ability to contextualise. We can assess examples in isolation, that is to say, but only by considering them relative to a normal context.

We shall now look at one of the major movement-rules, or syntactic variations relative to

[220]

Syntactic variation

a context, in the ensuing sections, and see how far it bears out the above predictions.

9.3 Syntactic effects: summary of predictions

The TCA constraint (set out in the preceding section) states that anaphoric elements occur to the left in sentence-structures. The so-called "stylistic inversions","optional movement rules", and the like, of the earlier generative literature, or the variation between structures in which the same lexical items occupy different positions or express different grammatical relations, are to be explained, we claim, in terms of their emphatic structures. Thus, R and C elements are anaphoric and occur at the beginnings of sentences, A elements are non-anaphoric and occur other than at the beginning, with the exception of discourse-initial sentences where none of the information is necessarily anaphoric.

The predictions for individual sentences in context, then, state in their strong form that R and C elements occur to the left, and A elements to the right. In their weak form, they state that R and C elements do not occur to the right, and that A elements do not occur to the left (with the exception of discourse-initial sentences, as we have seen).

In the following sections,these predictions will be tested in detail for one of the main movement-structures, by looking at "real, live" examples in the contexts in which they appeared (rather than in the customary isolation of linguistic examples). In doing this, we are not advocating a return to the "bad old days" of corpus-based grammar. In fact, some of our examples, though contextualized, are constructed. They are nevertheless to be assessed using the same criteria by which the actually-occurring examples are assessed. Our approach is still hypothetico-deductive, rather than inductive, in that hypothesis largely precedes evidence, rather than the reverse. However, the data we have chiefly scrutinized are naturally-occurring rather than artificially-constructed. Many of the contextualized examples come from Levine 1971. As a sort of control group, though, we will first look at sentences exhibiting NONE of the movement characteristics.

[221]

Syntactic variation

9.4 "Unmoved" structures

Preserving what may well be the fiction of movement rules, therefore, we may for the sake of argument assume that there exist structures in the derivation of which none of these rules have applied. These would be more or less equivalent to the "kernel sentences" of Chomsky 1957, and we refer to them here as "unmoved" structures.

The familiar notions of theme-rheme and topic-comment were developed in order to describe the semantic-rhetorical pattern of "unmarked" sentences: it is no accident, of course, that such sentences are so frequently those very same unmoved structures. However, the implications of the previous proposals require that sentences be assessed not in isolation, as is customary, but in context. The TCA constraint predicts that unmoved structures in context should exhibit an

$$\{R\}......A$$
$$\{C\}$$

pattern, or at least should not exhibit an

$$A......\{R\}$$
$$\{C\}$$

pattern. In other words, the former pattern is stable, and if movement exists and is influenced (not to say governed) by the emphatic pattern, then this stable pattern would not encourage movement. The reverse would be true of the latter, unstable, pattern, in that it would trigger movement or block the unstable pattern from surface-structure.

The claim is, then, that the stable emphatic structure discourages movement or the selection of alternative unstable structures, while the unstable emphatic structure encourages movement or equally the selection of alternative stable structures. However, with stable, unmoved structures, our only evidence for this assertion is the deployment of stress-patterns.

9.41 *Behaviour of stress in unmoved structures*

One of the well-known pieces of received knowledge about stress in English, and particularly, contrastive stress, is that it is more or less unrestrainedly variable in its sentence-position (cf. Halliday 1967b: 22 sqq. on "tonicity"; Kingdon 1958: 170sqq.). This is, however, actually fallacious: as we have seen, the occurrence of

[222]

Syntactic variation

emphasis — and here, stress — is very rigidly constrained by textual organization. Obviously, though, a grammar which does not take into account such data — that is, most current grammars — will by the same token overlook this entire area of restriction.

Let us, then, consider some unmoved Ss, examining the stress-possibilities each one exhibits.

4. (a) John writes poetry in the study
   (b) George collects parking tickets all year
   (c) The government announced its plan to the nation

The "tonicity" of English (cf. Halliday 1967, referred to above) allows practically any lexical item in these sentences to receive the nuclear stress. However, we are concerned not so much with the nuclear stress as with the occurrence of any stress at all (as opposed to its comparative non-occurrence). The unmarked pattern is generally said to have the nucleus on the final lexical item, though often little is stipulated about the rest of the sentence. Thus:

5. (a) John writes poetry in the *study*
   (b) George has collected parking tickets all *year*
   (c) The government announced its plan to the *nation*

However, we may well wonder what exactly is meant by "unmarked" in these examples? A sentence like (5a), for example, with a relatively heavy final stress, seems to be several-ways ambiguous in terms of the contexts it fits into (cf. Chomsky 1972 on "focus" and "presupposition", and our remarks in Ch. 6.7). It could, for instance, be an answer to a general question:

6. (a) What happens after lunch?

In this case, it displays the emphatic structure (6b):

   (b) John writes poetry in the study
       A   A   A   A

In (6b), <u>study</u> is perceived as nuclear merely

[223]

Syntactic variation

because it incorporates the intonational downturn.
Alternatively, (5a) might supply information to a more specific question:

7.(a) Where does John write his poetry?

This gives the emphatic structure (7b):

(b) John/he writes/does poetry/it in the
    R   R   R
    study
    A

Notice that it is not only the emphatic pattern which is constrained by the context. The possibilities for pronominalisation are similarly restricted: (7b) with pronouns cannot act as response to (6a) if (6a) is discourse-initial, i.e. non-anaphoric.
But consider the case if (6a) itself occurred in a context in which the poetic activities of John at various times of the day are under discussion:

8. A: Before breakfast, you know, John writes poetry in his bedroom, and after elevenses, in the dining-room.
   B: Really? How very interesting. And what happens after lunch?
   A: Oh, then he does it in the study

Then, as we can see, (7b) with pronouns (= B's question in (8)) can serve as a response to (6a), (= A's second contribution in (8)). However, in those circumstances, (6a) would itself be differently emphasized and specifically no longer non-anaphoric. In fact, given the n-anaphoric relationship of lunch to breakfast and elevenses, this item will bear Contrast (where the non-anaphoric version has Accent).
Another possibility is that (5a) might contradict a previous assertion, such as:

9.(a) So John writes poetry in the garage

This would provide the following emphatic pattern:

(b) No, he writes it in the STUDY
    R   R   R   C
Of the three patterns noted here, it will be seen that only (7b) actually conforms to the fully stable

Syntactic variation

pattern predicted; (6b) and (9b) are intermediate patterns. The most unstable pattern — which simultaneously has a non-anaphoric element to the left and an anaphoric to the right — does not occur here, though entirely anaphoric as well as entirely non-anaphoric structures are represented here. There are several corollaries, then, to our strongly-framed TCA constraint: we would predict that intermediate patterns may move, but need not, that stable patterns resist movement, and that the most unstable pattern actually requires to be moved. Thus context (6) should resist movement:

10.(a) (Where does John write his poetry?)
   (b) ??It's in the study that he writes it
   (c) ??In the study, he writes it

(10b) is perhaps not so much awkward as "overemphatic"; it seems to be violating some conversational principle of manner: "Don't be too eager". However, we shall see in section 9.6 below that cleft sentences such as (10b) in fact obey different conditions of use.

An ordinary informative sentence gives the clearest evidence of our claim:

11.(a) (What does John write?)
   (b) He writes poetry
        R   R   A
   (c) *Poetry is written by him
        A   R   R

The most unstable pattern, however, would have the form:

12.(a) John writes poetry in the study
        A   R   R   R

This could be, for example, the answer to the question:

   (b) Who writes poetry in the study?

But such a question-answer pair may readily be seen to be rhetorically marked: 12(a) is ironic or jocular or catechistic; (12b) is perhaps an echo-question or a teacher-question. Unmarked responses would be:

   (c) John (does)

Syntactic variation

```
        A       (R)
(d) The one who does that is John
        R       R   R     A
```

Of these, (12d) conforms to the predicted pattern; (12c) with _do_-proformation does not, (assuming that _does_ IS actually R here). In Chs. 6 and 7, we touched on the question of the emphatic status of pro-form elements, raising the problem that their normal Reduction-like status was not achieved by the usual emphatic means (as specified in (8), Ch. 6). (12c) seems to suggest that a proform like _does_ is not in fact Reduced, but rather non-stressed, its Contrastible properties coming from its intensional meaning.

Another possible contender as a response to (12b) would be the cleft form:

(e) It's John who writes poetry in the study

However, we would argue that (12e) has the same marked rhetorical properties as (12a) in this context, and as (10b). In section 9.6, we will show that the so-called "focal" element in clefts is usually Contrastive, so that (12e) would be more natural as a contradictory response to (12f), for example:

(f) George writes poetry in the *study*, doesn't he?

The most likely emphatic structure for (12e) would be, therefore, C...R...R...R rather than A...R...R...R. It follows from this that the unmoved form of this proposition would serve equally well as a response to (12f), if it had contrast on the same element, since this would give it the same intermediate emphatic structure:

```
(g) John writes poetry in the study
      C     R      R         R
```

Then in terms of actual realisation, both the cleft (12e) and the unmoved (12g) would have the same intonation pattern, which in RP would consist of a high fall on John (or perhaps a high rise-fall) plus a low rise on study.

Of all versions of (4a) investigated here, it is undoubtedly (6b) which represents the so-called unmarked case, since it presupposes the least context. Our predictions state that such an emphatic pattern may, but need not, exhibit movement.

[226]

Syntactic variation

Furthermore, since all of its major elements are Accented it should in theory allow all possible permutations of elements. It should therefore allow passivization, topicalization, dislocations, preposing of all kinds. However, in practice, this does not seem to be the case, perhaps for two reasons:

First, as has been suggested by Vennemann (1974), Vincent (1979), Lehmann (1976), Li and Thompson (1976 and elsewhere), there is a historical interaction between what on the synchronic dimension may be called topic-prominence and subject-prominence. The grammatical notion of subject seems to derive from the textual or rhetorical deployment of topic to the early part of the utterance, and its subsequent grammaticisation from "what the utterance is about" to the specific sentential function of "subject", with all its grammatical properties (cf. Keenan 1976). Thus, subject-prominent languages have at some stage grammaticised topicalisation, and institutionalised the topic as a first sentence-function. Sentence-types in which the grammaticised subject coincided with the still-mobile topic became the paradigm cases of sentence-patterning in the language. Thus the unmarked sentence-pattern in English is that form in which "what the sentence is about" coincides with the grammatically-specified bundle of properties called "subject".

"What the sentence is about", however, collapses two types of information: (i) the semantic structure of the proposition(s) underlying the sentence, and (ii) their emphatic structure, representing their deployment in the text. With regard to these, it seems that only certain combinations of semantic function and rhetorical deployment (topicalisation) will become grammaticised, e.g. Agent or Instrument ("Initiator"), or Experiencer. Location or Time, on the other hand, will rarely grammaticise into subject, though both are quite commonly topicalised (but cf. Keenan 1976: 330, for locative subjects in Bantu). The so-called "unmarked" structure of the active, declarative, transitive sentence, coinciding with the semantic sequence Initiator-Action-Experience is, therefore, to be explained by assuming that it represents an equally unmarked topicalisation arrangement. Why should this be so? One suggestion (see Kuno 1976) is "speaker empathy": all things being equal, the doer of an action is

Syntactic variation

psychologically prominent. One point to notice is that the unmarked-sentence type is normally assumed to be discourse-initial, i.e. context-independent. But as we have seen, the topic function implies anaphora, i.e. previous mention. We must conclude, therefore, that for the Vennemann et al. hypothesis to be correct, true unmarked sentences must occur in contexts (at least contexts of situation), enabling anaphoric topics. Conversely, discourse-initial sentences, or context-lacking sentences, of the type generally cited, must then be assumed to be unmarked only by analogy.

The second reason for the stability of such sentences as (6b) is complementary to the first reason. Since (6b) holds the semantic and (by analogy) rhetorical functions in stasis, any departure from its structural arrangement must be brought about by outside forces (prominent among which is anaphora). But if all the lexical elements of the sentence are first-mentions (viz. non-anaphoric), which of course they are in the context of the open question, (3a), then there is no pressure from outside, hence no need to re-arrange the structure of (6b). Thus the hypothesis of emphasis-related conditions on movement/variation will naturally explain the occurrence of unmarked sentences in which no movement has taken place (assuming, as the constant caveat, that sort of grammatical model).

Finally, the other intermediate pattern, (9b), is predicted to allow movement, but not require it. This is in fact entirely the case: (9b), with its final Contrast, is a prime candidate for clefting:

13.　　(Does John write poetry in the garage?)
　　(a) No, it's in the STUDY that he writes it

or pseudo-clefting, particularly of the inverted variety:

　　(b) No, (in) the STUDY is where he writes it

or even Y-movement:

　　(c) No, the STUDY, John writes poetry in,
　　　　not the garage

Note that (9b) is much more context-dependent (being

[228]

Syntactic variation

entirely anaphoric, in the sense developed in chapter 3) than (6b) is — hence its relatively greater freedom of movement.

9.42 *Heuristic for contrast with moved structures*

We can now express these facts as a further recognition-procedure for the contextual status of sentences. In other words, if the hypothesis about the interrelation between movement, emphatic structure (and hence context) and semantic structure is correct, then the mere fact of "movement" or "non-movement" may be used to predict the context of the sentence, at least to a significant extent. Thus, a non-moved structure is most likely to have leftward anaphora and rightward novelty: its leftward elements will therefore cohere anaphorically (cf. Ch. 8) with the common ground.

A somewhat less likely possibility is that such a structure might be either entirely novel (in which case it will have no relevant common ground), or else entirely anaphoric. In the latter case, it will either recapitulate elements of its common ground, as in Right Dislocation, for example; or else, more likely, it will include a Contrast, viz. an n-anaphora, as in (9b).

Types of sentence which display movement (or its equivalent) should follow these suggested patterns. Werth 1979 contains a survey of some of the major types. In the next section we take a close look at Passive sentences, to see if they display the predicted behaviour. They, as well as the other varieties, are strongly predicted to have leftward anaphora and rightward novelty (by the TCA constraint of section 9.21), so that their leftward elements will have picked up semantic relationships from preceding context. The corresponding unmoved (unpassivised) structures, on the other hand, will display an unstable emphatic pattern.

9.5 Passives: predictions of TCA constraint

Assuming a structure of the form $S-V-O_1-(O_2)$, i.e. transitive or ditransitive, the TCA constraint implies the following predictions:

14.(a) The most unstable active sentences, i.e.those most conducive to

Syntactic variation

passivisation, will have the emphatic structure:

A................{R}
{C}

(b) The most stable active sentences, i.e. those least conducive to passivization, have the emphatic structure:

{R}
{C}...............A

(c) Intermediate types, i.e. those fairly neutral on the possibility of passivization, will have the emphatic structure:

E.................E

where E = either A, or R/C.

In the latter case, the remarks in section 9.41 above apply.

In a non-transformational account, these conditions may be stated as output constraints providing degrees of markedness. Thus surface-structures having the emphatic structure of (14a) will be most heavily marked, those with (14b) will be unmarked (or least marked), while those with (14c) will have an intermediate degree of marking (including discourse-initial sequences).

Markedness in this case appears to mean unnaturalness in context of various kinds. Consider the heavily marked unstable structures:

15.(a) Justin kissed Maggie
A.............R

(b) Justin was kissed by Maggie
A...................R

These might occur as the respective answers to the following questions (and clearly are not equivalent to each other):

(c) Who kissed Maggie?
(d) Who was kissed by Maggie?

These questions, it is clear, might themselves have

[230]

Syntactic variation

any of a number of possible emphatic structures. A "genuine" question, reflecting the speaker's belief that *someone kissed Maggie, someone was kissed by Maggie*, respectively, would have the structure: R...A...A. An "echo-question", with preceding context similar to these speaker-beliefs (though with some affective addition of incredulity), would have the structure C...R...R. (15a,b) as answers to (15c,d) have the effect of "catechistical" responses, rather than natural ones.

This does not appear to be the case with the unmarked/stable equivalents:

    (e) (Who did Justin kiss?)
        Justin kissed Maggie
         R.............A
    (f) (Who was Justin kissed by?)
        Justin was kissed by Maggie
         R..................A

We shall review the treatment of passives in various contemporary accounts when we consider the problem of motivation in section 9.52.

9.51 *Contexts with and without passives*

The passages in (16) contain one or more examples where the option of passive has been chosen, irrespective of how this is handled in the grammar. The passages in (17) do not contain passives. The hypothesis that we shall examine is that these facts are to be explained as following from the different emphatic structures demanded by these contexts.

    16.(a) ...but success has brought its share of worry for Mr.and Mrs. Harrison...
           Since their mammoth win *tney have been plagued by an endless succession of callers and spongers.*
           (The People)

      (b) Positioning the lips is a problem that recurrently challenges the ingenuity of the embalmer... the lips tend to drift apart. (i) *Lip drift can sometimes be remedied by pushing one or two straight pins through...the lower lips* and then...between the two front upper teeth. If Mr. Jones happens to have no

[231]

Syntactic variation

teeth, (ii) *the pins can just as easily be anchored in his Armstrong Face Former and Denture Replacer.*
(Jessica Mitford)

(c)   Buckingham Palace has withdrawn its objection to the use of newsreel pictures of the Queen attending a State Opening of Parliament in 1970 in a commercial film, starring Rod Steiger, about an attempt to blow up Parliament. (i) *That was confirmed yesterday by Buckingham Palace* ...(ii) *The film has been banned by EMI...*(iii) Before *the film was made,* the company asked Buckingham Palace for permission to use parts of the relevant news film, (iv) and *that permission was granted...* (v) *one cut has been made...*(vi) *The film has been passed by the British Board of Film Censors.*
(The Times)

17.(a)   "...we wanted to revenge the damage Amin's soldiers had caused in Tanzania". *Amin's soldiers invaded and pillaged N.W. Tanzania last October.*
(The Guardian)

(b)The Reliant Robin is the only three-wheeler on the British market and is made by the Reliant Motor Company of Tamworth, Staffs. ...
Reliant started making three-wheeled cars and vans back in 1952...
(Motorists' Guide)

(c)...It was my first experience of doctors who handle you without speaking to you or, in a human sense, taking any notice of you... There was another treatment coming, the mustard poultice... *Two slatternly nurses had already got the poultice ready...*
(George Orwell)

The passive examples in (16) all have Reduced subjects (i.e. objects in the corresponding active sentences), and Accented or Contrastive predicates. In (16a), <u>they</u> is anaphoric (and may be counted as

[232]

Syntactic variation

Reduced), whereas <u>plagued</u> <u>with</u> <u>an</u> <u>endless</u> <u>succession</u> <u>of</u> <u>callers</u> <u>and</u> <u>spongers</u> is new, Accented material. In (16bi), <u>lip</u> <u>drift</u> is repeated (...*lips* ... *drift apart*), whereas most of the material from <u>remedied on</u> is Accented. In (16bii), <u>pins</u> is repeated, and in this case the predicate verb <u>anchored</u> is too, in that it semantically shares structure with <u>push...through</u>, presumably . However, the rest of this predicate is Contrastive with <u>teeth</u>. (16c) is a text containing a sequence of passives. (16ci) bears the emphatic structure (18a):

      18.(a) [That] was *confirmed yesterday* by
              R   A   A
             [Buckingham Palace]
                  R   R

However, an alternative explanation has C on <u>by</u>, giving a constituent-contrast, marking the change in grammatical relation of <u>Buckingham Palace</u> (cf. Ch. 7.1). Perhaps Kuno's notion of "empathy" has some bearing on this rather puzzling example.
　　(16cii) is a clearer case:

      (b) [The film] has been *banned* by *EMI*
           R   A   A

So also are (16ciii) and (iv), assuming that <u>before</u> stands in contrast to the current existence of the film:

      (c) BEFORE [the film] was *made*
           C   R   A
      (d) [That permission] was *granted*
           R   A
(16cv) is more difficult; we have to assume either that <u>permission</u> pragmatically entails 'entirety', i.e. 'no cuts', or that <u>banned</u> pragmatically entails 'nullity', i.e. 'no film', so that <u>one</u> might imply 'only one'. Given one of these assumptions, <u>one</u> would then be Contrastive, which fits the normal stress pattern of the sentence:

      (e) ONE cut has been made
           C   A   A

However, it should be said that this analysis is not very strongly supported by the facts, leaving us with the possibility that (18e) is an intermediate type. This receives some support from the fact that

[233]

Syntactic variation

the corresponding active (*Somebody has made one cut*) is reasonably acceptable too.

(16cvi), on the other hand, is perfectly regular:

  (f) [The film] has been *passed* by the *BBFC*
       R   A   A

(though the last phrase may contain some anaphoric material on account of the repetition —if such it is— of <u>censors</u>).

The indicated sentences in (17) are cases where the passive option might, on the face of it, have been taken, but was not. (17a) has the emphatic structure (19a):

  19.(a) [Amin's] [soldiers] *invaded* and *pillaged*
          R   R   A   A
          N.W. [Tanzania] *last October*
          A   R   A   A

However, <u>invaded</u> and <u>pillaged</u> might be R...R, depending upon how strong the implicational link with <u>caused</u>... <u>damage</u> is. <u>Amin's</u> <u>soldiers</u> and <u>Tanzania</u> are direct repetitions; everything else (with the possible exceptions mentioned above) is new.

Passivised, (17a) would have come out as:

  (b) *N.W.* [Tanzania] was *invaded* and *pillaged*

       A   R   A   A
       last October by [Amin's] [soldiers]
       A   A   R   R

This gives a marked/unstable structure, conforming to our predictions.

(16b) has the emphatic structure:

  (c) [Reliant] *started* [making] [3-wheeled]
       R   A   R   R
       [cars]   and   [vans]   back   in *1952*

       R   R   A

The equivalent passive would be of the same type (assuming that the temporal would remain final). Nothing would be gained, therefore, by choosing the passive option, which again is the stable sequence

[234]

Syntactic variation

predicted.

The subject of (17c) could be anaphoric (either Reduced because implied by the situation, or Contrastive, with <u>doctors</u> perhaps). Equally, it could be non-anaphoric, if it is new information. <u>Poultice</u>, however, is definitely Reduced, whereas <u>got...ready</u> is Accented. The emphatic structure of this non-passive is therefore an intermediate (14c) type:

```
          (d) Two slatternly nurses had already got

              A    A        R/C/A         A    A

              the [poultice] ready
                  R         A
```

The equivalent passive, however, would also be intermediate, though only if <u>nurses</u> is anaphoric (R or C); if <u>nurses</u> is Accented, then the passive would be of the predicted unmarked type:

```
          (e) The [poultice] had already been got
                  R              A          A

              ready by two slatternly nurses
              A     A      A         ?A
```

Of course, if our overall hypothesis is correct, it will allow us to deduce that, since the passive was NOT selected in (17c), <u>nurses</u> is probably not Accented, but anaphoric.

The active sentences which we may assume correspond to the passives of (16), all bear out the predictions of (14a):

```
      20.(a) An endless succession of callers and
                     A          A          A
             spongers has plagued [them]
                A        A       R
         (b) x can sometimes remedy [lip] [drift].
                   A         A       R     R
         (c) x can just as easily [anchor] [the pins]
                   A         A      R        R
             in his A.F.F.D.R.
                    C
```

Notice that the subject slots of (20b,c) contain the free variable x. We assume that the necessary agentive information can be filled in here from the common ground. Forms such as <u>one</u> or <u>people</u> have a function in natural language which is equivalent to

[235]

Syntactic variation

that of free variables in logical notation, and they are completely opaque to emphasis, being neither clearly Accentable, Reducible or, in this function, Contrastible. Nevertheless, as we saw in Ch. 6, there are good arguments for regarding them as Accented items. We will consider in the next section just what this sort of element contributes to passivisation.

Conversely, the active sentences of (17) correspond either to the optimally stable structures of (14b), or at worst to the intermediate structures of (14c).To sum up then: an object or oblique element marked R or C is much likelier to occur in grammatical subject position than one marked A. In such cases, it seems clear that an anaphoric element (R or C) is preferred in order to maintain the unmarked topic-comment structure of (14a).

9.52 *Why passivise at all?*

Robin Lakoff, in a 1971 paper, asks the question "why passivize a sentence at all?" and goes on to say:

> Passivization is one of the few rules I know of that, while apparently adding little semantic material to the 'basic' active sentence, considerably complicate it syntactically and morphologically. The linguist's task, then, in characterizing passivization - it would seem to me - is to ask why it is done, and done in this way, rather than, as usual, merely to ask what is done to the superficial configuration of lexical items   (1971: 2)

We have argued that the motivation for this somewhat unlikely construction is to be sought in the relationship between a given sentence and its context. Passives typically occur when the logical object is anaphoric and the logical subject is not. We may also add at this point, that this is particularly the case if the latter is a weak impersonal. We have seen that, on completely separate grounds, weak impersonals are Accented items, and thus non-anaphoric. When they function as logical subject, therefore, TCA functions quite regularly to encourage the passive.

Grammar-books often adduce reasons of the following kind for passivisation (cf., for example, Graver 1971, Stannard Allen 1959):

[236]

Syntactic variation

(1) Avoidance of weak impersonal subject;
(2) Stylistic: to maintain the same subject in a series of conjuncts;
(3) Suppression of agentivity: disclaimer of responsibility, evasion of personal involvement etc;
(4) Promotion of the predicate;
(5) "Focus of interest".

This particular list is in fact a summary of Graver 1971: 107sqq. It will be instructive to recast it into the terms we have been using.

First, the weak impersonals: these, as we have just said, are anomalously Accented elements, which however, may not be Reduced, since they normally lack stress anyway. Certain of them, such as you, one, meaning 'people in general', are, moreover, unContrastible, though most of the weak impersonals can be Contrasted. When Contrasted, they are anaphoric in our system, and are then candidates for the leftward position (e.g. as subjects), particularly if the predicate is Accented. Otherwise, however, though they are weakly-stressed, they are non- anaphoric; and since it is this which is the crucial property of leftward elements, they are unstable in that position, particularly with an anaphoric element to the right:

21. There have been many attempts to renovate Dingley Hall, none of them successful. After a particularly spectacular failure in 1981, *the [building] was eventually demolished/*(@Someone eventually demolished the [building])

Second, the so-called "stylistic" motive is in our view produced by the same pressure. Consider the typical situation here: there will be a series of conjoined sentences, cohering in the required way, perhaps anaphorically. One of these conjuncts, however, contains a verb whose controlled arguments are in the reverse order from those of the other conjuncts. Thus the topical argument is for the other conjuncts in subject position, but for the problem conjunct is in object or oblique position, the unstable situation as depicted in TCA. Selection of the passive at this point will clearly restore stability, as predicted by our constraint:

22. The Prime Minister arrived back in London last night, and *[__] was immediately*

[237]

Syntactic variation

besieged   by   reporters/(@reporters immediately besieged [her]) (Graver 1971)

Weiner and Labov 1983 find that "parallel structure" is a more significant factor in choice of passive than distribution of information. By our explanation, though, these are ultimately effects of the same impulse.

Thirdly, there are many possible motives for wishing to suppress mention of the agent, ranging from modesty to guilt, and including total predictability from context. Ultimately, this is a question of intentionality (with a t) and outside our scope. Yet, although there may perhaps be cases where the passive is motivated solely by evasion of responsibility, it is nonetheless noteworthy that the examples usually given fall under one of the other headings:

> 23. (a) You're fired!
> (b) The new working methods that are to be introduced... (Graver 1971)
> (c) Upon examination, the component was found to be faulty

(23a) seems to be a case where the predicate is accentuated (it is also, incidentally, Accented in the most likely context). But there is another important factor: if we compare it with the active (*I fire you!*), we may note that the latter begins and ends with situational pronouns, predictable from the very situation itself and thus R. Therefore, the emphatic structure of that active is R...A...R, an intermediate type. The passive, on the other hand, is R...A, a stable type, and therefore preferable. (23b) seems to be a case of the "stylistic" effect, or rather, as we have seen, of an R-marked item being moved from an unstable position at the right. (23c), a typical "scientific" use, would obviously be part of a discourse in which the referent of <u>component</u> had already been established, rendering that item anaphoric in (23c). Our explanation for suppression of agent is, therefore – questions of intentionality aside – that in such cases the passive without agent is a more stable form than active with agent. Since in these cases, the agent will always be contextually predictable, it will always be suppressed in the passive. (See also Comrie 1977).

Fourthly, the instances where the predicate, or some element of the predicate, is promoted, are clear cases of our constraint at work. Typical

[238]

Syntactic variation

contexts for this type would be scientific papers discussing, say, rat-reactions or particle-behaviour:

> 24. The subjects were 16 university students attending summer school. They were recruited by an advertisement and were paid $1.50 for their participation. They were tested individually, assigned in random alternation... The subject was told to learn 30 picture pairs which were shown to him at a rate of one every 12 sec. (Johnson and Solso 1978)

In (24), the equivalent actives would have <u>the subjects</u> in final position in the basic structure; but since this expression is anaphoric, the active would be unstable, or at least less stable than the passive.

Finally, the "focus of attention" cases will almost always turn out to be instances of anaphoric elements going to the left:

> 25. Finally, from the B.B.C. Sports Unit here is the latest news on today's international sporting events:
> Well, it's been an eventful day in the soccer world. Holland beat West Germany in the first leg of the World Cup Tournament last week, but was beaten 3-1 by Hungary this afternoon. Rugby football; and England was defeated by France after extra time

The second conjunct of the Holland sentence is clearly another instance where an anaphoric item happens to occur in non-subject position (or in a non-agentive role), whereas the agent is Accented. Hence the passive is more stable here than the active. The England sentence is rather more subtle, since neither England nor France has been mentioned before in this text. But this is the B.B.C., and we may assume that the community to which (presumably) both speaker and listener belong is always potentially prominent in the common ground. To that extent, it will be anaphoric in the broad sense. A member of a different community, though, will not presume the salience of this item: an American report, for example, would probably say "France beat England", which is an intermediate emphatic structure by (14). See Kuno 1976 on "empathy".

In general, therefore, we may consider that our hypothesis is strongly compatible with the facts of

[239]

Syntactic variation

passivisation in English. There are two related effects: firstly, an anaphoric item at the righthand end of any sentence is discouraged, particularly when there is a non-anaphoric item to the left at the same time, and even more particularly when this latter is a weakly-stressed impersonal. We may refer to this as a **drag-effect**, borrowing a term from historical linguistics. The second type of effect involves a Contrastive stress at the end of the sentence. Not only is this anaphoric and therefore in an unstable position, but in communicative terms, it may also be insufficiently distinct from the ordinary (Accented) nuclear stress normally occurring there. In order to make the Contrast more distinctive, therefore, it may be shifted away from its final position, or a syntactic variant may be selected in which the Contrastive element is non-final. This is then the corresponding **push-effect**.

9.6 "Emphatic" constructions

The **emphatic constructions** are those which, as compared with their ordinary non-emphatic equivalents, have an extra "topmost S" node, which is always copulative and, in English, attached to the rest of the sentence by what appears to be relativisation. We are referring primarily to **Clefts** and **Pseudoclefts** (P-clefts) such as:

26.(a)   Though Johnson stepped up the war in Vietnam, *it was Kennedy who first drew America into the conflict*

(b)   The involvement of "high culture" with Pop in the postwar era is a thing which has been much discussed. *What has been less thoroughly examined is the tendency of Pop to take what it needed from the avant-garde* (*The Times*)

As Quirk et al. 1972: 951sqq. point out, there are certain distributional restrictions on these forms. The cleft, as in (25a), allows constituents of most kinds in the top S position, but absolutely excludes verbs. (See also Culicover 1977). The P-cleft allows verbs, but tends to discourage (in some cases strongly) any element that cannot be introduced with <u>What</u>. However, we shall assume that, for example, the "human" P-cleft is introduced with <u>The</u> <u>one/man/person</u> <u>that</u>, rather than <u>Who</u>. (See also

[240]

Syntactic variation

Pinkham and Hankamer 1975, Higgins 1976).

The term 'cleft' (originally due to Otto Jespersen), and by derivation the more recent term 'pseudo-cleft' also, comes from the idea that a "more basic" sentence "splits" into two parts in order that one of them may be highlighted. This is clear enough with clefts, as we shall see, but with P-clefts there are two complicating factors: one, the <u>What</u>-part may with equal facility occur initially or finally; two, the highlighted element may occur either in the <u>What</u>-part or in the rest. Various emphatic structures are also possible:

27.(a) The [local] WINE is what I [miss] *most*
   (b) What I [miss] MOST is the *local wine*
   (c) The [local] [wine] is what I [miss] *most*
   (d) "Ah!" said Tigger, "HAYCORNS is what [tiggers] [like] *best* of all!" (A.A.Milne)

28.(a) What you HAVEN'T [mentioned] is the *economic crisis*
   (b) What we *want* is WATNEY'S

Clearly, if we are going to attempt an explanation of P-clefts, whether in terms of emphasis-marking and the TCA constraint, or in terms of some other mechanism, we first have to find out whether there is some system to this apparent variability.

According to the TCA constraint, our predictions for these structures would be essentially the same as for passives: that is, that the leftward element will be constructed upon anaphoric material (marked R or C), and that the rightward element will be Accented. It remains to be seen whether there are any special properties of these constructions which call for some modification to the predictions, and if so, whether they still fit the basic TCA hypothesis. In particular, we will be examining the positional variability of the <u>What</u>-part in P-clefts.

As far as our foregoing examples are concerned, we may swiftly check them for conformity to TCA. (26a) shows a typical cleft context, with a concession followed by a disclaimer. A first scrutiny, though, reveals that although the leftmost element (<u>Kennedy</u>) is Contrastive, as is normal with clefts, and in line with TCA, yet the rightmost element is Reduced, <u>conflict</u> being a virtual synonym of <u>war</u>. The whole construction is therefore an intermediate emphatic structure. This is fine — except that the corresponding non-clefted S is identical in the

[241]

Syntactic variation

order of its constituents, and therefore in the order of its emphases (Kennedy being the subject of the "relative clause"). Furthermore, this is a very general deployment in cleft sentences: the focal element is Contrastive, while the remainder is largely Reduced ("presupposed" in Chomsky's terminology). Thus clefts present *prima facie* evidence against the TCA constraint – evidently their function is different from the rearrangement of anaphoric material which TCA accounts for.

The rest of our preliminary examples are P-clefts. (26b) evidently has Contrasts on <u>less</u>, <u>Pop</u>, and <u>avant-garde</u> in the second, P-clefted S. The first of these takes <u>much</u> <u>discussed</u> and <u>thoroughly</u> <u>examined</u> to be virtual synonyms; <u>less</u> therefore Contrasts the EXTENT of the two activities. The Contrasts on <u>Pop</u> and <u>avant-garde</u>, on the other hand, demonstrate "reversed reciprocal Contrast" (cf. Lakoff 1971b, Oehrle 1981), a device used to signal reversal of case-roles established in the common ground. The first S of (26b) suggests that "high culture" borrowed from "Pop culture"; the second S suggests conversely that Pop borrowed from High culture, in the form of its representative, the avant-garde. Strikingly for our purposes, though, the P-cleft here is again an intermediate structure in terms of (14), and so is the corresponding non-P-clefted S. Again it seems that the motivation for a P-cleft must be different from that for a passive, for example.

The examples in (27) perhaps provide the first substantial hint that the emphatic constructions are not in fact motivated by TCA. What sort of context would (27a), (b) and (c) require? We suggest that contexts like (29a,b,c) respectively would be appropriate:

29. (a) The Camargue seafood and the delicious bread were hard to leave behind, but (27a)
   (b) I miss the Camargue wildlife and the beautiful sunsets a lot, but (27b)
   (c) O.K., you said you missed the wildlife and the sunsets, but if I know you, the local wine's got something to do with it as well! – Yeah, in fact (27c)

These seem to suggest that, given the appropriate context, the TCA constraint cuts across whatever

Syntactic variation

motivates the emphatic constructions, i.e. the two impulses are separate and perhaps independent. Thus, (29a) mentions members of the set {food-and-drink}, while (27a) singles out the local wine as being superlative (hence unique) with regard to the predicate. <u>Wine</u> is thus anaphoric, whereas the superlative quality is a new element. TCA thus operates here, we may suppose, to rearrange anaphoric and non-anaphoric elements, giving a reversed P-cleft, but a P-cleft all the same. (In fact, a cleft would appear to be exactly equivalent in this case). (29b) places more prominence on the function of missing certain things which are in themselves not particularly connected (except through location). In (27b) accordingly, the degree of "missingness" is anaphoric, whereas the wine is Accented, since it coheres in the text-world, but shows no identity. (29c) is somewhat similar, except that it actually mentions the wine, which is therefore Accented in (29c) for the same reasons as in (27b). In (27c), however, it is Reduced, being a straight repetition. Since it is therefore anaphoric, the TCA constraint cuts in as predicted⁴. (27d) appears to behave like (27a), while (28a) is comparable to (27b). (28b) is a bit of a mystery. This is a well-known and very old advertising slogan, which is never spoken, so it is difficult to judge what the stress pattern might be. Assuming, however, that the purpose of an advert is to contrast that product with all others in the set (in this case, beer), we have put C on <u>Watney's</u>. The emphasis on the rest of this short sequence is rather difficult to be certain about, but similar examples in context, such as (30), appear to have another C in the <u>What</u>-part:

30. (a) They keep on giving us free tickets, when what we WANT is the MONEY
    (b) Don't be fobbed off with flowers. What you NEED is RESPECT

We will discuss such "double-Contrast" examples in a subsequent section.

9.61 *Examples of emphatic constructions in context*

Our further examples are all taken from Svartvik and Quirk 1980. On the whole, we have not

[243]

Syntactic variation

reproduced their notation, except to indicate relevant stress-information. We have also tended to simplify the texts so as to cut out the "performance-features", since on the whole we are more interested in the contextual content. However, our complete references will enable readers to check the original transcription, if they suspect that any distortion has occurred[7].

31.(a) A: Well – may I ask what goes INTO that paper now, because I have to advise a couple of people who are doing the...

B: Well, what you DO is to <...> what you DO is to *make sure* that your own *candidate* <...> that <...> there's something that your own [candidate] can *handle*...

(b) A: I DID get a postcard from him saying that the thing is now ready and that he will send it by the end of June. [That]'s what he SAYS

(c) A: Now, what was the OTHER [thing] I wanted to ask you? Is it THIS year that *Nightingale goes*?

B: No, NEXT [year]
              <...>
A: So it's not until NEXT [year] that the [job] will be ADVERTISED?

(d) B: He was saying for example that these questions three and four didn't make any difference really to the result of the examination.

A: But they DO, I think.

B: Well, I'm quite CERTAIN that they [do] <...> I said straight out at the meeting, if you take a statistical analysis of the people who pass, you'll find that it is <THIS [question]> which <...> they're <*passing* on>
(All from text S.1.1, pp. 34–52)

(e) B: Well, Mallet is hopping MAD about all this because Mallet sees a hundred and fifty thousand pounds for a building and various other things

[244]

Syntactic variation

going down the drain. What I think
he doesn't REALIZE is that it's
<very *largely* BECAUSE> he's been
building this kind of *peripheral*
[thing] in *Appleby* that it HAS [gone
down]
(Text S.1.2, First subtext (TU
1-885), p. 58)

(f) B: Is that the actual terms of
reference? I thought that it was
more <...> if you want to have
Philosophy and Mathematics as your
two possible subjects as an
undergraduate, then you can do
those.
A: Oh, no!
B: Then this isn't your chore.
A: No. It's not IRRELEVANT to it, but
it's the *academic structure* of the
UNIVERSITY that WE're [concerned]
about.
(Text S.1.2, subtext S.1.2b (TU
1214-1463), p.80)

(g) A: It's simply UNTRUE that there's been
another big row since I was there,
then, is it?
B: <...> There hasn't been another big
row, no <...> That's the ONE <...>
What has [happened] <SINCE [then]>
is that there has been ANOTHER
[meeting] of the *executive committee*
at which it was quite clear that
Mallet and I did not see eye to eye

(h) A: ... and what about the immediate
future? What about for next year? Is
there a continuation grant, or
anything?
B: Not at the moment. Not as it stands,
no. <...> What *really sank* the
<*whole* [thing]> as far as *Thame* is
concerned, the [whole] *existing*
[one], *including* a [continuation] on
the *same basis*, was when they came
to look at the *detailed accounts*
(Both from S.1.2, First subtext (TU
1-885) pp. 57, 68)

[245]

Syntactic variation

(i) B: Two years ago now, three years ago, I
brought cups and saucers, and a
coffee and tea pot, and I haven't
[done] anything ELSE.
A: But have you got a KETTLE?
B: Well, what I would *use* is one of
those *little solid-fuel* [jobs].
They're awfully good, and they're
QUICKER than the [kettle]
(S.1.4, p. 121)

(j) B: <...> I should ask him if there are
any seminars you ought to go to
<...> He has a way of having them at
a horrible time <...> like
five-fifteen, when you want to go
home.
<...>
<...> Beryl Martin <...> she used to
come in late in the MORNING, and
he'd say "Good AFTERNOON, Beryl",
which used to make her terribly
worried.
<...>
THAT's all right, 'cos the trouble
is, he'll be there HIMSELF soon
after <...> nine, isn't he, and he
expects everybody else to do
likewise. What he DOESN'T [realize]
is that <not EVERYBODY else> can
work quite as *hard* as HE can
(S.1.5, p. 130)

(31a,b) are P-clefts, the latter an inverted
type, (31c,d,f) are clefts, while (31e) is a cleft
embedded in a P-cleft. (31g-j) are all P-clefts. A
preliminary survey of this material seems to reveal
that clefts always contain a contrOstive element in
the "It-part" (usually known as the focal element,
indeed). In fact, as Quirk et al. 1972: 951 point
out (their comments being based on this same
corpus):

the highlighted element has the full
implication of contrastive focus: the rest of
the clause is taken as given, and a contrast is
inferred with other items which might have
filled the focal... position in the sentence

A typical example of this account would be (31c),

[246]

Syntactic variation

in which the fact that Nightingale is going is presupposed, as well as, naturally, that the event will take place one of these years. We should, however, be careful to distinguish between "taken as given" as Quirk et al. evidently mean it — i.e. "presupposed" — and as it would more naturally be interpreted in the light of such accounts as Chs. 3, 4, and 6 above, where it means "already present in the common ground", a much wider set of propositions. Nevertheless, both of the propositions we have distinguished in (31c) are presumably part of the mutual knowledge of the speakers: it is enough for speaker A to mention the name Nightingale for speaker B to activate the relevant section of his knowledge. The fact that such events are related to academic years is part of another more general store of knowledge, perhaps. The contrast, too, is based on a conventionally recessive item, namely the current time span, which is a member of a set of possible time-references. The second cleft of (31c), though, is rather less dependent upon common ground knowledge. Here, the contrast is on another member of the set of possible time-references. The remainder of the sentence coheres by inference: 'when Nightingale goes, there will be a job-vacancy; if there is a vacancy, you usually fill it without delay; you have to do this by advertising the job'. Since this entire inferential chain is, presumably, present in the relevant knowledge-store, i.e. belongs to that knowledge-frame evoked by the subject-matter, all of the items in it (including job) are pragmatically presupposed, and therefore anaphoric when explicitly expressed. However, since the constituent advertised...(same) year occurs in the scope of a negative, the normal inference chain is contradicted, and a constituent-Contrast is appropriate here.

The other examples of cleft, however, although they all have a Contrastive focal element, also have a Contrast in the rest of the sentence. Furthermore, in these same cases, the rest of the sentence often ends with a Reduced element. This, on the face of it, is rather puzzling: some clefts, that is to say, behave in precisely the reverse way, apparently, to the predictions of the TCA constraint (cf. our brief discussion in the previous section). If we consider equivalent non-clefted sentences, we find that the situation is not obviously clearer:

[247]

Syntactic variation

```
32.(c) Does Nightingale [go] THIS [year]
            A        R    C    R
       So the [job] won't be <ADVERTISED
              R                C
       until NEXT [year]>
             C    R

   (d) You'll find that [they]'re passing on
                         R         (A)
       THIS question
       C    (A)

   (e) [it] HAS [gone down] largely BECAUSE
       R    C    R          (A)     C
       [he's] been building this [kind] of
       R          A              R
       peripheral [thing] in Appleby
       A          R         A

   (f) WE're [concerned] about the academic
       C      R                         A
       structure of the UNIVERSITY
       A                C
```

The bracketed As in (32d,e) represent renewals of information, rather than completely new information. They also correspond to the propositional-bracketing introduced in this section to denote a semantic/intonational tie-up.

If we regard the structures of (32) as representing the syntactically unmarked alternatives to those of (31), contextual effects aside, then we have the apparent relationships with regard to TCA as shown in (33); (the first set in each case is for the unmarked, "unmoved" example of (32)):

```
33.(c) A...A...C...R → C...R...A...A

   and R...A...C...R → C...R...R...A

   (d) R...(A)...C...(A) → C...(A)...R...(A)

   (e) R..C..R..(A)..C..R..A..R..A..R..A
       → (A)..C..R..A..R..A..R..A..R..C..R

   (f) C...R...A...A...C → A...A...C...C...R
```

In the terms of the TCA constraint, (33c) goes from unstable to stable in the first case, and from intermediate to stable in the second. (33d) goes from stable to stable, (33e) from stable to

[248]

Syntactic variation

unstable, and (33f) from intermediate to unstable. What, then, is going on here?

In our view, the answer is bound up with the function of the two Contrasts, which need not be on a single lexical item, as our notation appears to suggest, but may in fact be on a whole anaphoric constituent. In such cases, we have to look at the discourse-function of the whole Contrastive constituent. Take (31f), for example: here, speaker B has been describing the function of a committee which he believes speaker A to be a member of. That is to say, he knows that A is on a committee, and believes it to be the one he is describing. He therefore tries to negotiate A's acceptance into the common ground of his description. A, however, rejects B's account — not on the grounds of falsity, but on the grounds that it does not refer to his committee. A's clinching contradiction occurs in cleft form, and the clinchingly contradictory part of it is the section stating the terms of reference of the committee that he actually is on. This is the whole constituent <the *academic structure of the university*>, which, as a statement of the terms of reference of a committee, belongs to the same semantic set as B's explanation, though remains, of course, distinct from it. We may call this the **primary Contrast**, in terms of its communicative motivation, which in this case is contradiction or correction of the main textual theme at that point. The **secondary Contrast**, on the other hand, picks up the point that though B's description may refer to some existing committee, it does not refer to the set of committee-members of which A is one.

(31e) is a rather more complex case, but shows essentially the same effect: B introduces the proposition that £150,000 has "gone down the drain" (or at any rate is in the process of doing so) in the view of a certain "Vice-presbyter Mallet". The speakers evidently share a large amount of community knowledge about this man, who according to the wider context (e.g. p. 66) is the head of the institution, and about his exploits, his character, his behaviour, and so on — including the fact that he has been building something in Appleby. In the opinion of speaker B, this last activity is the chief cause of the loss referred to (the loss of a building grant, perhaps). The reference to this activity, forming a constituent with <u>because</u>, is thus Contrasted with Mallet's presumed attribution of blame for the loss of the money. (Two pages previously, the speakers discuss a row over the

[249]

Syntactic variation

status of subdepartments of the "School of Yiddish". Mallet presumably regards the resulting delay in reaching agreement as contributing to the loss of this money). The primary Contrast in this case, then, is on ⟨*very largely because he's been building... in Appleby*⟩. The secondary Contrast is on the polarity of the constituent ⟨*has gone down the drain*⟩, which also displays repetition and zero-anaphora.

(31d) is a much simpler case with only one Contrast, on the constituent ⟨*this question*⟩, referring back to ⟨*these questions three and four*⟩ (the explanation of the singular in our extract is probably that only one of questions three and four has to be chosen by the examinees). The two clefts in (31c) follow a similar pattern.

Before attempting a synthesis of our account for clefting, let us look at the behaviour of P-clefts. Again, we may look at equivalent non-P-clefted forms:

```
34.(a) You make sure that there's something
           A    A                   ?A
       that your own candidate can handle
              A    A              A

   (b) He says that
       R  C     R

   (d) He doesn't realise that (32d)
       R           C           R...A

   (g) ANOTHER [meeting] of the executive
       C            R              A
       committee has [happened] SINCE [then]
           A          R          C     R

   (h) When [they] came to look at the detailed
       R     R/A          R/A               A
       accounts it really sank the whole thing
           A        A      A        A      ?R

   (i) I would use one of those little solid
                A                A      A
       fuel [jobs]
        A    ?R

   (j) He DOESN'T [realize] that not EVERYBODY
       R    C         R              A      C
       else can work quite as hard as HE can
            A              A          C
```

[250]

Syntactic variation

The first three examples are apparently immune to TCA requirements. (34a,d) are both stable emphatically; (34b) is completely anaphoric, hence intermediate, but with no hope of ending up stable. (34g,j) are both intermediate; (34h) is stable, and (34i) is unstable. Clearly, as with the cleft examples, there is something more going on here than the TCA constraint alone can account for. To consult the whole picture again, let us compare the emphatic structures of the non-P-clefted and the P-clefted versions:

```
35.(a) A...A...?A...A...A...A
    ➔ (R)...A...A...A...?A...A...A...A

   (b) R...C...R ➔ R...(R)...R...C

   (d) R...A...C...R...<...>...A
    ➔ (R)...R...A...C...R...<...>...A

   (g) C...R...A...A...R...C...R
    ➔ (R)...R...C...R...C...R...A...A

   (h) R..R/A..R/A..A..A..A..A..A..?R
    ➔ (R)..A..A..A..?R..R..R/A..R/A..A..A

   (i) A...A...A...A...?R
    ➔ (R)...A...A...A...A...?R

   (j) R...C...R...A...C...A...A...A...C
    ➔ (R)...R...C...R...A...C...A...A...A...C
```

From this, we can see that (35a) is intermediate emphatically in the non-P-cleft, and stable in the P-cleft; (35b) goes from intermediate to intermediate; (35d) from stable to stable (and in fact the order of elements is identical); (35g) from intermediate to stable; (35h) from intermediate to intermediate; (35i) from unstable to intermediate; and (35j) from intermediate to intermediate. Like (35d), the last two retain the identical element-order in both versions.

Now in all of these cases, the P-cleft is never worse than intermediate: but this is because we have always marked the What-element itself as (R), ensuring that, except in the inverted case, the construction always begins with an anaphor. What, though, is the evidence for the anaphoricity of what?

[251]

Syntactic variation

The first point is that the antecedent of <u>what</u> usually follows it (except in the inverted type): nevertheless, it makes sense to think of the relationship between <u>what</u> and the semantic material following the copula as one of anaphor-antecedent, since paraphrases of these sentences into conjoined or separate-sentence forms invariably produce a clearly anaphoric equivalent to <u>what</u>:

36.(a)   What he doesn't realise is that not everybody else can work quite as hard as he can
   (b)   Not everybody else can work quite as hard as he can, and he doesn't realise <u>it</u>
   (c)   What really sank the whole thing was when they came to look at the detailed accounts
   (d)   They came to look at the detailed accounts, and <u>this</u> sank the whole thing
   (e)   What I love is misty weather
   (f)   Misty weather, I love <u>it</u>
   (g)   What you have to do first is to get in touch with the Complaints Section
   (h)   Get in touch with the Complaints Section. You have to do <u>that</u> first

Secondly, we note that the <u>what</u>-phrase introduces a presupposition of existence upon the element corresponding to <u>what</u>, the rest of the <u>what</u>-phrase then predicating something upon the presupposed element (which is eventually filled in by the rest of the sentence). This is so, whatever the existential status of the antecedent:

37.(a)   What John doesn't believe in are unicorns
   (b)   Unicorns? John doesn't believe in <u>them</u>

Thus the components of the generalised P-cleft structure (38a) are always interpretable as in (38b):

$$
\text{38.(a)} \quad \text{What} \begin{Bmatrix} \text{VP} \\ \text{NP V} \end{Bmatrix} \text{be} \begin{Bmatrix} \text{S} \\ \text{VP} \\ \text{NP} \\ \text{PP} \end{Bmatrix}
$$

[252]

Syntactic variation

$$
\begin{aligned}
&\quad\qquad\qquad\qquad\qquad\langle\{S\ \}\rangle \\
&\quad\qquad\qquad\qquad\qquad\langle\{VP\}\rangle \\
\text{(b)}\quad Exists\ x{:}\ x\ \{\ VP\ \}\ \ \&\ \langle\{NP\}\rangle \\
&\quad\qquad\qquad\{NP\ V\ \}\quad\langle\{PP\}\rangle_{*}
\end{aligned}
$$

Here, as is normal in the discourse-semantic system we are employing, the existential operator has scope across the world elaborated in the common ground of the discourse. However, because the normal antecedent-anaphor order is reversed, the resulting suspense (cf. de Beaugrande 1980: 123) gives a highlighted rhetorical effect to the construction, rather similar to that achieved by so-called "backwards pronominalisation", left-dislocation, and other forms of cataphora. The anaphoricity of such constructions, that is to say, is parasitic upon ordinary anaphora in that it foregrounds an expected anaphoric relationship for rhetorical effect.

9.62 *Why cleft or pseudo-cleft?*

Unlike passives, we shall argue that the emphatic constructions are essentially **rhetorical** in nature, in that they are used to highlight semantic material, rather than to merely redeploy it. This is most clearly to be seen with the cleft construction, in which a Contrast-marked item occurs in the focal position, and the remainder of the sentence is, by definition, at least partly given (though it may contain some new, Accented material). In certain, contextually-defined circumstances, the sentence-remainder is absent:

> 39.   A: Which President first drew America into
>   the Indochina conflict, Eisenhower,
>   Kennedy, or Nixon?
>   B: It was Kennedy __

Where the sentence-remainder of the cleft is completely repeated material, then often it is the case that only the focal part will appear. Where the sentence-remainder contains Accented material, however, then this option is not available.

In other cases, our data show that when the sentence-remainder is only partly given (i.e. in all cases except those of complete anaphora), it often contains a second Contrast. This suggests that one purpose of the cleft construction may be to separate two Contrasts from each other, in order to enhance their saliency. Furthermore, the "primary Contrast"

[253]

Syntactic variation

(in focal position) often carries with it new Accented material, while the "secondary Contrast" (in sentence-remainder position) will usually be accompanied by repeated and Reduced material, including zero-anaphora. **It is this reversal of the expected TCA order, we may assume, which gives the construction its heightened rhetorical effect.**

P-clefts, on the other hand, tend to maintain the expected TCA order more often than not, in that they place anaphoric material before non-anaphoric material. However, as we have seen, the non-anaphoric material in P-clefts includes or constitutes the antecedent of the anaphoric material, the resulting tension providing the heightened rhetorical effect in this case. With P-clefts, too, a reversed order is possible, which allows both the TCA redeployment and the rhetorical heightening simultaneously. However, the fact that, in non-reversed cases, the P-cleft constituent order is often identical to the non-P-cleft constituent order, shows that TCA-type redeployment is not the function of the construction.

Higgins 1976 (following Akmajian 1970) makes a distinction between **Specificational** P-clefts and **Predicational** P-clefts, the latter more or less equivalent to Hankamer's (1974) "Headless Relative". The Specificational is what we have in fact been calling the P-cleft, and fills in some information signalled by the empty slot <u>what</u>. The Predicational, in our view, is not a P-cleft at all; it provides a predicate for a complex Subject NP which also begins with <u>what</u>:

> 40. (a) What annoyed him was John's refusal to talk (SPECIFICATIONAL)
>   (b) What annoyed him was quickly dealt with (PREDICATIONAL)

Specificationals have regular simplified equivalents lacking <u>what</u> and the copula verb; predicationals do not:

> (c) John's refusal to talk annoyed him
> (d) *Quickly dealt with annoyed him

Higgins also distinguishes, however, a third type, which he calls Identificational, and which he regards as a subtype of Predicational:

> (e) What Mr. Weems is is a teacher

[254]

Syntactic variation

We can see why Higgins placed this type in the same category as his Predicationals: a teacher is a predicate nominal. Nevertheless, (40e) is arguably Specificational, in that it fills in the semantic gap signalled by what, and is paraphrasable by a simple sentence omitting what and be:

    (f) Mr. Weems is a teacher

In fact, (40e) also has a Predicational meaning, though it is rather difficult to grasp. We may perhaps suggest what it is by way of a different example:

    41.(a) What Mr. Weems is is important

As a Specificational, (41a) is equivalent to (41b); as a Predicational, it is equivalent to (41c):

      (b) Mr. Weems is important
      (c) Mr. Weems' profession (i.e. what he is) is important

For sense (b), therefore, (41d) is contradictory; for sense (c), it is perfectly coherent:

      (d) What Mr. Weems is is important, but Mr. Weems himself isn't important

We shall assume, therefore, that the Identificational type is a true P-cleft also. The difference between Specificationals and Identificationals is then, in our view, a difference of emphatic structure. Compare the following two texts:

    42.(a) Paris is a city of sights for the dedicated tourist who, with limited time available, is faced with an embarrassment of choice: l'Etoile, the Louvre, the Eiffel Tower, the Rodin Museum, Napoleon's Tomb. With only two hours between trains, John had time for just one landmark.
What he visited eventually was the
(R) R   R   A
EIFFEL TOWER
   C

[255]

Syntactic variation

    (b)   "Was the Eiffel Tower that sort of arch
          thing?" enquired Granny, who had never
          been   very good at Geography. "No,
          Granny", we explained patiently,
          "What we visited yesterday was the
           (R)   A   A
          [Eiffel Tower]"
                 R

(42a) is Specificational, filling in the "what" from
a set of possibilities: it is, therefore,
essentially Contrastive. (42b) is Identificational,
reidentifying a description with a name: here, the
name is repeated, hence Reduced. But this is not
necessarily the case: the identification can be new
information, hence Accented:

    (c) A: So, what have we seen so far?
        B: Well, what we visited YESTERDAY was
             (R)   R   C
           the *Eiffel Tower*...
                 A

      There is a third possibility for P-clefts, and
as is evidenced by Svartvik and Quirk 1980, a very
common one. This is the Presentative type (Hetzron
1975), in which a proposition is "presented" to the
listener, in the context of a performative or verb
of propositional attitude (cf. Ch. 6.23 above).
Examples of this type which we have already used are
(31e,h) above; in Svartvik and Quirk we find many
more beginning, for example: *"What I mean is..."*,
"What I want to say is...". A related subtype
contains generalising verbs of events, states,
actions etc. (31a,g,i) above provide examples. Thus,
presentation consists of the sequencing of the main
proposition after an introductory lead-in which
states the speaker's attitude or intention relative
to the proposition. Generalising to all P-clefts, we
can say that the What-part functions as a "bridge"
between the common ground of the discourse, and the
new proposition which the speaker is negotiating for
entry. Since to this extent, its function is to draw
attention to itself, and to the propositional
attitude etc. which it conveys, we may also regard
it as rhetorical.

[256]

Syntactic variation

NOTES TO CHAPTER NINE

1. The terms 'topic' and 'comment' are due to Hockett (e.g. 1958: 201).
2. Halliday (1967a: 200 etc.) points out that topic and comment are normally used misleadingly to conflate "given-new" in information structure, and "theme-rheme" in thematic structure. The cases where this becomes crucial for him are those where there is a Contrast early in the sentence, e.g. (using our notation):

    (i) JOHN [saw the play yesterday]

    Here, John is the theme, but since for Halliday it is not "given" here, it must be the comment. Halliday therefore avoids the terms 'topic' and 'comment'. Notice, though, that the Reduced part of (i) is equivalent to (and rather less likely than) a proform:

    (ii) JOHN did

    or an elliptical form

    (iii) John __

    Moreover, (i) could take alternative forms:

    (iv) It was JOHN who [saw the play yesterday]
    (v) It was JOHN __
    (vi) The one who [saw the play yesterday] was JOHN

    These assume a contradictory context, such as (vii) for (i)-(iii), and (viii) for (i) and (iv)-(vi), but not (ii) and (iii):

    (vii) Nobody saw the play yesterday, did they? (i.e. $\langle Not \langle Exists\ x \rangle \langle x$ saw play$\rangle \rangle$)
    (viii) Tony saw the play yesterday (i.e. $\langle Exists\ x \rangle \langle x$ saw play$\rangle$)

    On the distinction theme-rheme (Mathesius's *basis* and *nucleus*), see Vachek 1966: 111.
3. In fact, we are often talking about fairly subtle degrees of acceptability or probability

[257]

Syntactic variation

in many of these cases, rather than anything that could be represented as downright ungrammatical or unsayable. For some discussion of the question of grammaticality in D-grammar, cf. Ch. 2 above, and Werth 1976: 29 sqq.

4. Hetzron (1975: 348) doubts that it is the novelty of the element which is at issue here, but rather "what the speaker intends to build up in the discourse", i.e. its import. Nevertheless, this information too is subject to first-mention, or may be renewed in a subtext, so the question of motivation, while ultimately important, may probably be dispensed with at the level we are concerned with.

5. See also Creider 1979 for an account of the relationship between movement and stress which has many affinities with our own. Empirical evidence for this sort of position may be found in Tannenbaum and Williams 1968, and Most and Saltz 1979.

6. It should be said, though, that variants of (27a,c,d) with a final C appear to be possible, giving an intermediate structure. However, in two of these cases, we then get a double-Contrast P-cleft - see discussion below.

7. The notation for emphasis here is as before, though we introduce some new notational devices to handle irrelevant features in the transcribed passages. Omitted text - sometimes only hesitation features, sometimes lengthy but irrelevant digressions - is marked <...>; sequences of lexical items which represent a single proposition in semantic structure are sometimes enclosed in <> brackets, too, since they often manifest some sort of linking intonation effect, such as step-down (cf. Ch. 6, fn. 2), or constituent-Contrast (cf. Ch. 7.1). As is generally true of our notation in this book, we only mark that which is germane to the issue under discussion.

[258]

Conclusions

Chapter Ten

CONCLUSIONS

10.1 Summary

We have tried to provide evidence in support of the thesis that an extension of grammatical theory in the direction of discourse will solve many of the problems of sentence-grammar in a unified and natural way. As we see it, a **D-grammar** is not a device equivalent to an S-grammar except that it has texts rather than sentences as its output. This view would have to be founded on the untenable premiss that texts display the same sort of structural constraints as do sentences. Instead, we propose that a D-grammar is a S-grammar, with additional constraints making it sensitive to sequential properties of sentences in texts. As for the S-grammar in question, we assume that any of the current models, insofar as it can express the basic syntactic properties of sentences, will be adequate.

We demonstrate that **textuality** is indeed a comprehensible property, i.e. that there are real differences between texts and mere sequences of sentences. These differences resolve themselves into the single principle of **coherence**, which states that every proposition in a text has a semantically- or pragmatically-definable relationship with at least one other proposition in the discourse. By 'discourse', we refer not only to the text (the verbal context) but also to the situational and community knowledge shared by the speakers, and specifically informing a given text. The total set of propositions which have been expressed in the text so far, and accepted by the participants, plus the relevant properties of the situation and items of backgound knowledge, also expressed in the form of propositions, together with all inferences which can be drawn from all these propositions, constitute the **common ground** of the discourse. This is equivalent to the notion of (Pragmatic) Universe of Discourse (cf. Kempson 1975: 167sqq.). The coherence constraint, then, requires that any proposition in a text (including the proposition currently being

[259]

Conclusions

uttered) should be related to at least one of the propositions in the common ground. We demonstrate that this takes several forms in surface-structure. Notable among these is **anaphora**, which in our view is based on the specific relationship of identity between elements of propositions, elements which may denote individuals, sets or subsets, or a part or implication of one of these. We also argue that an important function of any discourse is to set up one or several conceptual frameworks — the **"world(s)" of the text** — within which anaphora and other processes operate. These worlds form an important part of the common ground for that discourse, and tracing their interaccessibility is an essential task for discourse semantics.

The machinery of the coherence constraint, we suggest, is the far-reaching device of **emphasis**. Emphasis is a semantic/pragmatic notion which responds to the coherence relationships between propositions, depending on whether they are anaphoric or not, and if anaphoric, whether this is positively or negatively. This system is actually a refinement of the notions 'given' and 'new', as commonly understood in the literature. We may therefore think of emphasis as monitoring the flow of information through a discourse, and tagging items which have cropped up before in some form, as distinct from those which, while cohering generally, have not occurred previously.

We then go on to argue that this emphasis-marking is responsible for some of the processes which hitherto have found their way into sentence-grammars. In particular, we examine sentence-stress, anaphora, and various types of syntactic variation. For the last of these, we can apparently distinguish between two kinds. There is a fairly automatic type of variation which ensures that anaphoric elements occur to the left in a sentence in context, and non-anaphoric elements to the right, and a rhetorically-marked variety which divides a highlighted part of a sentence from a recessive part. In all of these cases, and several more which we do not have the space to discuss, the discursive machinery of emphasis plays a vital role.

10.2 Implications

On the whole, the methodology of this book has

Conclusions

been to demonstrate that its approach is technically feasible and internally consistent. The question of empirical justification will be discussed in the final section. However, at this point we should like to briefly consider the possible implications of our approach, in two areas: **linguistic theory**, and **psychological reality**.

Linguistic theory. We would contend that the approach we have outlined allows at last a reconciliation between "competence" and "performance". When Chomsky first drew this distinction, it was clear that he meant to separate the proper matter of linguistic scrutiny from the "pathology" of language in use: mistakes, false starts, hesitations, memory limitations, lapses of attention and concentration etc. In the climate of the day, this was a necessary corrective to the avowed (and unworkable) ideals of corpus-based linguistics, which in practice made the same exclusions, though covertly. In the words of Katz and Bever (1974: 23):

> linguistic competence is distinguished from linguistic performance primarily in a negative way by the fact that the latter involves matters not relevant in the explanations of such intuitions [i.e. about aspects of sentence structure], e.g. limitations stemming from the nature of the organism's psychological mechanisms, which restrict immediate memory, computation time, and information access.

If such limitations did not exist, if human beings never made mistakes, were unfailingly fluent, and so on, the original notion of performance would have been quite unnecessary: "competence is reflected by ideal performance" (Chomsky 1965: 4). This notion of performance, it seems to us, is perfectly valid and in fact absolutely essential, as long as it is used to exclude only the unsystematic "perturbations" in the organism. However, from very early on, it became clear that performance was turning into a dustbin for systematic facts of language in use, inconvenient because they did not fit into the current theories of grammar. As early as 1963, Katz and Fodor were excluding from linguistic theory information about "settings in linguistic discourse (written or verbal) or in nonlinguistic contexts (social or physical)" (p.

[261]

Conclusions

484). By 1974, this had hardened into principle: Katz and Bever 1974 is a criticism of several contemporary attempts to include such information, together with participant-beliefs etc. into linguistic theory.

What we have tried to provide in the foregoing pages, however, is an account which relates relevant features of "settings" to features of grammatical surface structure in a direct and natural way. We do not claim that the isolation of what is "relevant" in the common ground is necessarily simple in any given case. What we do claim to have provided, however, is a framework to capture these facts in principle. Further analysis of a great many real discourses along the lines suggested here will reveal how viable the system is, and how much modification it requires.

A second theoretical implication of this work is that it appears to offer a practical basis for the notion of 'rule constraint'. We do not claim that the coherence constraint or the TCA constraint are in any sense the "real-world" correlates of c-command, Binding Theory, or any other components of REST/GB, not to mention equivalent constraints in GPSG, LFG or any other acronymic schools of thought. What does seem plausible, though, is that all such constraints are at base fossilised versions of semantic requirements on textuality. Reinhart 1983: 198sqq. offers some interesting speculations for c-command which appear to amount to just such a proposal. The notion of 'Dominance' in Erteschik-Shir and Lappin (e.g. 1983) is another example of a discourse-based processing principle with implications for syntactic structure. A third example of this kind of approach is Givòn 1979, and especially his Ch. 5.

Another potential advantage of our approach is that it facilitates the descriptive distinction between relatively fixed syntactic structuring on the one hand, and relatively flexible syntactic selectability, on the other. The set of so-called "stylistic transformations" in generative grammar have always had the status of unmotivated alternative locutions, the tacit assumption being that extraposed or topicalised structures are chosen not for any intrinsic reason, but for "mere stylistic reasons", such as harmony, euphony, parallelism, etc. We have taken the contrary view that syntactic variation of this kind is motivated, by its sensitivity to the flow of information

[262]

Conclusions

through the text. In general terms, we claim to have captured at least part of the relationship between functional purposes and syntactic output.

Psychological reality. Like democracy, this is a quality which all current theories claim to possess. Nevertheless, it is difficult to see how any theory can claim psychological reality which, for example, has several different kinds of empty category, or indeed, empty categories at all, or which ignores in principle any type of connection outside the boundary of the sentence. Our claim to psychological reality, though, is based on a number of hard facts:

(i) **Textuality** is a fact, as we demonstrate in Ch. 2, and as is shown also in Grimes 1975, Frederiksen 1977, Kintsch 1977, Enkvist 1978, Van Dijk 1980, Hoey 1983, to name just a few references in the burgeoning literature in this field.

(ii) **Information-salience** is a fact: see Ch. 6 above, and cf. also contemporary work by Taglicht 1979, Gussenhoven 1983, in linguistics, and by Bock and Brewer 1974, McKoon 1977, Bock 1977, Bock and Irwin 1980, Engelkamp and Krumnacker 1978, Cutler and Fodor 1979, Lesgold et al. 1979, Yekovich et al. 1979, etc., in psychology. There is a great deal of evidence available (see, e.g. Bock and Irwin 1980: 468) that conceptualisation processes assemble information from memory in terms of knowledge-frames etc., while structural processes retrieve this information and assemble it in an order which is partly determined by syntactic regularities in the language (e.g. the choice of SVO, VSO etc.) and partly by the status of the information retrieved (in terms of such distinctions as given-new, entailed, inferrable, and so on). This latter characteristic is, of course, of some importance in the approach we have taken in the foregoing chapters. Thus, givenness appears to be a function of availability in short-term memory, whereas entailment and inference appear to reside in the longer-term storage and cataloguing facilities.

(iii) **Coherence** is a fact: see Chs. 4 and 5 above, and the references therein, together with work by Keenan and Klein 1975, Keenan and Schieffelin 1976, Dascal 1977, Reichman 1978, Hobbs 1979, Dascal and Katriel 1979. See Van Dijk 1980: Ch. 6, for a useful survey of psycholinguistic work in this area.

Conclusions

(iv) **Common ground.** The use of backgound knowledge and accumulated textual information in the production and comprehension of discourse has received extensive coverage in the literature of the last decade or so. We may consider two crucial aspects of this: **inferencing** and **negotiated reality.** Recent work on inferencing probably began with the study by Haviland and Clark 1974 on "bridging assumptions". Subsequent work includes: Clark and Haviland 1977, Rochester and Martin 1977, Linde 1977, Harris and Monaco 1978, Yekovich and Walker 1978, Noordman 1979, Crothers 1979, and Maclaran 1981. All of this work emphasises the active role of the listener in drawing inferences, both logical and pragmatic, from what has already accumulated in the common ground and specifically from the current contribution. The notion of "negotiated reality" refers to the gradual construction of a text-world by the participants in a discourse as an essential component of the common ground. We have already referred to the work of Van Dijk 1977 and Clark and Marshall 1981 on the more theoretical aspects of this process (though both approaches are very aware of the practical restrictions of cognition). For further work, see Kratzer 1980, Johnson-Laird 1981, and the references in de Beaugrande 1980: 24sqq.

In general, we claim that there is ample independent evidence for the view that the semantic structure of sentences is not an autonomous entity (*pace* the work of Katz since 1963), but is a totality derived from:

(i) the intensional meanings of the linguistic expressions used, together with their logical entailments (i.e., roughly speaking, the subject-matter of Katzian semantics);

(ii) the extensional references of these expressions in the text-world built up by the context in which they occur;

(iii) the context, or common ground, which is an artefact derived from the propositions making up the preceding text plus all relevant knowledge-frames in the memory of the participants, (also expressed propositionally).

[264]

Conclusions

10.3 Empirical evidence for emphasis

In this section we report on a research project which is in progress. The aim of the project, which is being carried out by Kitty Jacobs, and is supported by the Belgian Fonds Nationale de la Recherche Scientifique, is to test our characterisation of Accent, Reduction, and Contrast. The specific notions tested are:

(i)   antecedent (cf. Ch. 8);
(ii) semantic relatedness, or "similarity" (cf. Ch. 5);
(iii) set-membership (cf. Ch. 7);
(iv) denial of identity (cf. Chs. 5 and 7).

Test (i) is to confirm that Accented items have no antecedents, whereas both Reduced and Contrastive items do have antecedents. A number of short written texts are presented to subjects with certain words (x) underlined. The underlined items have been chosen on the basis of independent judgements of their emphasis — whether Accented, Reduced, or Contrastive. Subjects are asked to indicate from the text *"What, if anything, does x connect up with?"*. They are, in addition, encouraged to explain their response. The predicted result is that Reduced items will always have an antecedent reference, that Contrastive items will be linked to a co-member of a set, while Accented items will have no clear connections (we expect responses to be divided between various collocational possibilities and a negative answer). One of the texts used in this first test is given here:

1. By the window, a <u>mirror</u> hung over the sink, and she stood in front of <u>it</u> winding her <u>rollers</u> out one by one, dropping <u>them</u> on to a <u>chair</u>, running her <u>fingers</u> quickly through the <u>rolls of</u> hair, piling and pinning <u>it</u> high. Then she tried on her <u>hats</u>, and stepped back to get a proper view of <u>each of them</u>. <u>Neither</u> looked quite like funeral <u>wear</u>, although the <u>green one</u> had a <u>black underside</u> to the <u>brim</u> and the <u>red one</u> was trimmed with a <u>narrow black ribbon</u>. But <u>one of them</u> would certainly do.
   (Dee Phillips 1980, slightly altered)

[265]

Conclusions

Test (ii). This is a small battery of tests designed to assess the notion of "similarity" (up to identity) in the relationship between anaphor and antecedent. The main test in the battery consists of short written texts which are presented to the subjects, with final sentences containing a blank in a position which invites anaphora. A choice of four possible completions is offered in random order, selected as follows: (a) is a pronoun, (b) is a virtual synonym, (c) is an implicationally related term, either by part-whole, set-subset, or strong association, and (d), as far as can be arranged, is an unrelated item. The first sentence in each text contains the antecedent item, the second sentence is a buffer, containing no interfering references, and the third and final sentence contains the blank anaphor spot. Subjects are invited to rank the four choices in order of preference, and to justify the link they make for the fourth item, if they make one (half of these have been selected on the basis that a link might be forced, but a great deal of extra context would be necessary; for the other half, even this possibility has been avoided). A control group is presented with the texts and blanks, but without the multiple-choice response. They are asked to suggest three possible completions for each blank, and rank them for preference. The prediction in these cases is that the order of preference will reflect the order in which we have described the possible choices above, i.e. (a)-(d). For (d) items, it is predicted that the linkable items will generate a Contrast rather than a Reduction, and will require extra explanatory context. An example text for test (ii) is:

2. Do you remember the day I found you inside our bedroom cupboard? You nearly gave me a heart attack. When I asked you what on earth you were doing, you said something was wrong with _____.

      (a) the wardrobe
      (b) it
      (c) the dog
      (d) the hinges

Test (iii) is also concerned with the question of similarity, but this time in connection with Contrastive items. This being the case, the tested notion is that of the 'set'. As we have seen, sets

Conclusions

may be paradigms of items sharing many of their semantic properties (e.g. cooking containers, flowers), they may be more loosely related in semantic fields (e.g. political words, words connected with psychoanalysis), or they may be related ad hoc, for the purposes of the current text-world only (e.g. the many disparate items which might happen to find themselves together in the description of a junk-shop). Furthermore, there perhaps exist items which cannot be set co-members under any circumstances. Subjects are presented with a number of Contrastively-structured pairs of items bearing one of the above types of set-relationship to each other, and are asked to assess each sentence for contextualisability on a five-point scale. A control group is asked to suggest a context for each sentence. Our predictions are that the order of assessment will reflect the closeness of the set-type in the order of the descriptions given above (i.e. paradigm, field, text-world, unrelated). Some example-sentences are:

3. (a) I like strawberries, but I don't like blackcurrants
   (b) I like strawberries, but I don't like lawn tennis
   (c) We can still use the strawberries, but the cats have passed their best
   (d) I like strawberries, but I hate philosophy
   (e) Strawberries are fine. Heidegger isn't
   (f) I hear you like strawberries. No, it's doing crosswords that I like

Test (iv) examines the second main property of Contrast, namely its negative anaphora, or "denial of identity". This property, as we saw in Chs. 5 and 7, may take various more or less explicit forms, ranging from overt negation (<u>not</u> <u>like</u>) through morphologically-expressed negation (<u>dislike</u>) and negative lexical items (<u>hate</u>) to implicational forms (<u>prefer</u>). This task presents lists of Contrasted structures, showing the various non-overt negative possibilities, sometimes in the antecedent part, sometimes in the subsequent (anaphoric) part. Subjects are asked to rewrite each sentence with an overt negative form, but preserving the meaning. A control group will be asked to match the corresponding overt and non-overt negative sentences from groups of four, their reaction-time being

[267]

Conclusions

measured. The prediction in this case is that the further away from overt negation the original sentence is (in the order presented above), the more varied will the answers be, and the longer the reaction time in their comprehension. Examples are:

4. (a) I like jazz but I detest classical music
   (b) I hate Mozart but I rather like Bach
   (c) All boys are noisy. Alan is rather quiet, though
   (d) All little boys are adorable, but Sam is an absolute angel
   (e) Given the choice between a bad democracy and a benign dictatorship, I'll take the democracy every time

Such tests are valuable in that they help to reveal a few of the types of decision that speakers and hearers make during every moment of their linguistic activities. In the foregoing chapters, we have tried to suggest the range and complexity of the information which is actively available to the language-user, most of it normally accessible only through introspection. The central principle binding texts together, we have argued, is coherence. By concentrating on the system of emphasis, which is in our view the executive machinery of this principle, we claim to have provided a fairly direct means of probing the hidden sources of discourse production and control.

[268]

BIBLIOGRAPHY AND AUTHOR-INDEX

Abbreviations:

ACLS	American Council of Learned Societies	Lang&Sp	Language and Speech
AmAnth	American Anthropologist	LACUS	Linguistic Association of Canada and the United States
AmSp	American Speech	LAUT	Linguistic Agency University of Trier
AP	Academic Press		
API	Association Phonétique Inter- nationale	Lg	Language
		LI	Linguistic Inquiry
ArchLing	Archivum Linguisticum	Ling	Lingua
BLS	Berkeley Linguistic Society (Proceedings)	Ling&Phil	Linguistics and Philosophy
		LingB	Linguistische Berichte
CAL	Center for Applied Linguistics	Lings	Linguistics
CH	Croom Helm	LRI	Linguistic Research Inc.
CLS	Chicago Linguistic Society (Proceedings)	MITP	Massachusetts Institute of Technology Press
Cog	Cognition	NHP	North-Holland Press
CogPsy	Cognitive Psychology	OUP	Oxford University Press
CogSc	Cognitive Science	P-H	Prentice-Hall
CornUP	Cornell University Press	PhilRev	Philosophical Review
CUP	Cambridge University Press	PM	Pragmatics Microfiche
EUP	Edinburgh University Press	PsyRes	Psychological Research
FL	Foundations of Language	PTL	Poetics and Theory of Literature
GUP	Georgetown University Press	RAIP	Rapport d'Activités de l'Inst- itut de Phonétique, Bruxelles
GURT	Georgetown University Round Table		
		S&S	Syntax and Semantics
HRW	Holt, Rinehart, Winston	SEL	Studies in English Linguistics
IULC	Indiana University Linguistics Club	Sem	Semiotica
		SIL	Summer Institute of Linguistics
IUP	Indiana University Press	SocRev	Sociological Review
JExPsy	Journal of Experimental Psychology: General	SUP	Stanford University Press
		UCalP	University of California Press
JL	Journal of Linguistics	UCSD	University of California San Diego
JPhil	Journal of Philosophy		
JPrag	Journal of Pragmatics	UIP	University of Illinois Press
JPsyRes	Journal of Psycholinguistic Research	ULond	University of London
		UMP	University of Michigan Press
JSocI	Journal of Social Issues	UPennP	University of Pennsylvania Press
JVLVB	Journal of Verbal Learning and Verbal Behavior		
		USC	University of Southern California
LA	Linguistic Analysis		
LA&B	Linguistic Association of Great Britain	UTP	University of Texas Press

NOTE: The final set of figures after each entry refers to pages in the present volume.

[269]

Bibliography

Abercrombie D. 1967 *Elements of general phonetics* Edinburgh: EUP. 98

Adams C. 1979 *English speech rhythm and the foreign learner* The Hague: Mouton. 98

Akmajian A. 1970 On deriving cleft-sentences from pseudo-cleft sentences, *LI*1: 149-68. 120,254

Allerton D. and Cruttenden A. 1979 Three reasons for accenting a definite subject, *JL*15: 49-54. 125

Austin J.L. 1962 *How to do things with words* Oxford: OUP. 70,127

Behagel O. 1923 *Deutsche Syntax* (4 vols.). 218sq

Bennett D.C. 1975 *Spatial and temporal uses of English prepositions* London: Longman. 165

Bever T.G. 1970 The cognitive basis for linguistic structures, in J.R.Hayes *Cognition and the development of language* London: Wiley, 279-352. 127

Bock J.K. 1977 The effect of a pragmatic presupposition on syntactic structure in question answering, *JVLVB*16: 723-34. 263

Bock J.K. and Brewer W.F. 1974 Reconstructive recall in sentences with alternative surface-structures, *JExPsy*103: 837-43. 263

Bock J.K. and Irwin D.E. 1980 Syntactic effects of information availability in sentence production, *JVLVB*19: 467-84. 263

Bolinger D. 1958 Stress and information, *AmSp*33: 5-20. 124

Bolinger D. 1961 Contrastive accent and contrastive stress, *Lg*37: 83-96. 124

Bolinger D. 1972 Accent is predictable (if you're a mind-reader), *Lg*48: 633-44. 124

Bolinger D. 1977 *Meaning and form* London: Longmans. 84

Bolinger D. 1978 Intonation across languages, in J.Greenberg *Universals of human language*, vol.2, Stanford: SUP. 98

Bolinger D. 1979 Pronouns in discourse, *S&S*12: 289-309. 15,94,179

Bossuyt A. 1981 Mutual knowledge and relevance, *RAIP*15: 21-30. 59

Brainerd B. 1976 On the Markov nature of texts, *Lings*176: 5-30. 33

Bradley R. and Swartz N. 1979 *Possible worlds* Oxford: Blackwell. 174

Brame M.K. 1977 *Conjectures and refutations in syntax and semantics* Amsterdam: NHP. 79

Brame M.K. 1979 Realistic grammar, in M.K.Brame *Essays towards realistic syntax* Seattle: Noit Amrofer. 176

Brazil D. 1975 *Discourse intonation* English Language Research:

[270]

Bibliography

University of Birmingham. 127

Brazil D. 1978 *Discourse intonation II* English Language Research: University of Birmingham. 127

Bresnan J. 1978 A realistic transformational grammar, in Halle *et al. Linguistic theory and psychological reality* Cambridge: MITP, 1-69. 214

Brugman C. 1981 *Story of Over* Bloomington: IULC (1983). 135

Bühler K. 1934 *Sprachtheorie* Jena: Fischer. 79

Carden G. 1982 Backwards anaphora in discourse context *JL18*: 361-87. 15,94

Cazden C.B. 1970 The situation: a neglected source of social class differences in language use *JSocI26*: 35-60. 38

Charniak E. 1975 Organisation and inference in a framelike system of common-sense knowledge, in R.C.Schank and B.L.Nash-Webber *Theoretical issues in natural language processing* Cambridge, Mass: Bolt, Beranek and Newman. 6

Chomsky N. 1957 *Syntactic structures* The Hague: Mouton. 222

Chomsky N. 1965 *Aspects of the theory of syntax* Cambridge, Mass: MITP. 66,77,163,261

Chomsky N. 1972 Deep structure, surface structure and semantic interpretation, in N.Chomsky *Studies on semantics in generative grammar* The Hague: Mouton, 62-119. 15,120,122sqq,130,163,164,223

Chomsky N. 1973 Conditions on transformations, in S.Anderson and P.Kiparsky *Festschrift for Morris Halle* New York: HRW, 232-86. 213

Chomsky N. 1975 *Reflections on language* London: Temple Smith (1976). 83

Chomsky N. 1976 Conditions on rules of grammar *LA2*: 303-51. 193,213

Chomsky N. 1977a *Essays on form and interpretation* Amsterdam: NHP. 70,176

Chomsky N. 1977b On wh-movement, in Culicover *et al. Formal syntax* New York: AP, 71-132. 176,213

Chomsky N. 1980 On binding *LI11*: 1-46. 101,188,191,213

Chomsky N. 1981 *Lectures on government and binding* Dordrecht: Foris. 61,63,65,80,130,163,176,187sqq,213

Chomsky N. 1982a *The generative enterprise* Dordrecht: Foris. 59

Chomsky N. 1982b *Some concepts and consequences of the theory of government and binding* Cambridge, Mass: MITP. 61,63,65,80

Clark H. and Haviland S.E. 1977 Comprehension and the given-new contract, in R.O.Freedle *Discourse production and comprehension* New Jersey: Ablex, 1-40. 264

Clark H. and Marshall C.R. 1981 Definite reference and mutual knowledge, in A.Joshi *et al. Elements of discourse understanding* Cambridge: CUP, 10-63. 47,55,115,264

[271]

Bibliography

Cole P. 1978 On the origins of referential opacity *S&S9*: 1-22. 171

Coleman H.O. 1914 Intonation and emphasis, in P.Passy and D.Jones *Miscellanea Phonetica* Bourg-la-Reine: API, 6-26. 98,119

Comrie B. 1977 In defense of spontaneous demotion: the impersonal passive *S&S8*: 47-58. 238

Contreras H. 1976 *A theory of word-order with special reference to Spanish* Amsterdam: NHP. 124

Creider C. 1979 On the explanation of transformations *S&S12*: 3-22. 258

Cromack R.E. 1968 *Language systems and discourse structure in Cashinawa* Ph.D. thesis, Hartford. 33

Crothers E.J. 1979 *Paragraph structure inference* New Jersey: Ablex. 264

Cruse D.A. 1976 Three classes of antonyms in English *Ling38*: 281-92. 94,164

Culicover P. 1977 Some observations concerning pseudo-clefts *LA3*: 347-75. 240

Dahl ö. 1976 What is new information? in N.Enkvist and V.Kohonen *Reports on text linguistics: approaches to word order* Abo: Abo Akademi, 38-50. 126

Daneš F. 1974a *Papers on functional sentence perspective* The Hague: Mouton. 214sq

Daneš F. 1974b Functional sentence perspective and the organisation of tne text, in Daneš 1974a: 106-28. 215

Dascal M. 1977 Conversational relevance *JPrag1*: 309-27. 263

Dascal M. 1981 Contextualism, in H.Parret et al. *Possibilities and limitations of pragmatics* Amsterdam: Benjamins, 153-78. 38

Dascal M. and Katriel T. 1979 Digressions: a study in conversational coherence *PTL4*: 203-32. 87,263

De Beaugrande R. 1980 *Text, discourse and process* New Jersey: Ablex. 15,43,253,264

De Beaugrande R. and Dressler W.U. 1981 *Introduction to text linguistics* London: Longmans. 33,43

Dickinson L. and Mackin R. 1969 *Varieties of spoken English* Oxford: OUP. 96

Dogil G. 1979 *Autosegmental account of phonological emphasis* Edmonton: LRI. 143

Donnellan K.S. 1966 Reference and definite descriptions *PhilRev75*: 281-304. 171

Donnellan K.S. 1978 Speaker reference, descriptions and anaphora *S&S9*: 47-68. 150,171

Dorrity T. 1981 Problems with <u>Do so</u> *RAIP16*: 31-42. 174

Dougherty R. 1970 A grammar of coördinate conjoined structures I *Lg46*: 850-98. 197

[272]

Bibliography

Dougherty R. 1974 The syntax and semantics of <u>each other</u> constructions *FL*12: 1-47. 205,210

Ellis J. 1966 On contextual meaning, in C.E.Bazell *et al. In memory of J.R.Firth* London: Longmans, 79-95. 38

Emonds J. 1976 *A transformational approach to English syntax: root, structure-preserving and local transformations* New York: AP. 213

Engelkamp J. and Krumnacker H. 1978 The effect of cleft sentence structures on attention *PsyRes*40: 27-36. 263

Enkvist N. 1978 Coherence, pseudo-coherence and non-coherence, in J-O.östman *Reports on text linguistics: cohesion and semantics* Abo: Abo Akademi, 109-130. 87,263

Erteschik-Shir N. and Lappin S. 1983 Under stress - a functional explanation of English sentence stress *JL*19: 419-54. 118,262

Esau H. 1975 Focus again *LACUS*II: 350-69. 124

Fiengo R. 1977 On trace theory *LI*8: 35-61. 176

Fiengo R. and Lasnik H. 1973 The logical structure of reciprocal sentences in English *FL*9: 447-68. 210

Fillmore C. 1975 An alternative to checklist theories of meaning *BLS*1: 123-31. 26,42,43

Fillmore C. 1982 Towards a descriptive framework for spatial deixis, in R.J.Jarvella and W.Klein *Speech, place and action* Chichester: Wiley. 6,26,43

Firbas J. 1974 Some aspects of the Czechoslovak approach to problems of functional sentence perspective, in Daneš 1974a: 11-37. 215sq

Firth J.R. 1950 Personality and language in society *SocRev*42: 37-52. 37

Firth J.R. 1951 Modes of meaning *Essays and Studies* N.S.4: 118-49. 19

Firth J.R. 1957 *Papers in linguistics* London: OUP. 37

Frederiksen C.H. 1977 Semantic processing units in understanding text, in R.O.Freedle *Discourse production and comprehension* New Jersey: Ablex, 57-88. 263

Gazdar G. 1979 *Pragmatics: implicature, presupposition and logical form* New York: AP. 176

GivónT. 1979 *On understanding grammar* New York: AP. 187,262

Goffman E. 1964 The neglected situation *AmAnth*66: 133-6. 38

Graver B. 1971 *Advanced English practice* London: OUP. 236sqq

Greenbaum S. 1969 *Studies in English adverbial usage* London: Longmans. 69sqq

Grice H.P. 1975 Logic and conversation *S&S*3: 41-58. 21,57,60

[273]

Bibliography

Grimes J. 1975 *The thread of discourse* The Hague: Mouton.15,263
Grimshaw J. 1979 Complement selection and the lexicon *LI*10: 279-326. 163
Grinder J. and Postal P. 1971 Missing antecedents *LI*2: 269-312. 176
Gussenhoven C. 1983 Focus, mode and the nucleus *JL*19: 377-418. 263

Halliday M.A.K. 1966 Lexis as a linguistic level, in C.E.Bazell *et al. In memory of J.R.Firth* London: Longmans, 148-62. 19
Halliday M.A.K. 1967a Notes on transitivity and theme in English, part 2 *JL*3: 199-244. 119sqq,257
Halliday M.A.K. 1967b *Intonation and grammar in British English* The Hague: Mouton. 222
Halliday M.A.K. 1972 *Explorations in the functions of language* London: Arnold. 38
Halliday M.A.K. and Hasan R. 1976 *Cohesion in English* London: Longmans. 15,45,60sqq
Hankamer J. 1973 Unacceptable ambiguity *LI*4: 17-68. 93
Hankamer J. 1974 On the non-cyclic nature of wh-clefting *CLS*10: 221-33. 254
Hankamer J. 1976 The semantic interpretation of anaphoric expressions *GURT*1976: 15-57. 176sq
Hankamer J. and Sag I. 1976 Deep and surface anaphora *LI*7: 391-426. 62,174,177
Harris R.J. and Monaco G.E. 1978 Psychology of pragmatic implication: information processing between the lines *JExpPsy*107: 1-31. 264
Harris Z. 1963 *Discourse analysis reprints* The Hague: Mouton. 33
Haviland S.E. and Clark H. 1974 What's new? Acquiring new information as a process of comprehension *JVLVB*13: 512-21. 264
Hawkins J. 1978 *Definiteness and indefiniteness* London: CH. 132,174,205
Healey A. 1958 Notes on Yogad *Oceanic Linguistics Monograph* 3: 77-82. 129
Heny F. 1978 Why there aren't any transformations, paper given to the Hull Linguistic Circle. 213
Hetzron R. 1975 The presentative movement, in C.N.Li *Word-order and word-order change* Austin: UTP, 346-88. 95,256,258
Hetzron R. 1977 Emphasis vs. contrast, paper given to the L.A.G.B., Walsall. 164
Higgins F.R. 1976 *The pseudo-cleft construction in English* Bloomington: IULC. 151,240,254sqq
Hinds J. 1978 *Anaphora in discourse* Edmonton: LRI. 64
Hobbs J. 1978 Resolving pronoun references *Ling*44: 311-38. 213

Bibliography

Hobbs J.R. 1979 Coherence and coreference *CogSc3*: 67-90. 87,263

Hockett C.R. 1958 *A course in modern linguistics* New York: Macmillan. 171,257

Hoekstra T. *et al.* 1980 *Lexical grammar* Dordrecht: Foris. 163

Hoey M. 1983 *On the surface of discourse* London: Allen and Unwin. 15,16,263

Hope E.R. 1973 Non-syntactic constraints in Lisu noun phrase order *FL*10: 79-109. 124

Householder F.R. 1972 *Syntactic theory I: Structuralist* Harmondsworth: Penguin. 129

Huddleston R.A. 1978 On classifying anaphoric relations *Ling*45: 333-54. 62

Hughes G. and Cresswell M.J. 1968 *Introduction to modal logic* London: Methuen. 59,173

Hyman L.M. 1977 *Studies in stress and accent* Los Angeles: USC. 98

Hymes D. 1964 Towards ethnographies of communication *AmAnth*6: 12-25. 38

Hymes D. 1971 *On communicative competence* Philadelphia: UPennP. 38

Jackendoff R. 1972 *Semantic interpretation in generative grammar* Cambridge, Mass: MITP. 77,120,143

Jackendoff R. 1975 Morphological and semantic regularities in the lexicon *Lg*51: 639-71. 213

Jackendoff R. 1976 Towards an explanatory semantic representation *LI*7: 89-150. 106,213

Johnson H.H. and Solso R.L. 1978 *An introduction to experimental design in psychology: a case approach* New York: Harper and Row. 239

Johnson-Laird P. 1981 Mental models of meaning, in A.Joshi *et al. Elements of discourse understanding* London: CUP, 106-26. 264

Jones D. 1967 *An outline of English phonetics* (9th ed.) Cambridge: Heffer. 120

Karttunen L. 1971 Discourse referents, Bloomington: IULC. 33

Karttunen L. 1977 Presupposition and linguistic context, in A.Rogers *et al. Proceedings of the Texas conference on performatives, presuppositions and implicatures* Arlington, Va: CAL, 149-60. 53

Karttunen L. and Peters S. 1979 Conventional implicature, in *S&S*11: 1-56. 54

Katz J.J. 1966 *The philosophy of language* New York: Harper and Row. 76

Katz J.J. 1972 *Semantic theory* New York: Harper and Row. 76

Katz J.J. and Bever T.G. 1974 The fall and rise of empiricism, Bloomington: IULC. 261sq

Bibliography

Katz J.J. and Fodor J.A. 1963 The structure of a semantic theory *Lg*39: 170-210. 76,261

Katz J.J. and Postal P.M. 1964 *An integrated theory of linguistic descriptions* Cambridge, Mass: MITP. 6,76

Keenan E.L. 1976 Towards a universal definition of "subject", in C.N.Li *Subject and topic* New York: AP, 303-33. 227

Keenan E.O. and Klein E. 1975 Coherency in children's discourse *JPsyRes*4: 365-80. 263

Keenan E.O. and Schieffelin B. 1976 Topic as a discourse notion, in C.N.Li *Subject and topic* New York: AP, 335-84. 263

Kempson R. 1975 *Presupposition and the delimitation of semantics* London: CUP. 259

Kempson R. 1977 *Semantic theory* London: CUP. 88,94,127

Keyser S.J. and Postal P.M. 1976 *Beginning English grammar* New York: Harper and Row. 197

Kiefer F. 1967 *On emphasis and word order in Hungarian* Bloomington: IUP. 143

Kimball J. 1973 Seven principles of surface-structure parsing in natural language *Cog*2: 15-47. 127

Kingdon R. 1958 *The groundwork of English intonation* London: Longmans. 98,120,222

Kintsch W. 1977 *Memory and cognition* New York: Wiley. 42,263

Kratzer A. 1980 Possible-world semantics and psychological reality *LingB*66: 1-14. 264

Kreckel M. 1981 *Communicative acts and shared knowledge in natural discourse* London: AP. 55

Kripke S.A. 1972 Naming and necessity, in D.Davidson and G.Harman *Semantics of natural language* Dordrecht: Reidel, 253-355. 59,174

Kuno S. 1972 Functional sentence perspective: a case study from Japanese and English *LI*3: 269-320. 15,94

Kuno S. 1976 Subject, theme and the speaker's empathy, in C.N.Li *Subject and topic* New York: AP, 419-44. 93,227

Kuno S. 1978 Generative discourse-analysis in America, in W.U.Dressler *Current trends in textlinguistics* Berlin: de Gruyter, 275-94. 93,129

Ladd D.R. 1980 *The structure of intonational meaning* Bloomington: IUP. 127

Lakoff G. 1968a *Counterparts* Bloomington: IULC. 174

Lakoff G. 1968b *Pronouns and reference* (2 parts) Bloomington: IULC. 113

Lakoff G. 1971a On generative semantics, in D.D.Steinberg and L.A.Jakobovits *Semantics* London: CUP, 232-96. 78sqq,120,130,213

[276]

Bibliography

Lakoff G. 1971b Presupposition and relative well-formedness, in D.D.Steinberg and L.A.Jakobovits *Semantics* London: CUP, 329-40. 180,242

Lakoff G. 1972 Hedges: a study in meaning-criteria and the logic of fuzzy concepts *CLS8*: 183-228. 25,128

Lakoff G. 1973 Some thoughts on transderivational constraints, in B.Kachru *et al. Issues in linguistics* Urbana: UIP, 442-52. 33,78sq,82

Lakoff G. 1975 Pragmatics in natural logic, in E.L.Keenan *Formal semantics of natural language* London: CUP, 253-86. 85,94,103

Lakoff G. 1977 Linguistic gestalts *CLS13*: 236-87. 6

Lakoff G. 1982 Categories and cognitive models, Trier: LAUT. 26,28,52,135

Lakoff R. 1971 Passive resistance *CLS7*: 149-63. 236

Leech G. 1969 *Towards a semantic description of English* London: Longmans. 165

Leech G. 1974 *Semantics* Harmondsworth: Penguin. 88,94

Lehman C. 1977 A reanalysis of givenness: stress in discourse *CLS13*: 316-24. 127

Lehmann W.P. 1976 From topic to subject in Indo-European, in C.N.Li *Subject and topic* New York: AP, 445-56. 227

Lehrer A. and Lehrer K. 1982 Antonymy *Ling&Phil5*: 483-501. 94

Lesgold A.M. *et al.* 1979 Foregrounding effects on discourse comprehension *JVLVB18*: 291-308. 9,263

Levine A. 1971 *Penguin English reader* Harmondsworth: Penguin. 221sqq

Lewis D. 1968 Counterpart theory and quantified modal logic *JPhil65*: 113-26. 174

Lewis D. 1972 General semantics, in D.Davidson and G.Harman *Semantics of natural language* Dordrecht: Reidel, 169-218. 103

Lewis D. 1973 *Counterfactuals* Oxford: Blackwell. 59,173

Lewis D. 1981 Index, context and content, in S.Kanger and S.öhman *Philosophy and grammar* Dordrecht: Reidel, 79-100. 47

Li C.N. and Thompson S.A. 1976 Subject and topic: a new typology of language, in C.N.Li *Subject and topic* New York: AP, 457-89. 227

Lightfoot D. 1976 Trace theory and twice-moved NPs *LI9*: 75-89. 176

Lightfoot D. 1977 On traces and conditions on rules, in P.Culicover *et al. Formal syntax* New York: AP, 207-38. 176

Lightfoot D. 1979 Trace theory and explanation *S&S13* (1980): 137-66. 176

Linde C. 1977 Information structures in discourse *GURT1977*: 226-36. 264

Lindner S. 1981 *A lexico-semantic analysis of verb-particle*

[277]

Bibliography

constructions with *up* and *out* Bloomington: IULC (1983). 135

Longacre R. 1983 *The grammar of discourse* New York: Plenum. 15

Lyons J. 1977 *Semantics* (2 vols.) London: CUP. 62,72,87sqq,94,152sq,180

Maclaren R. 1981 Demonstratives: the role of focus in discourse comprehension, paper given to LAGB, Manchester. 264

Malinowski B. 1930 The problem of meaning in primitive languages, in C.K.Ogden and I.A.Richards *The meaning of meaning* London: Kegan Paul, Trench, Trubner, 296-336. 37

Mangold M. 1975 *Phonetic emphasis* Hamburg: Buske. 144

Marslen-Wilson W. and Tyler L.K. 1980 Towards a psychological basis for a theory of anaphora, in J.Kreimen and A.E.Ojeda *Papers from the parasession on pronouns and anaphora* Chicago: CLS, 258-86. 212

McCawley J.D. 1971 Where do noun phrases come from? in D.D.Steinberg and L.A.Jakobovits *Semantics* London: CUP, 217-31. 66

McCawley J.D. 1975 Review of Chomsky 1972 *SEL3*: 209-311. 124

McCawley J.D. 1976 Some ideas not to live by *Die neueren Sprachen75*: 151-65. 58

McCawley J.D. 1979 Presupposition and discourse structure *S&S11*: 371-88. 66

McCawley J.D. 1981a *Everything that linguists have always wanted to know about logic* Oxford: Blackwell. 25,29,171,173,174,193,207

McCawley J.D. 1981b Fuzzy logic and restricted quantifiers, in S.Kanger and S.öhman *Philosophy and grammar* Dordrecht: Reidel, 101-18. 25

McIntosh A. 1961 Patterns and ranges *Lg37*: 325-37. 19

McKoon G. 1977 Organization of information in text memory *JVLVB16*: 247-60. 263

Miller G.A. 1972 English verbs of motion: a case study in semantics and lexical memory, in A.W.Melton and E.Martin *Coding processes in human memory* Washington D.C: Winston, 335-72. 128

Miller G.A. and Johnson-Laird P. *Language and perception* London: CUP. 128sq

Minsky M.A. 1975 A framework for representing knowledge, in P.Winston *The psychology of computer vision* New York: McGraw-Hill, 211-77. 6,42

Mitchell T. 1971 Linguistic 'goings on': collocations and other lexical matters arising on the syntagmatic record *ArchLingN.S.2*: 35-69. 19,77

Most R.B. and Saltz E. 1979 Information structure in sentences: new information *Lang&Sp22*: 89-95. 258

Bibliography

Neijt A. 1980 *Gapping: a contribution to sentence-grammar* Dordrecht: Foris. 93

Nesfield J.C. 1918 *Outline of English grammar* (2nd ed.) London: Macmillan. 86

Noordman L.G.H. 1979 *Inferring from language* Berlin: Springer. 264

O'Connor D.J. 1975 *The correspondence theory of truth* London: Hutchinson. 27

O'Connor J.D. and Arnold G.F. 1961, 1973 *Intonation of colloquial English* (1st and 2nd eds.) London: Longmans. 120

Oehrle R. 1981 Common problems in the theory of anaphora and the theory of discourse, in H.Parret et al. *Possibilities and limitations of pragmatics* Amsterdam: Benjamins, 509-30. 242

Pike K.L. 1945 *The intonation of American English* Ann Arbor: UMP. 98,120

Pike K.L. 1954 *Language in relation to a unified theory of the structure of human behavior* (part I) Glendale: SIL. 26

Pike K.L. 1963 A syntactic paradigm, in Householder 1972: 195-214. 129

Pike K.L. 1964 Discourse analysis and tagmeme matrices *Oceanic Linguistics* 3: 5-25. 33

Pinkham J. and Hankamer J. 1975 Deep and shallow clefts *CLS11*: 429-50. 240

Postal P.M. 1969 Anaphoric islands *CLS5*: 205-39. 182

Postal P.M. 1971 *Cross-over phenomena* New York: HRW. 180,213

Postal P.M. 1974 *On raising* Cambridge, Mass: MITP. 197

Postal P.M. and Pullum G.K. 1978 Traces and the description of English complementizer contraction *LI9*: 1-29. 176

Pullum G.K. and Postal P.M. 1978 On an inadequate defense of "trace theory" *LI10*: 689-706. 176

Quirk R. et al. 1972 *A grammar of contemporary English* London: Longmans. 240,246sq

Reichman R. 1978 Conversational coherency *CogSc2*: 283-327. 263

Reid A.A. et al. 1968 *Totonac: from clause to discourse* Norman, Ok: SIL. 33

Reinhart T. 1979 Syntactic domains for semantic rules, in F.Guenthner and S.Schmidt *Formal semantics and pragmatics for natural languages* Dordrecht: Reidel, 107-30. 189

inhart T. 1983 *Anaphora and semantic interpretation* London: CH. 64,176,189,212,262

cher N. 1964 *Hypothetical reasoning* Amsterdam: NHP. 173

[279]

Bibliography

Rescher N. 1975 *A theory of possibility* Oxford: Blackwell.59,174

Rochester S.R. and Martin J.R. 1977 The art of referring: the speaker's use of noun phrases to instruct the listener, in R.O.Freedle *Discourse production and comprehension* New Jersey: Ablex, 245-70. 264

Rosch E. 1973 Natural categories *CogPsy4*: 328-350. 52

Rosch E. 1975 Cognitive reference points *CogPsy7*: 532-47. 52

Rosch E. 1977 Human categorization, in N.Warren *Advances in cross-cultural psychology* New York: AP, 3-49. 52

Rosch E. 1978 Principles of categorization, in E.Rosch and B.B.Lloyd *Cognition and categorization* New Jersey: Erlbaum. 52

Ross J.R. 1967 *Constraints on variables in syntax* Bloomington: IULC. 213,220

Ross J.R. 1975 Parallels in phonological and semantactic organization, in J.F.Kavanagh and J.E.Cutting *The role of speech in language* Cambridge, Mass: MITP. [Preface]

Sanders G. 1969 On the natural domain of grammar, Bloomington: IULC. 35

Sanford A.J. and Garrod S.C. 1981 *Understanding written language* Chichester: Wiley. 42

Schank R.C. and Abelson R.P. 1977 *Scripts, plans, goals and understanding* New Jersey: Erlbaum. 6,42

Schmerling S. 1974a A re-examination of normal stress *Lg50*: 66-73. 124,143

Schmerling S. 1974b Contrastive stress and semantic relation' *CLS10*: 608-16. 164

Schubiger M. 1935 *The role of intonation in spoken Engl* St.Gallen: Fehr'schen Verlag. 98,119

Searle J. 1983 *Intentionality* Cambridge: CUP. 118

Seiler H. 1970 Semantic information in grammar: the prob syntactic relations *Sea2*: 321-34. 40

Sgall P. *et al.* 1973 *Topic, focus and generative s* Kronberg: Scriptor. 216sq

Sinclair J.McH. and Coulthard M. 1975 *Towards an ? discourse* London: OUP. 37sq

Slama-Cazacu T. 1961 *Langage et contexte* The Hague

Smith N.V. 1982 *Mutual knowledge* London: AP. 55,

Soames S. and Perlmutter D.M. 1979 *Syntactic arg/ the structure of English* Berkeley: UC

Sperber D. and Wilson D. 1982 Mutual knowledge theories of comprehension, in N.V. 55

Stannard Allen W. 1954 *Living English speec* 120

Stannard Allen W. 1959 *Living English str*

Bibliography

London: Longmans. 236

Stockwell R. 1977 *Foundations of syntactic theory* New Jersey: P-H. 218sq

Sussman G. 1973 *A computer model of skill acquisition* Cambridge, Mass: MIT dissertation. 42

Svartvik J. and Quirk R. 1980 *A corpus of English conversation* Lund: Gleerup. 243sqq, 256

Taglicht J. 1982 Intonation and the assessment of information *JL*18: 213-30. 263

Tannenbaum P.H. and Williams F. 1968 Generation of active and passive sentences as a function of subject or object focus *JVLVB*7: 246-50. 258

Thrane T. 1980 *Referential-semantic analysis* Cambridge: CUP. 181

Trager G. and Smith H.L. 1957 *An outline of English structure* Washington D.C: ACLS. 120

Vachek J. 1966 *The linguistic school of Prague* Bloomington: IUP. 130,257

Van Dijk T.A. 1972 *Some aspects of text grammars* The Hague: Mouton. 32,73,82,89

Van Dijk T.A. 1973 Text-grammar and text-logic, in J.S.Petöfi and H.Reiser *Studies in text grammar* Dordrecht: Reidel, 17-78. 79,83

Van Dijk T.A. 1977 *Text and context* London: Longmans. 51,173,264

Van Dijk T.A. 1980 *Macrostructure* New Jersey: Erlbaum. 73,263

Vendler Z. 1967 Each and every, any and all, in Z.Vendler *Linguistics in philosophy* Ithaca: CornUP, 70-96. 207

Vennemann T. 1974 Topics, subjects and word-order: from SXV to SVX via TVX, in J.Anderson and C.Jones *Historical linguistics* Amsterdam: NHP, 339-76. 227

Vincent N.B. 1979 Word-order and grammatical theory, in J.Meisel and M.D.Pam *Linear order and generative theory* Amsterdam: Benjamins, 1-22. 227

Wasow T. 1979 *Anaphora in generative grammar* Ghent: Story-Scientia. 15,63,176,181

Weiner E.J. and Labov W. 1983 Constraints on the agentless passive *JL*19: 29-58. 238

Werth P.N. 1968 On the analysis of discourse in English, paper given to the LAGB, Cambridge. 35

Werth P.N. 1974 Some thoughts on non-restrictive relatives *Lings*142: 33-68. 26

Werth P.N. 1976 *On the semantic representation of relative clauses in English* London: ULond Ph.D. thesis. 29,33,43,75,84,95,258

Werth P.N. 1977 Focus-pocus, in *PM*2.3: F3-G14. 15,77,95

[281]

Bibliography

Werth P.N. 1979 If linear order isn't in the base, then where is it? in J.Meisel and M.D.Pam *Linear order and generative theory* Amsterdam: Benjamins, 187-251. 95,97,182,229

Werth P.N. 1980a Towards a text-linguistics for English *RAIP*14: 17-41. 15,95

Werth P.N. 1980b Universals of emphasis, paper given to Linguistic Workshop on Language Universals, Trier. 15

Werth P.N. 1980c Articles of association, in J.Van der Auwera *The semantics of determiners* London: CH, 250-89. 65,75,87,132,174,196

Werth P.N. 1981a The concept of 'relevance' in conversational analysis, in P.N.Werth *Conversation and discourse* London: CH, 129-154. 57,95,107,168,186,209

Werth P.N. 1981b Tense, modality and possible worlds *RAIP*16: 17-30. 174

Williams E. 1977 Discourse and logical form *LI*8: 101-39. 177

Wilson D. and Sperber D. 1979 Ordered entailments: an alternative to presuppositional theories *S&S*11: 229-324. 57,115

Wilson D. and Sperber D. 1981 On Grice's theory of conversation, in P.N.Werth *Conversation and discourse* London: CH, 155-78. 57,209

Yekovich F.R. and Walker C.H. 1978 Identifying and using referents in sentence comprehension *JVLVB*17: 265-77. 264

Yekovich F.R. et al. 1979 The role of presupposed and focal information in integrating sentences *JVLVB*18: 535-48. 263

Yule G. 1979 Pragmatically-controlled anaphora *Ling*49: 127-35. 15

Index

SUBJECT-INDEX

Accent (A) 8, 9, 10, 15, 83, 95sq, 105, 108, 109, 115sqq, 119, 120, 122, 126, 127, 130, 179sq, 182, 217, 219sqq, 224, 227, 232sqq, 265
- attention a. 9, 10, 122, 129
- information a. 9, 122, 129
Accessibility 48, 49, 50, 51, 59, 91, 168, 173, 208, 211
Actual world: see World
Adequacy 97
Adverb-preposing 12
Agent, -ive 235
- non-a. 239
- suppression of a. 237, 238
AGR 190sq
Ambiguity 79
American structuralists 120, 214
Analytic 150sq
Anaphora,-ic 9, 14, 15, 18, 20, 22, 23, 29, 61sqq, 66, 67, 75, 79, 81, 93, 109, 129, 132, 137sq, 148, 166sqq, 179sq, 210, 216, 218sq, 228, 243, 260
- anaphor 20, 61sqq, 83
 - bound (standard) a. 189, 195, 196
 - full (overt) a. 187, 192
- a. indeterminacy: see Indeterminacy
- a. island 182, 199
- anaphoricity of P-cleft <u>what</u> 252
- Backwards A. 94, 253
- discourse (D-) a. 63, 184, 187, 206
 - distributive (d-) a. 194sq, 196, 198, 206sq

- identity of reference a. 64, 86, 174, 176, 177, 182, 183, 187
- identity of sense a. 64, 86, 176, 177, 183sq, 187, 211sq
- negative (n-) a. 193, 196, 199, 204, 206, 207, 224, 229, 267
- non-a. 102, 109, 179, 186, 220sq, 224, 229, 235
 See also: Accent
- pragmatically-controlled a. 62, 166, 177, 187
- R and C as a. 95
- sentence a. 182, 187
- standard a.: see anaphor: bound a.
- syntactically-controlled a. 62
- zero-a. 2, 18, 29, 64sq, 79, 176sq, 182, 187
 See also: Cohesion, Information: given i., Pronoun, Repetition
Antecedent 22, 29, 61sqq, 82, 137sq, 209, 265
- a. binding: see Binding
- a. set 175, 195, 196, 197, 207, 208
- remote a. 191
Antonymy 76, 87sqq, 90, 109sqq, 152sqq, 158
Appropriateness 3
 See also: Relevance
Arbitrary reference: see Reference
Argument 28, 106
 See also: Predicate, Proposition
Artificial intelligence 13
Aspectual adjunct 71

[283]

Index

Artificial intelligence 13
Aspectual adjunct 71
Attitudinal
- a. disjunct 70sq
- a. predicate 127sq, 256
Attributive 150, 171
 See also: Referential
Autonomous syntax 34
Auxiliary 133sq

Back-channel feature 54
Backwards   Anaphora: see
 Anaphora
Backwards   Pronominalisation:
 see Anaphora
Base 11
Binding 63, 64, 167, 176,
 184, 187, 188sq, 192
 - antecedent (A-) b.   63,
 192, 207
 - argument b. = antecedent b.
 - B.Theory   80, 82, 188sqq,
 193, 262
 - mutual b. 195, 196, 204
 - operator (A--) b.   194, 207
 - quantifier b. = operator b.
Bloomfield, Leonard 4, 36
Bound anaphor: see Anaphora

Case
 - c. frame: see Frame
 - c. marking 192
 - c. role 29
Cataphora 62, 253
Categories 51sq
Causality 69
C-command 63, 64, 80, 188,
 189sq, 192sq, 262
Church, Alonzo 25
Citation-form 151
 - c. Contrast: see Contrast
Cleft   11, 148sq, 225, 226,
 228, 240sqq, 246sqq, 253
 - non-c. 242
Coherence (= positive c.)   7,
 10, 13, 14, 32, 51, 58, 60,
 69, 72sqq, 81, 83, 87,
 89sqq, 93, 124, 145sq, 164,
 168, 181, 186sqq, 218, 229,

Coherence (cont.) 259sq, 263
 - c. chain 116
 - c. constraint   32, 72, 73,
 75sq, 80sqq, 89sqq, 102,
 105, 115, 117, 137, 146,
 151,   184,   186, 207sqq,
 259sq, 262
 - negative c.   87sqq, 109,
 137, 147, 151sqq, 160, 260
Cohesion 21, 60sq, 72, 73,
 175, 216
 See also: Anaphora
Co-indexation 63, 187, 192
 See   also: Reference:
 co-reference
Collocation 19, 20, 24, 60,
 65sqq, 72
 - c. chain 66, 75
Comment 214, 222
 See also: TCA, Topic
Common ground 45, 46, 53sqq,
 57sq, 72, 73, 76, 85sqq,
 90sq, 92, 94, 105, 112,
 115, 118, 122sq, 134, 146,
 149,   156, 167sq,   186sq,
 196, 200, 204, 205, 206sqq,
 218,   219,   229, 236, 239,
 247, 249, 253, 256, 259sq,
 262, 264
 - "grounded" 217sq
 - ground-establishing 168
 - ground-referring 168
Communicative 61, 167sq
 - C. Dynamism (CD) 215sq
 - c. function 103
Community   knowledge: see
 Knowledge
Competence 5, 34, 261
Complementary 88, 158sq
Complement(is)ation 1,   65,
 139, 163
 - COMP 139sqq
Comprehension 42, 73, 91
Conceptual focus 51
Concession 69
Conditional 49, 54
Conjunction: see Connectivity
Connectivity 5, 6, 7, 8, 13,

[284]

Index

Connectivity (cont.) 17, 60sqq, 126
- connective 32, 134
- connector 60, 69sqq, 72, 73
  - discourse (D-) c. 71sq
  - logical c. 69
  - sentence (S-) c. 69sq
- conjunction 70, 134sq
  - c. reduction 65, 176
  - co-ordinating c. 134
  - subordinating c. 134
Constant 28
Constituency 66, 124
- constituent-Contrast: see Contrast
Constraint 78, 213
- derivational c. 78
- global c. 78sq, 176sq
- local c. 78sq
- pragmatic c. 203
- rule c. 14, 32, 78sqq, 188, 262
- transderivational c. 78sqq, 80, 82sq, 93, 94, 177
See also: Coherence c., TCA c.
Content word 99, 110
See also: Form word
Context 2, 6, 7, 8, 11, 13, 20, 32, 34sqq, 53, 57, 85, 90, 123, 264
- extralinguistic c. 34, 35
  See also: Situation
- linguistic c. 34, 35, 38, 57
  See also: Discourse
- theory of c. 80, 216
- contextual boundness 216
- contextuality 5, 6, 7, 13, 32
- contextualisability 35, 58, 128, 220, 267
Contingent: see Implication: pragmatic i.
Contradiction 148, 155sq, 224, 249

Contrast (C) 8, 9, 10, 14, 15, 83, 87, 90sqq, 95sq, 105, 109sq, 113, 118sq, 120, 122, 125, 126, 127, 131sqq, 179sq, 182, 183, 187, 211sq, 214, 219sq, 224, 226, 228, 232sqq, 265sq
- citation-C. 143sq
- constituent-C. 142, 233, 247, 258
- double C 243, 248sqq, 253, 258
  - primary C 249sq, 253
  - secondary C 249, 254
- reversed reciprocal C. 242
- sentential C. 139sqq, 142
Control 65, 202, 237
- C.Theory 80
Conventionally recessive 107, 238, 247
Converse 88, 153, 159sq
Co-operation 54sq, 160
- Co-operative Principle 21, 55
Co-presence 47
Co-reference: see Reference
Counterpart 173sq, 211sq
Cross-reference: see Reference
Culture 19, 145, 164
Current file: see Proposition: current p.
Cycle 58

Dative-movement 12
Definite
- definite description 23, 54, 61, 64, 65, 112sq, 115
- definitisation 174sq, 177, 187
Definition 151
Deixis 8, 82, 112, 168, 210
Deletion 177
Dependency-rules 32
De re/de dicto: see Reference
Descriptive indeterminacy: see Indeterminacy
Designator 28

Index

Determiner 131
Dimension-term 152
Discourse 5, 6, 8, 10, 11, 12, 13, 15, 16, 17, 24, 33, 35, 37, 42, 43, 50, 53, 54, 55, 57, 61, 90sq, 95, 126, 205, 259
- d. anaphora: see Anaphora
  - d. connector: see Connectivity
- d. (D-) grammar 3, 11, 13, 14, 31, 35, 80sq, 125, 209, 216, 258, 259
  See also: Sentence-grammar
- d. initial 224, 228
  See also: First mention
See also: Context, Text
Disjoint reference: see Reference
Displacement 171, 173
Distributive anaphora: see Anaphora
Distributive quantification: see Quantification
Dominance 118, 262
Drag-effect 240

Each 193sqq, 200, 206sqq
Ellipsis 61
See also: Anaphora: zero-a.
Empathy: see Speaker-empathy
Emphasis 8, 10, 13, 14, 32, 61, 65, 83, 84, 95sqq, 128, 151, 179sqq, 217sq, 222sq, 260
- e. placement (e. marking) 95, 103sqq, 182, 213sq, 241
  - e. p. rules 105, 130
- emphatic structure 33, 218, 220sq, 224, 226, 227, 231, 234sq, 238, 251, 255
- intensity e. 133
Endophora 62
Entailment 57sq, 85, 86, 115, 263, 264
- pragmatic e. 233
Epithet 64sq, 113, 167, 175sq, 177, 187

See also: Synonymy: virtual s.
Equivalence 58, 82
See also: Identity, Repetition, Synonymy
Evaluative term 152
Exhaustive 204, 206sqq
- e. listing focus: see Focus
- non-e. 204, 205
See also: Binding: mutual b.
Existence 87, 169sq, 173, 252
Exophora 62, 166
See also: Anaphora: pragmatically-controlled a.
Extended Standard Theory (EST) 66, 130, 213
Extension 73, 146, 168, 194, 264
See also: Intension, Reference
Extraposition 12

Factive 159
Fictional 50
See also: Literary studies
First-mention 167, 228, 258
See also: Discourse-initial, Previous-mention
Focus 7, 9, 15, 119sqq, 127, 129, 130, 180, 223
- exhaustive listing f. 129
- focal element 226, 242, 246sq, 253sq
- focal subset 204, 206
See also: Residue subset
Foregrounding 179
Form word 99, 110
See also: Content word
Frame 6, 7, 42, 146, 187, 247, 263, 264
- case f. 43
- f. semantics 6
- propositional f. 43
Free reference: see Reference
Frege, Gottlob 25
Function 37
- functionalism 13, 263
See also: Communicative

[286]

Index

Function (cont.)
- Functional Sentence Perspective 214sqq
  See also Communicative Dynamism
Fuzzy: see Multivalent

Gap 2, 9, 65, 145, 176, 184
- gapping 65, 93, 176
Gender 152sq
Generative grammar 14, 63, 80, 120
Generic 52, 75, 131sq, 152sq, 169, 195
Gestalt 6
Given: see Information
Government-Binding (GB) 58, 63sq, 65, 80, 130, 141, 176sq, 183, 187sqq, 196, 213
  See also REST
- Government Theory 80
Gradable 88, 152, 158, 160sqq
Grammatical
- g. category 131, 143, 147
  See also: Form word
- grammaticality 16, 35, 58, 660, 84, 145, 258
    See also: Context: contextualisability
- g. relation 19, 68
  - r. changing rule 32
- g. subject 67, 227, 237
Ground
- "grounded": see Common ground
- g. establishing: see Common ground
- g. referring: see Common ground

Headlinese 41
Head-modifier 30
Hearer (H) 49
Hedge 70, 128
House-keeping rules 58
Hyponymy: see Inclusion

Idealized Cognitive Model (ICM) 6, 43, 204
Identity
- full i. 18, 22, 62, 75, 93, 167sq, 181, 183, 266
- i. of reference: see Anaphora
- i. of sense: see Anaphora
- intensional i. 86
- non-i. 83
- partial i. 72, 76, 148, 167sq, 181, 183sq, 187, 211, 265sq
- sloppy i. 171
  See also: Equivalence, Synonymy
Idiom 64
Impact 12
Implication 58, 74, 76, 94, 108, 113sqq, 117, 155, 166sq, 183, 185, 266
- logical i. 113sq
- negative i. 154sq, 158
- pragmatic i. 113sq, 116, 145, 156, 164, 185
  See also: Entailment, Implicature, Presupposition
Implicature 60, 178
Inclusion 58, 74, 82
  See also: Set-membership
Incompatibles 89
Incrementation 53sqq, 74
- temporary i. 54, 72
Indeterminacy 20, 22sq
- anaphoric i. 22
- descriptive i. 20
- polysemic i. 21
Inert forms 8, 29, 100, 110
Inference 73, 75, 118, 263, 264
Inferrables 97, 99
Information 8, 9, 12, 18, 22, 32, 54sqq, 95, 126, 186, 238, 260, 262
- given i. 111, 123, 125, 129, 247, 257, 263
- i. accent: see Accent

[287]

Index

Information (cont.)
- i. gap: see Gap
- new i. 118, 121, 127, 257, 263
- renewed i. 9, 95, 248, 258
Intensional meaning (sense) 22, 62, 66, 67, 68, 69, 72, 73, 106, 113, 146, 166sq, 168sq, 200, 207, 227, 264
See also: Extension, Semantic
Intensity-emphasis: see Emphasis
Intentionality 98, 116, 118, 121, 238
Interpretation strategy 22
Intonation 126sq, 223, 226, 258
- i. centre 122, 124, 125, 126

Jespersen, Otto 241

Knowledge
- community k. 55, 115, 146, 164, 209, 249
- k. frame: see Frame
- mutual k. 47, 55, 115, 247
- pragmatic k. 22, 24, 71
See also: Common ground

Language
- l.-specific 39
- l. theory: see Theory of language
L-dislocation 12, 253
Lexical
- l. category 144sq, 147
  - See also: Content word, Grammatical category
- lexicalism 11, 213
- lexicon 65, 67
Linguistic theory: see Theory of language
Literary studies 33, 73
See also: Fiction
Location 47sqq
Logic: see Standard logic
See also: Multivalent logic

Logical operator 26, 133, 136, 253

Manner, Maxim of 219, 225
Many-member set: see Multiple taxonomy
Markedness 152sq, 166
Meaning 8, 103
    See also: Extension, Intensional meaning, Reference, Semantic
Membership: see Set-membership
Message 8, 55, 56
Middle ground 158, 161sqq
Modal 133sq
- modality 69
Movement 11, 14, 32, 65, 96, 110, 177, 210, 213sqq
- move-alpha 58, 63, 141, 188
Multiple taxonomy 88, 153, 156
Multivalent 28, 92
- m. logic 25, 70, 113, 164
See also: Standard logic
Mutual
- m. binding: see Binding
- m. disjoint reference: see Reference: disjoint r.
- m. exclusion 148sqq
- m. knowledge: see Knowledge

Narrative inserts 10
Negation 153sq, 267sq
Negative
- n. anaphora: see Anaphora
- n. attraction 154
- n. coherence: see Coherence
- n. implication: see Implication
- negativity: see n. coherence
Negotiation 48, 54, 249, 256
- negotiated reality 264
New information: see Information
Nominative Island Condition (NIC) 190, 192

[288]

Index

Non-actual world: see World
Non-anaphoric: see Anaphora
Non-cleft: see Cleft
Non-deterministic: see
  Probability: probabilistic
Non-exhaustive: see Exhaustive
Non-meaning-bearing element:
  see Inert form
Non-P-cleft: see Pseudo-cleft
Non-prominence: see Prominence
Non-unique: see Unique
Notation 25, 31
NP
 - -anaphora 182, 187
  See also: Anaphora
 - -movement 177
  See also: Movement
Nuclear
 - n. stress/tone (= tonic)
  119, 120
 - N. Stress Rule (NSR) 107

Observables 97, 99
Operator: see Logical operator
 - o. binding: see Binding
Oppositions 88sq, 94
Other 196sq, 200, 206sqq
Overt anaphor: see Anaphora:
  full anaphor

Particle 138sq
 - p. movement 12, 84
Part-whole 168
Passive 12, 110, 227, 229sqq
Pending file: see
  Incrementation: temporary
  i.
Performance 5, 34, 35, 261
 See also: Competence
Performative 27, 70, 100sq,
  102sq, 104, 110, 127sq,
  160, 256
Personal experience 44sq
Phrasal vs. periphrastic: see
  Reciprocal
Plans 6, 42
Polarity
 - predicate p. 161

Polarity (cont.)
 - propositional p. 161
Polysemic indeterminacy: see
  Indeterminacy
Position 12
Possible-world Theory 46, 59,
  171sqq, 180
 See also: World
Pragmatic,-s 13, 66, 68, 69
 - p. assumptions 75
 - p. constraint: see
  Constraint
 - p. entailment: see Entail-
  ment
 - p. implication: see
  Implication
 - p. knowledge: see Knowledge
 - p. presupposition: see
  Presupposition
 - pragmatically-controlled
  anaphora: see Anaphora
 - pragmatically-controlled
  reciprocal anaphora: see
  Reciprocal
Prague School 124, 214sqq
Predicate 28, 29, 106, 108,
  134, 147
  See also: Argument,
  Proposition
Predictable 107, 238
Preposition 135, 165
Presupposition 79, 123sqq,
  130, 148sq, 223
 - pragmatic p. 8, 30, 53,
  247
Previous mention 94, 228
 See also: First mention
Principle of co-operation: see
  Co-operation
Probability 44sq, 103, 257
 - probabilistic 35, 58, 68
Processing 43, 44, 92
 See also: Comprehension
Production 42, 73
 - p. constraint 92
 See also: Comprehension
Projection
 - P. Principle 163

[289]

Index

Projection (cont.)
- p. rule 66
Prominence 8, 9, 98, 120, 178
- non-p. 8
- relative p. 119sq
Pronoun 2, 14, 22, 24, 28, 61, 64, 67, 79, 82, 101, 136sq, 174, 177, 182, 183sqq, 187, 212, 224, 266
- Backwards Pronominalis- ation: see Anaphora: Backwards A.
- PRO 65, 190sq
- proform 136sqq
- p. anaphora: see Anaphora
- p. of laziness 171
- relative p. 138
See also: Anaphora
Proper noun 23, 112sq, 156
Proposition,-al 8, 22, 23, 24, 25, 28, 29, 46, 53, 54, 70, 71, 76, 102, 105sqq, 186
- current p. 9, 57sq
- p. attitude: see Attitud- inal predicate
- p. frame: see Frame
- p. function (PF) 28, 29, 43, 76, 85sq, 90, 105sqq, 136
- p. relationship 69
Prototype theory 52
Pseudo- (P-) cleft 12, 228, 240sqq, 250sqq, 254
- identificational P. 254sq
- inverted P. 241sqq, 246, 254
- non-P. 250sq
- predicational P. 254sq
- presentative P. 256
- specificational P. 151, 254sq
Pseudo-relative 12
PS rules 32, 65
Psych-movement 12
Psychological reality 261, 263sqq
Push-effect 240

Quantification 29, 194
- distributive q. 193
- universal q. 163, 169, 174, 193, 197
Quantifier 28, 101, 135sq, 163, 193sq, 195, 198, 208
- q. binding: see Binding
- q. floating 197sqq

R-dislocation 12, 229
Reading aloud 10
Reception: see Comprehension
Reciprocal 64, 184, 187sqq
- periphrastic r. 193, 198, 204sq, 210, 212
- phrasal r. 193, 204sq, 206, 207, 209, 212
- pragmatically-controlled r. anaphora 205sq
Recoverability Principle 82, 176
Reduction (R) 8, 9, 10, 14, 32, 65, 83, 86, 87, 90sqq, 95sq, 105, 106sq, 109sq, 111sqq, 115sqq, 122sq, 125, 126, 130, 145, 179, 182, 183, 212, 217sqq, 232sqq, 265sq
See also: Anaphora
Reference 8, 23, 24, 28, 29, 49, 62, 72, 82, 85, 87, 166sq, 168sqq, 180
- arbitrary r. 191
- co-r. 22, 180sq, 185
See also: Co-indexation
- cross-r. 18
- de re/de dicto r. 171
- disjoint r. 181, 187, 188sq, 196
- distributed d.r. 197, 198
- mutual d.r. 196
- free r. 63, 64, 187, 188sq, 191
- r. chain 24, 75
- r. link 86
- referential 150, 171
See also: Attributive

[290]

Index

Reference (cont.)
- non-r. 169, 175sq, 180
See also: Extension, World
Reflexive 64, 184, 187, 206
Reichenbach, Hans 25
Relation-changing rule: see Grammatical relation
Relation, Maxim of 57, 218
Relative pronoun: see Pronoun
Relevance 13, 37, 38, 48, 54, 55, 59, 186, 209, 262
See also: Coherence
Remainder (in clefts and P-clefts) 241sq, 253sq
Renewed information: see Information
Repair 143
Repetition 32, 64sq, 83, 89, 91, 95, 107, 112, 138, 167, 177sqq, 187, 239, 253
See also: Anaphora, Reduction, Synonymy
Residue subset 204sq, 206sq
See also: Focus: focal subset
REST 63sq, 65, 80, 177
See also Government Binding
Rheme 215, 222, 257
- rhematisation 12
Rhetorical 225, 227sq, 253, 260
See also: Stylistic
Rule-constraint: see Constraint

Salience 132, 156, 161, 239, 253, 263
Scenario 42
Scene 42, 43, 44, 46, 49, 53, 146, 187, 204, 211
Scheme 42
Script 6, 42
Selectional restriction (SR) 65sqq, 72, 76sq
Semantic,-s 6, 17, 19, 22, 23, 25, 32, 66, 69
- discourse s. 69
- s. field 19, 24, 85, 187

Semantic (cont.)
- s./pragmatic 104sqq, 110sq, 118
- s. relationship 41
- s. set: see Set
- semantically central 116sq
See also: Intensional, Pragmatic, Proposition
Sense: see Intensional meaning
Sentence 5, 6, 7, 11, 15, 16, 25
- S-connector: see Connectivity
- s. (S-) grammar 1, 3, 5, 7, 11, 34, 35, 36, 39, 58, 63, 67, 76, 79, 123, 193, 205, 259, 260
- s. stress: see Stress
See also Discourse, Proposition
Sequence of tenses 81
Sequentiality 5, 6, 7
Set (= Semantic set) 85, 119, 144sq, 147sqq, 167, 175, 187, 194, 201sq, 210, 266
- many-member s.: see Multiple taxonomy
- s. membership 82, 147, 168, 211
- s. specification 149
- s. subset 168, 197
- single-member s. 150
See also Focus: focal subset, Inclusion, Residue subset
Setting 261sq
Short-term memory 219
Situation,-al 6, 10, 13, 17, 19, 36, 39, 40, 43, 45, 46, 47sqq, 81, 210
- immediate s. 37
- s. anaphora: see Anaphora: pragmatically controlled a.
- s. context 41, 42
- s. pronoun: see Conventionally recessive
Speaker (S) 49
- s. attitude 70

[291]

Index

See also Attitudinal, Intentionality
- s. empathy 227, 233, 239
Specific 75, 148, 150sq
- specificational: see P-cleft
Specified Subject constraint 76
Spoken data 9
Stable pattern: see TCA constraint
Standard anaphora: see Anaphora: bound a.
Standard logic 13, 28, 30
See also: Multivalent logic
Standard Theory (ST) 11, 34, 35, 66, 176, 213
State-of-affairs 44sqq
See also: World
Stipulative 49, 169
Stress 14, 65, 98sq, 126sq, 179, 222sq, 244, 258
- contrastive s. 125, 126, 164, 122
- sentence-s. 98sq, 119, 260
- s. placement 120
- s. reduction: see Reduction
- word s. 98
See also: Intonation, Nuclear, Tonicity
Style,-istic 23, 33, 94, 177sq, 236sqq, 262
- s. disjunct 71
- s. variant 12, 112
Subcategorisation 140sq, 163
Subject: see Grammatical subject
- SUBJECT 190sq
- s. prominence 227
Subset: see Set
Surface-structure 25, 97sqq, 103sq, 124
- s.-s. parsing 127
Syllable-timing 98
Synonymy 74, 83sqq, 87, 90, 110sq
- absolute (complete, full) s. 111sq, 117

Synonymy (cont.)
- partial s. 74, 85, 87, 89, 109, 112, 117sq
- virtual s. 23, 112, 175, 266
See also: Antonymy, Equivalence, Identity, Repetition
Syntax,-ctic 6
- syntactically-controlled anaphora: see Anaphora
- syntacticisation 187, 227, 262
- s. variation 11, 32, 96, 213sqq, 260
See also: Autonomous syntax, S-grammar

Tarski, Alfred 25
Text 5, 6, 7, 11, 13, 32, 33, 46, 71, 81
- t. grammar: see Discourse grammar
- t. structure 179, 186
- textuality 16, 259, 263
- t. world: see World
Theme 215, 222, 257
- thematically-central 116sq
See also: Semantic: semantically-central
See also: Rheme
Theory
- t. of grammar 34
- t. of language 13, 261sqq
- t. of situation 44
Time 47sqq
- temporality 69
Tonicity 222sq
See also: Nuclear, Stress
Topic 214, 222
- topicalisation 11, 227
- T. Comment Articulation (TCA) 214sqq, 254
- TCA constraint 94, 218sqq, 229sq, 241sqq, 248, 262
- intermediate TCA pattern 225sqq, 230, 236, 248sqq

[292]

Index

Topic (cont.)
- stable TCA pattern 222, 224, 230sq, 234, 236, 238, 248sqq
- unstable TCA pattern 222, 225, 229sq, 237, 248sqq
- t. prominence 227
See also: Comment
Tough-movement 12
Trace 65, 82, 176
Transformations 11, 32, 176
Truth
- t.-conditional semantics 25, 103, 127sq
- t. value 26, 27, 70, 71, 128

Unique 132, 175
- non-u. 148, 149sq
Universal
- U. Grammar 39
- U. Situation Theory 39
See also: Theory
Unmarked
- u. emphasis: see Inert forms
- u. topic-comment order 220
Unmoved structures 222sqq, 229
See also: Movement
Unstable TCA pattern: see Topic
Utterance 5, 6, 8, 11, 24, 25, 34, 53, 57, 76

Variable 28, 29, 176, 193, 235sq

See also: Argument, Constant, Predicate, Proposition
Verb control: see Control
VP anaphora 187
See also: Anaphora, Pronoun: proform
Verification 26, 194
Virtual synonym: see Synonymy

Weak impersonal 14, 100sqq, 104, 110, 127, 236, 237, 240
What-part (in P-clefts) 241, 243
Whitehead, Alfred North 25
Wh-movement 11
Word-order 1
World 46sqq, 91, 92sq, 208sq, 253
- actual w. 46sqq, 59
- non-actual w. 47, 50
- text-w. 51, 52, 53, 59, 61, 87, 146, 168, 182, 187, 211sq, 243, 260, 264, 267
- w. shift 173
See also: Accessibility, Counterpart, Frame, Possible-world Theory
Written texts 10

X-bar notation 106sq, 139sq, 195

Y-movement 11, 228

Zero-anaphora: see Anaphora